THE MAKING OF GLOBAL ENTERPRISE

The Making of Global Enterprise

Edited by

GEOFFREY JONES

FRANK CASS

First published in 1994 in Great Britain by
FRANK CASS AND COMPANY LIMITED
Gainsborough House, 11 Gainsborough Road,
London E11 1RS, England

and in the United States of America by
FRANK CASS
c/o International Specialized Book Services, Inc.
5602 N.E. Hasssalo Street, Portland, Oregon 927213–3640

Transferred to Digital Printing 2004

British Library Cataloguing in Publication Data

Making of Global Enterprise. – (Business
History Series, ISSN 0007–6791)
I. Jones, Geoffrey II. Series
338.8

ISBN 0–7146–4554–0(hbk)
ISBN 0–7146–4103–0(pbk)

Library of Congress Cataloging-in-Publication Data

The Making of global enterprise / edited Geoffrey Jones.
p.   cm.
"This group of studies first appeared in a special issue of
Business history, vol. XXXVI, no. 1, January 1994 "— —T.p. verso
Includes bibligraphical references and index.
ISBN 0–7146–4554–0. — — ISBN 0–7146–4103–0 (pbk.)
1. International business enterprises— —History. 2. International
business enterprises— —Case studies. I. Jones, Geoffrey.
HD2755.5.M345   1994
338.8′8— —dc20   93–5942
CIP

This group of studies first apppeared in a Special Issue of *Business History*,
Vol. XXXVI, No. 1 (January 1994), [The Making of Global Enterprise].

Contents

ABSTRACTS

Comparative Hosts, *by Mira Wilkins*

This paper explores ways of comparing industrial and developing nations that are and have been 'hosts' to multinationals. General problems in doing this included: defining multinational enterprise; acknowledging the formidable number of hosts; finding appropriate measures; clarifying the meaning of impacts; and recognising the 'truncation problem' (that of slicing into the fabric of the multinational firm). The activities of multinational enterprises are considered through time in individual host countries. Since corporate decision making is the point of departure, parameters of corporate choices (those related to opportunities, political conditions, familiarity, third-country considerations, and specific corporate style) are developed. Various rankings by countries are introduced to establish impact comparisons. The evidence shows that impacts differ by country and period. The paper demonstrates the historical importance of industrial countries as hosts and argues that students of economic growth and development should pay attention to all aspects (not simply the direct investment ones) of multinational enterprise impact through time.

International Financial Capital Transfers: A Transaction Cost Framework, *by Jean-François Hennart*

This paper argues that a number of non-conventional types of foreign direct investments – such as free-standing firms – that fit awkwardly in models where multinational firms arise to exploit abroad their firm-specific advantages, can be explained by looking at the role of these institutions in the international transfer of financial capital. The paper develops a theory to explain why a particular form of transfer will be used based on the choice between price and hierarchical transfer on one hand, and intermediated versus non-intermediated transfer on the other. Hierarchical transfer (equity) will be favoured when transaction costs in the market for investible funds are high. Intermediation will take place when there is considerable asymmetry between savers and investors. Non-intermediated equity transfers (free-standing firms) will

arise to finance projects offering no collateral (hence equity) but of low
scale and known technology (hence non-intermediated).

Britain's Overseas Investments in 1914 Revisited, *by T.A.B. Corley*

By 1914, over 35 per cent of Britain's net national wealth was held
abroad: a proportion unequalled by any country before or since. This
essay suggests that this substantial volume of overseas investment was
by no means as harmful to the British economy as many earlier scholars
have maintained. If the modern definition of foreign direct investment is
used, namely that which involved control over the assets acquired,
getting on for half of Britain's overseas investment stock turns out to
have been direct, and hence the result of positive entrepreneurial effort,
for example to secure raw materials abroad or to surmount tariff barriers. This general discussion is supplemented by estimates of the industrial and geographical composition of Britain's foreign direct
investment.

Foreign Multinationals in British Manufacturing, 1850–1962, *by Frances
Bostock and Geoffrey Jones*

This essay draws on a new database to describe the dimensions and
characteristics of 685 foreign companies which established British manufacturing subsidiaries between 1850 and 1962. The numbers of foreign
companies grew from the 1890s, expanded rapidly in the inter-war
years, and even more rapidly from the 1950s. The majority were
American, and were clustered in chemicals, mechanical and electrical
engineering, metal goods, motor vehicles and food products. The majority of foreign firms established greenfield plants in Britain, but there
were a significant number of acquisitions from 1900, and this became an
important mode of entry from 1950. Many foreign investors were of
modest size, and a considerable number of investors were short lived.
The majority of factories were always in the south-east of England, but
there was a surge of investment in Scotland and Wales after 1945.
Foreign-owned companies began to undertake R & D activity in Britain
from the inter-war years, and had a notable propensity to engage in
foreign trade.

**Negotiating Technology Transfer Within Multinational Enterprises:
Perspectives from Canadian History**, *by Graham D. Taylor*

This essay examines the processes through which technology and technological capabilities were transferred by parent companies to their

foreign affiliates in Canada, focusing on three companies covering the period from the 1880s to the 1950s. The three companies are: Bell Telephone Co. of Canada, which was affiliated with American Bell/ American Telephone & Telegraph during this period; Canadian Vickers Ltd, a wholly-owned subsidiary of the British firm, Vickers Ltd, from 1910 to 1927; and Canadian Industries Ltd (CIL) which was jointly owned by the American firm, Du Pont, and the British company, Imperial Chemical industries Ltd, from 1910 to 1952. In each case the major factors affecting decisions involving transfers of technology were: the general strategic objectives of the parent firm(s); the role played by managers in the affiliated firm in negotiating for these transfers; and the degree of control exercised by the parent company over the Canadian enterprise.

I.G. Farben in Japan: The Transfer of Technology and Managerial Skills, *by Akira Kudo*

Before the Second World War, I.G. Farben, the giant German chemical firm, extended its operations to the Far East. It exported goods, licensed its technologies and made direct investments in Japan. Through these forms of international business activities, I.G. Farben transferred its production technology and managerial skills to the Japanese chemical industry. This article, using company archives, examines the background, motives, process and results of the transfer activities. It concludes that I.G. Farben exerted a significant influence on the production technology, marketing policy, and distribution system of the Japanese chemical industry.

After Henry: Continuity and Change in Ford Motor Company, *by Alan McKinlay and Ken Starkey*

Since 1979 the Ford Motor Co. has attempted to introduce fundamental changes in its corporate strategy, management structure and labour relations. This article focuses on the impact of corporate restructuring on the management of Ford UK. Significant changes in industrial relations and work organisation have been tempered by strong continuities with Ford's maintenance of its traditional management prerogative. The most profound changes have been achieved in product development which has moved from functional hierarchy towards project management. Ford's interpretation of Japanese 'lean production' has been a significant factor shaping Ford's corporate agenda in America and Europe.

The Making of Global Enterprise

GEOFFREY JONES
University of Reading

The essays in this collection provide new and important insights on the history of international business. Research on this subject has proliferated over recent years. The literature is now so extensive that compilations of the most important writings are being published.[1] A series of literature surveys have also been published to guide non-specialists through the topic.[2] However, it is perhaps less the number of publications on the history of multinationals, than their impact, which has made it such an interesting area of business history research. As Donald Coleman observed in 1987, the subject has been one of the few in which business historians and economists have had a fruitful dialogue, resulting in substantial cross-fertilisation of ideas between the two disciplines.[3]

The result has been that research on the history of multinationals has, like the work of Chandler on management structures and strategies, escaped to some extent from the confining world of economic history to reach a wider academic audience. Mainstream conferences on international business have begun to feature business history sessions: examples include recent meetings of the Academy of International Business in the United States and the 1992 meeting of the European International Business Association.[4] The recent textbook on multinationals by John H. Dunning, the doyen of British economists in the field, includes a long chapter on their historical evolution which makes extensive use of business history literature.[5]

Considerable attention in this literature has been devoted to researching the determinants of the growth of multinational enterprise over the last century. Following the work of Dunning and other economists, business historians have explored the 'ownership advantages' possessed by firms that undertake foreign direct investment (FDI), such as superior managerial skills and technology; they have observed the locational factors in host economies that favour overseas production, such as tariffs and other types of trade restraints; and they have applied transactions cost theory to the growth of multinationals by showing how internalisation factors have been important.[6] The essays in this volume make further contributions to their understanding of the determinants of international business, but they also address less well-researched topics; these are the dimensions and characteristics of international business over time, and the impact of international business. And while much of the earlier business history literature has dealt with multinationals from a home country perspective, many of the articles published here adopt a host country perspective.

The studies of Wilkins, Corley and Bostock and Jones are all concerned with the historical dimensions of international business. The need for research on this matter arises from the paucity of historical data on FDI. The United States was the first country to publish FDI statistics, but the US Department of Commerce estimates for US outward FDI only begin in 1929. Official European statistics appeared much later. Britain only began to collect and publish statistics on inward and outward FDI in the 1960s, while the first official Swiss statistics on FDI were only published in 1985. One important reason why FDI statistics were not collected was that modern concepts of 'portfolio' and 'direct' types of foreign investment were slow to develop. Until well into the twentieth century most governments and economists saw only foreign investment, and paid no regard to whether that investment was accompanied by managerial control from abroad. As Corley shows, when British authors used the term 'direct' they were not referring to the issue of managerial control, but meant that the investment had not been made through the capital markets. The term 'multinational' itself only started to be used around 1960. Before that date, there was no established economic theory of multinational or foreign direct investment,[7] and only the US government collected any systematic data about the phenomenon.

Over the last three decades the main outline of the historical evolution of multinational enterprise have been established. It has been demonstrated that manufacturing multinationals appeared in the world economy in the mid-nineteenth century, and that firms such as Singer and Siemens were among the pioneer corporations. By the time of the First World War, multinational enterprise was a well-entrenched feature of the world economy, active in the manufacturing, extractive and service sectors. International business activity grew vigorously in the 1920s, slowed down in the depressed and war-torn 1930s and 1940s, and then staged a heroic recovery in the 1950s, when it began a period of rapid growth which (albeit with fluctuations) has been sustained to the present day. The names of the business enterprises involved, and the circumstances in which they went abroad, have been mapped in the pioneering two-volume history of American multinational enterprise by Mira Wilkins, and in her latest study of foreign investment of the United States before 1914.[8] After an initial period when far more was known about the American experience than that of other countries, a great deal has now been published also about European-based multinational enterprise. The large role played by German, British and other western European firms in the early growth of the multinational firm before 1914 has been convincingly demonstrated, as has the continuing importance of European multinationals in the twentieth century.[9] The history of Japanese multinational activity – which was modest before the 1970s – and of Canadian multinationals have also been explored.[10]

While it has proved possible to make considerable progress in describing the multinational growth of firms and industries, the precise quantification of that growth has remained more elusive. Two broad approaches have been taken. The first approach has been concerned to construct historical estimates of the size and structure of FDI. The second approach has concentrated on counting multinationals.

The pioneering study of Cleona Lewis published in 1938 was the first major attempt to estimate levels of FDI since the nineteenth century. Lewis provided estimates of the level of foreign investment in the American economy, and of US FDI according to sector and host region.[11] Wilkins makes considerable use of the Lewis data in all three of her major books, while noting (as have many others) their limitations. Over the last 25 years, Dunning has made a series of attempts to estimate world FDI before official figures began. His views have changed considerably over the period. The early estimates were based on the view that 90 per cent of all international capital movements took the form of portfolio investment, 'the acquisition of securities by individuals or institutions issued by foreign institutions, without any associated control over, or participation in their management'.[12] However, as Corley notes in his article in this collection, by the mid-1970s Dunning had come to the conclusion that over a third of world foreign investment was direct before 1914. The result was a series of estimates of world FDI in 1914, 1938 and 1960 by home and host country. The Dunning data established what has become the conventional wisdom about the historical evolution of FDI. Pre-1945 FDI originated in the developed world and was largely invested in the developing world in the exploitation of primary products and services. The United Kingdom was the world's largest direct investor, accounting for around 40 per cent of world FDI in 1938, followed by the United States. After the Second World War, a dramatic restructuring of world FDI occurred, alongside its equally dramatic growth. The relative importance of the developing world as a host region fell sharply. Increasingly FDI flowed between developed market economies, particularly in the manufacturing sector. Meanwhile, the United States replaced the United Kingdom as the world's largest direct investor, accounting for around 50 per cent of the stock of world FDI in 1960.[13]

The Dunning estimates are evidently of the order of magnitude variety which need further refinement, but research in this area has been very limited, reflecting the daunting problems of methodology and empirical evidence. It is striking that Wilkins, in her comprehensive study of foreign investment in the United States before 1914, finally declined to provide a portfolio/FDI breakdown of the $7 billion figure which she accepts as the most likely estimate for total foreign investment in the United States by 1914.[14] Nevertheless, some work has been undertaken at home country level. To date, the most important revisions to, or supplements of, the Dunning data have been for Germany and the Netherlands. Verona Schröter raised the Dunning estimate of German FDI in 1914 from $1,500 million to $2,600 million.[15] On this estimate, Germany's FDI emerges as the same size in 1914 as that of the United States, and thus in joint second place to Britain. For the Netherlands, Gales and Sluyterman have calculated FDI stock for 1900, 1914, 1938 and 1947.[16] Their figures for 1914 and 1938, of $925 million and $2,700 million respectively, are considerably higher than might be expected from Dunning, whose estimates for *combined* Belgian, Dutch, Italian, Swedish and Swiss FDI in those years only amounted to $1,250 million and $3,500 million.

Corley's article provides a revised estimate for British FDI in 1914. He goes back to the well-known Paish estimates of British overseas investments before the First World War, and reclassifies them according to modern definitions of FDI and portfolio investment. He also re-examines the Dunning figures, and adjusts them to allow – for example – for the overseas branches of domestic British companies. The upshot is a revisionist interpretation that Britain held a large stock of FDI. Indeed, it is suggested that no less than 45 per cent of the huge British foreign investment abroad before 1914 was direct. The resulting stock figure is calculated at £1,681.4 million, or around $8,172 million. Corley thereby joins Schröter and Gales and Sluyterman in raising the Dunning estimate for his country in 1914. The Corley estimate is almost $1,700 million – or £344 million – higher than the earlier Dunning one.

As in her previous work, Wilkins is altogether more sceptical of numbers than Corley. Her wide-ranging paper begins by confronting the paucity of our knowledge about the size of FDI in host economies at different time periods. As she notes, because there have been relatively few really significant home economies for multinational enterprise, it is easier to estimate FDI from that side of the equation rather than that of the host economies, which have been numerous and varied over the last century. Dunning's historical estimates for FDI stock held by host economies are much broader than those for host economies: for 1914, 1938 and 1960 he provides figures only for broad regional categories such as western Europe, Australasia and South Africa, and Latin America. Asia, which Dunning believed held 25 per cent of world FDI stock in 1938, is broken down only into China and India and Ceylon.

Although eschewing detailed figures, Wilkins makes a bold attempt to rank individual host economies by size of FDI in 1914 and 1929, as well as in the more recent past. This exercise appears to show the importance of developed economies as hosts, even before the Second World War, and it also demonstrates the very high place of the United States and Canada throughout the twentieth century. These are highly significant observations, but in reality Wilkins is not in the business of generating new FDI estimates. Indeed, her article is subversive of the whole approach. She shows that even today international FDI statistics are plagued with inadequacies, but the real thrust of her argument is that FDI figures alone say surprisingly little about the impact of multi-nationals on host economies.

Wilkins' views on the impact of multinational enterprise will be discussed below, but meanwhile it is necessary to introduce the second approach to quantifying the growth of international business over time, which has concentrated on firms rather than FDI stock. The first and, to date, most ambitious research on these lines was that of the Multinational Enterprise Study project at Harvard Business School directed by Raymond Vernon. This project compiled data on the 10,000 foreign subsidiaries of 187 US manufacturing multinational parents active between 1900 and 1967. The sample of 187 US multinationals was chosen by two criteria: (1) the enterprise appeared in Fortune 500 Largest US Industrial Corporations for the year 1964, published in 1965, or for the year 1964, published in 1964; (2) at the end of 1963, the US parent held equity interests in manufacturing enterprises located in six or more foreign countries, such equity interest in each case amounting to 25 per cent or more of the total equity. Two volumes of historical data resulted from the project,[17] and the database has been used by Chandler among others to document the growth of American multinational manu-facturing operations.[18] The later stages of the Harvard project studied non-American multinationals; the pioneering studies of the history of British and continental European multinationals by Stopford and Franko were the two most important results.[19]

The Vernon methodology of tracing backwards the antecedents of contemporary multinationals has been widely criticised, for it obviously failed to document the many multinational investments which were made but did not, for one reason or another, continue up to the contemporary period. Subsequent researchers preferred not to work backwards, but to count multinationals active at particular time periods. Nicholas, for example, has constructed an ever-expanding database of British multinationals, which he has used to test models concerned with the determinants of multinational growth and to explore the performance of British multinationals. Nicholas' first major study, in 1982, used a database of 119 British manufacturing firms which made a direct investment between 1870 and 1939. A decade later the Nicholas database had expanded to 448 pre-1939 British multinationals.[20] A database of such a size enables a clear delineation of the geographical and industrial distribution of British manufacturing multinational activity before the Second World War, even if there is a dispute about the relevance of such data to debates about the performance of British multinationals.[21]

Harm Schröter has also employed the methodology of counting companies and plants to explore the growth of German and other Continental European multinationals. In a study of the multinational growth of the German chemical industry, he identified 51 German chemical companies with a total of 153 production subsidiaries abroad in 1913. This figure was far above the level that had previously been imagined. Even in 1930, despite the well-established collapse of German FDI following the First World War, Schröter identified 85 German-owned foreign production subsidiaries in the chemical sector. A subsequent study of German chemical industry after 1930 tracked its further multinational expansion in the 1930s – by 1939 German chemical firms had 144 foreign production subsidiaries; its collapse because of the Second World War; and its revival from the mid-1950s. By 1965 Schröter calculated that German chemical firms had 150 production subsidiaries abroad.[22] Schröter's research on the early history of Swiss multinationals, employing a similar methodology, also revealed surprisingly high levels of direct investment. Some 160 Swiss firms controlled 265 foreign production subsidiaries in 1914: two-thirds of these were in Germany and almost another fifth in France.[23]

Schröter's most extensive attempt to quantify early multinational development to date was his *Habilitationsschrift* on the multinational enterprises from small European states between 1870 and 1914. Schröter examined multinational firms owned in Denmark, Sweden, the Netherlands, Belgium and Switzerland, assembling much information on their characteristics as well as providing extensive case study material. Schröter was able, using his population of firms, to establish periods of particularly rapid growth – such as the 1890s – as well as the main industrial sectors in which they were active, which were textiles, machinery, electrotechnicals, chemicals, food and other consumer goods, and various raw materials. However the Schröter thesis also demonstrates one of the methodological problems which hinder research in this area: the problem of definition. In his thesis, unlike the earlier articles, Schröter defines a 'multinational' very specifically as a firm which has at least two production facilities in two foreign countries or three production facilities in one foreign country. Investments in colonies are also excluded.[24] One consequence of this approach is that the Schröter estimates of multinationals are not compatible with those of – say – Nicholas, who counted as a multinational any firm which had one production plant abroad. Schröter would also eliminate the three-quarters of Dutch FDI in 1914 estimated by Gales and Sluyterman which was located in the Dutch East Indies.[25]

The essay by Bostock and Jones published here represents a further addition to the literature counting multinational investments over time, but unlike Nicholas and Schröter, and like Wilkins, they adopt a host country perspective. Over the last 100 years, Britain has been characterised by its prominence as both a major home and a host economy. In Wilkins' various tables on FDI stock levels, Britain is shown as the largest host economy in western Europe at all her benchmark dates. Britain also figures highly in her other measures of the importance of multinationals: for example, foreign affiliates accounted for a noteworthy 38 per cent of British exports in the 1985–90 period.

Bostock and Jones map the growth of foreign multinationals in British manufacturing from the first investments from the 1850s to 1962, when the first official British statistics become available. They show the growth of foreign investments, with particular peaks in the 1900s, the 1920s, and from the 1950s. The prominent role of US-owned enterprises is confirmed, especially after the First World War, as well as the clustering of inward investment in particular industries and products.

This methodology permits the analysis of certain elements of the growth of multinational enterprise which cannot be investigated using aggregate FDI stock estimates. Bostock and Jones are able to show that many of the foreign companies established in Britain passed into British hands over time, for a variety of reasons. They also reveal that many direct investments were on a small scale, and/or made by small foreign companies. This latter characteristic, however, illustrates some of the drawbacks involved in counting foreign companies without regard to their importance in terms of employment, sales and asset size. Such supplementary data is much harder to locate for the historical period, but without it the aggregate evidence derived from simply counting numbers of firms, though informative in some respects, can also be misleading.

The attempt to quantify the historical dimensions of international business is further complicated by a number of other factors. Far more is known about FDI in the manufacturing sector than in services or primary products. This is a particular problem because manufacturing FDI formed only a modest part of total FDI before the 1950s. A great deal remains to be discovered about the history of multinational activity in the service sector, although certain subjects – such as Japanese trading companies, European multinational banking and Canadian public utilities in Latin America and the West Indies – have received considerable attention recently.[26] The history of the extensive FDI in the primary product and extractive sectors before 1945 is also slowly being explored.[27]

A further set of difficulties arise from the variety of institutional forms used to make FDI in the past. American multinational enterprise was typically undertaken by an enterprise which grew in its domestic market and then established subsidiaries abroad. This may also have been the pattern of German FDI. However, many European multinational enterprises often assumed different corporate forms, especially before 1914.[28] Belgian, French and other European enterprises often invested abroad through holding companies involving complex international cross-holdings. Financial intermediaries, especially Continental 'mixed' banks, often 'controlled' substantial direct investments in utilities and manufacturing. It is often hard to establish where 'control' lay in such groups, and even the country of origin of the capital being used. The significance of such extensive cross-border business activity cannot be captured either in FDI estimates or through counting subsidiaries.[29] More generally, international business activity over the last 100 years has regularly involved joint ventures and various forms of equity and non-equity collaboration – whose influence and impact are hard to quantify.[30]

The 'free-standing' firm provides an example of the difficulties caused by the diversity of institutional forms used in the early period of FDI, especially before 1914. It has always been known that thousands of British companies were established before 1914 to undertake business activities abroad. Stopford, writing in 1974, called these firms 'expatriate investments', which had to be 'distinguished from direct investments in that they had at best a financial "shell" located in Britain'.[31] During the 1970s Dunning came to the conclusion that there was sufficient managerial control from Britain in such firms to count them as FDI. This argument has been taken further by Wilkins in her concept of the free-standing company – 'probably the most typical mode of British direct investment abroad'.[32] Corley's high estimate for British FDI published here rests fundamentally on the inclusion of this type of business enterprise as FDI.

The article by Hennart addresses the institutional complexities found in the history of international business. As he notes, the economic theory of the multinational enterprise has concentrated in explaining the determinants of a particular type of enterprise: 'a large firm with a clean structure of wholly-owned subsidiaries exploiting internally-generated advantages overseas'. The problem is that the theory does not really fit the many other types of corporate enterprise which existed historically, especially outside the US, including the free-standing firms, trading companies, and investment groups which were so prominent in British and other European international business activities before 1914.

Hennart uses transactions cost theory to explain some of these 'non-American incarnations' of the multinational enterprise. There was no question of free-standing companies – for example – internalising knowledge advantages derived from their non-existent domestic operations. Rather, Hennart suggests, if financial capital is regarded as an intermediate factor equivalent to knowledge, free-standing firms can be seen as arising from the internalisation of capital markets. The various modes of international financial capital transfer are identified, and a model is developed to explain why a particular form of transfer was adopted in particular situations. The reason why British free-standing firms were disproportionately involved in colonial plantations and mining before 1914 is explained by the high risk levels and, especially, the problems of collateral in such sectors. Conversely, nineteenth-century European, American and Russian railways were generally financed by loans rather than by FDI. In the case of the US, the land owned by the railways provided good collateral, thereby considerably reducing the risk of default.

The second major theme of this collection, after the dimensions and characteristics of international business, is its impact on host economies. The study of multinationals or direct investment from a host country perspective attracted some major studies in the inter-war years.[33] In the 1960s and 1970s a large and often controversial literature appeared on the impact of multinational enterprises on developing economies.[34] The modern historical literature on the impact of multinationals is not enormous, but valuable studies now exist on both developing and developed economies. Some of these take the form of business history case studies of the role of one or two multinational enterprises in host economies. Important examples include Fieldhouse's study of the role

of Unilever in a number of developing countries; Cochran's work on
BAT in China before 1930; Carstensen's book on Singer and
International Harvester in imperial Russia; and Tignor on two British
textile firms in Egypt between 1930 and 1956.[35] There has also been
research on the impact of FDI on such diverse topics as the extractive
industries of Spain in the late nineteenth century; at the strategies, and
their consequences, pursued by foreign oil companies in Latin America;
and at the impact of foreign banks in Iran.[36] The business history
literature on the impact of foreign multinationals on Latin America
includes studies of the cigarette industry and the Brazilian car
industry.[37] The role of multinationals in Japan's early economic development has been investigated.[38] This literature has generally pointed to
a positive impact of foreign companies on developing host economies,
and it has also been shown that the rewards from such investment for
the companies were not always as great as might have been imagined.

Major publications have also appeared on the historical impact of
multinationals on more developed economies. Studies by economists
from the late 1950s often contained historical reviews, and have now
become important sources of historical data themselves.[39] More recently, business historians have addressed this subject. Wilkins' work on
foreign investment in the US before 1914 contains a great deal of
information.[40] The impact of foreign multinationals on the industrial
development of Italy and the southern European economies generally
has been researched.[41] There have been a number of studies of the
historical impact of foreign business on the economies of Britain and
Germany. Fritz Blaich, for example, examined in detail the impact of
American machinery firms on Germany between 1890 and 1918. His
research is particularly interesting in showing the reaction of indigenous
firms to the Americans, which involved both imitation of American
technology and production and distribution methods, and diversification into other products when it was impossible to match the
Americans.[42]

Wilkins, in the essay published here has utilised this existing literature, and her own research over many years, in an ambitious attempt to
explore the impact of multinationals on host economies on a comparative historical basis. As noted above, her starting point was the absolute
size of inward investment received by countries, but she quickly reaches
the conclusion that such data – even if completely 'reliable' – is only of
limited value in exploring impact issues. What follows is a challenging
survey of the problems of assessing the impact of foreign enterprise,
and various means by which they might be resolved. At the very
least, Wilkins suggests, absolute FDI figures need to be related to

population size and gross national product, but other measures such as the share of 'foreign-owned firms' in various economic activities, such as exporting or employment, may provide better insights, if the historical data exists. The multinational enterprise and FDI are not the same thing. Some economic influences – such as technology transfer – are not amenable to easy quantification, let alone cultural, social and political impacts. Moreover, the real and the perceived impact of foreign firms might differ, as might the short- and long-term impacts.

Among the major insights of the Wilkins article is the need for historians to avoid a linear approach to this subject. The impact of multinationals on countries varied very considerably at different time periods, and did not simply grow and grow over time. This point is most vividly made in the cases of Russia and India: foreign-owned companies accounted for very significant shares of their economic activity before the First World War, but at the present day they account for very little.

The remaining essays in this collection confine their attention to individual host economies, but both explore many of the issues raised by Wilkins, and provide new empirical evidence for future comparative historical research. The concern of Bostock and Jones is to describe the growth and characteristics of foreign multinational investment in British manufacturing rather than to analyse its impact, but nonetheless their data provides a number of pointers on the impact issue. They explore the geographical location of foreign-owned companies in Britain. They demonstrate the willingness to appoint British nationals to the most senior managerial positions within British subsidiaries. They also show the long-term export propensities of foreign-owned firms in Britain, and their readiness to undertake R & D there, at least from the inter-war years. The role of foreign firms in introducing new processes and products is confirmed: these included not only high-technology products such as chemicals and electricals, but breakfast cereals, non-alcoholic drinks and many other food products. In some instances, at least, the British response to foreign enterprise – which Wilkins identifies as a particularly important impact issue – was dynamic. An outstanding example was in pharmaceuticals, where the R & D activities of foreign firms in Britain after 1945 exercised a demonstration effect on British firms, encouraging them to undertake large-scale research themselves.

The articles by Taylor and Kudo focus on one of the most discussed features of the impact of multinationals on host economies – their role in technology transfer. This subject has stimulated considerable controversy, and a whole range of issues have been raised. While it has always been recognised that multinationals potentially provide a major source of up-to-date technology, there has been considerable discussion about the cost and appropriateness of transferred technologies, especially to developing economies. There has also been a considerable debate about the degree to which investors adopt their technology to local conditions. As early as 1974, Wilkins raised the matter of the ability of host economies to absorb transferred technologies. She suggested that there was a difference between the transfer and absorption of technology within host countries, postulating the existence of an 'absorption gap' consisting of the time between the introduction of a new technology and when that new technology was used by nationals of the country.[43] Much recent economics literature has explored the absorption, utilisation and diffusion of transferred technologies in host economies, and the reasons why different countries have displayed differing abilities to absorb modern technologies transferred by multinationals.[44]

These technology transfer issues are often discussed at an aggregate or abstract level, and Taylor makes a singular contribution to the literature by exploring them using three, archivally based, historical case studies. The chosen host economy is Canada, one of the world's largest recipients of inward investment over a long period of time. Taylor explores the process of technology transfer, and identifies the key variables which affected decisions on the kind of technology which was transferred. He shows the considerable importance of the managers of the foreign affiliates. The foreign parents' willingness to transfer technology, especially advanced technology, was also closely linked to the degree of control exercised by the foreign part over the Canadian subsidiaries: the more control exercised by the foreign company, the more willing it was to transfer technology to the subsidiary. Taylor also shows how, as in the case of the Vickers operations in Canada between 1910 and 1927, a poorly performing FDI in financial terms can nevertheless result in considerable technology transfer to its host economy.

Twentieth-century Japan provides a particularly interesting host country case study for students of the impact of multinationals. Throughout the twentieth century Japan has held a low level of inward investment stock, the precise reasons for which, and consequences, have been explored in several recent studies.[45] The correlation between Japan's phenomenal economic success and its low level of inward investment – and the resulting contrast with a country like Britain, which has combined extensive inward investment and poor economic performance since 1945 – might raise doubts about the benefits of liberal policies which permit extensive foreign multinational control over a country's business. In fact, as Wilkins observes in her essay, matters are not so simple, for although the stock levels were low, at certain stages of the development of particular Japanese industries, such as cars and electricals, foreign multinationals did exercise a considerable impact. This impact was especially positive because Japanese business exhibited a considerable capacity to absorb foreign technological and managerial practices.

Kudo's article demonstrates that foreign multinationals also had a significant impact on the Japanese chemical industry in the inter-war years. The author shows that through a number of different modes – exporting, licensing and FDI – I.G. Farben transferred both production technology and managerial skills to the inter-war Japanese chemical industry. The Germans were initially reluctant to license any technology to the Japanese – and so feed their 'almost morbid ambition' – but the growth in the 1930s of the Japanese market and of Japanese chemical companies, and the strengthening of international cartel agreements, prompted I.G. Farben to change course. The licensing of the Haber–Bosch process to a number of Japanese companies in particular resulted in considerable technology transfer in fertiliser production to Japan.

McKinlay and Starkey, in the last essay in this collection, take the discussion up to the more recent past. Like Taylor, they are concerned with relationships within the multinational enterprise. Their concern is the global Ford Motor Co., and more especially the process of change which has occurred inside the American parent and in its largest foreign subsidiary, Ford of Europe. The latter entity was created in 1967, and over the following years it became the decision-making focus in Europe of the American firm, stripping power away from the national manufacturing companies such as Ford UK and Ford Werke. It is with the former company that McKinlay and Starkey are principally concerned.

During the 1980s McKinlay and Starkey show that both Ford US and Ford UK underwent radical change in their production methods, but through different routes. Between 1980 and 1982 the American firm passed through a disastrous crisis, which led to a wholesale rejection of past Fordist practices which reached down all levels of the company. The result was 'one of the greatest turnarounds in corporate history'. In contrast, Ford of Europe remained very profitable during the early 1980s, providing vital support to its ailing American parent, but it was galvanised by the realisation by its executives of the scale of Japanese manufacturing superiority in car production. The process of change was more ambiguous in Europe, with Ford UK's management adopting an aggressive attitude to the labour force which stood in marked contrast to the new emphasis on employee involvement seen in Ford US.

The essays published here explore the dimensions over time of international business activity, and its impact on host economies. They supply rich new empirical evidence, but also show the complexities faced by those seeking to use it to provide clear-cut answers. They demonstrate some of the crucial insights that historians can make to the study of international business. FDI and multinationals did not just grow and grow, exercising an ever-greater influence on the world economy. Business history shows that their impact varied according to time, place and circumstance. Different institutional forms flourished at different times. There were many divestments as well as investments. Flows of technology were influenced by relationships within multinational enterprises at particular junctions. The making of global enterprise was far from a linear process.

NOTES

1. M. Wilkins (ed.), *The Growth of Multinationals* (Aldershot, 1991); G. Jones (ed.), *Transnational Corporations: A Historical Perspective* (1993).
2. For example, M. Wilkins, 'The History of European Multinationals: A New Look', *Journal of European Economic History*, Vol.15 (1986); idem, 'European and North American Multinationals, 1870–1914: Comparisons and Contrasts', *Business History*, Vol.30 (1988); J.P. Daviet, P. Hertner, G. Jones and M. Wilkins, 'La storia delle imprese multinazionali', *Passato e Presente*, Vol.13 (1987); K.E. Sluyterman, 'Onderzoek van historici naar multinationale ondernemingen', *Orgaan voor de economische geschiedenis in Nederland*, Vol.4 (1990).
3. D. Coleman, 'The Uses and Abuses of Business History', *Business History*, Vol.29 (1987), p.152. The opening stages in the dialogue between economists and business historians can be seen in M. Casson (ed.), *The Growth of International Business* (1983) and P. Hertner and G. Jones (eds.), *Multinationals: Theory and History* (Aldershot, 1986).
4. The articles by Corley and Hennart in this collection were first presented at the EIBA conference held in Reading, UK in December 1992.
5. J.H. Dunning, *Multinational Enterprises and the Global Economy* (Wokingham, 1993), Ch. 5. A historical interest is also evident in other studies on contemporary international business, such as C. Dupuy, C. Milelli and J. Savary, *Stratégies des multinationales* (Montpellier-Paris, 1991).
6. For important contributions, from different perspectives, to the literature on the determinants of British multinational enterprise, see S.J. Nicholas, 'British Multinational Investment before 1939', *Journal of European Economic History*, Vol.11 (1982) and G. Jones (ed.), *British Multinationals: Origins, Management and Performance* (Aldershot, 1986). The theoretical literature can be approached in Dunning, *Multinational Enterprises*. There is an excellent survey of the recent empirical literature on determinants in United Nations Centre on Transnational Corporations, *The Determinants of Foreign Direct Investment. A Survey of the Evidence* (New York, 1992).
7. Dunning, *Multinational Enterprises*, p.68.
8. M. Wilkins, *The Emergence of Multinational Enterprise* (Cambridge, MA, 1970); idem, *The Maturing of Multinational Enterprise* (Cambridge, MA, 1974); idem, *The History of Foreign Investment in the United States before 1914* (Cambridge, MA, 1990).
9. In addition to the work of Wilkins cited above, the most significant publications which have established the main outlines of the history of European multinationals include L. Franko, *The European Multinationals* (1976); P. Hertner, 'Fallstudien zu deutschen multinationalen Unternehmen vor dem Ersten Weltkrieg', in N. Horn and J.

Kocka (eds.), *Law and the Formation of the Big Enterprises in the 19th and early 20th Centuries* (Gottingen, 1979); A. Teichova and P.L. Cottrell (eds.), *International Business and Central Europe, 1918–1939* (Leicester, 1983); Hertner and Jones (eds.), *Multinationals: Theory and History*; G. Jones (ed.), *British Multinationals*; A. Teichova, M. Lévy-Leboyer and H. Nussbaum (eds.), *Multinational Enterprise in Historical Perspective* (Cambridge, 1986); idem (eds.), *Historical Studies in International Corporate Business* (Cambridge, 1989); and G. Jones and Harm G. Schröter (eds.), *The Rise of Multinationals in Continental Europe* (Aldershot, 1993).

10. The best English-language introduction to the history of Japanese multinationals are M. Wilkins, 'Japanese Multinational Enterprise before 1914', *Business History Review*, Vol.60 (1986); idem, 'Japanese Multinationals in the United States: Continuity and Change, 1879–1990', *Business History Review*, Vol.64 (1990). The Canadian literature can be approached in the Special Issue on 'Canadian Multinationals and International Finance', *Business History*, Vol.32 (1992).

11. C. Lewis, *America's Stake in International Investments* (Washington, DC, 1938).

12. J.H. Dunning, *Studies in International Investment* (1970).

13. J.H. Dunning, 'Changes in the Level and Structure of International Production: The Last One Hundred Years', in Casson (ed.), *Growth*, pp.87–8; idem, *Explaining International Production* (1988), pp.74–5; idem, *Multinational Enterprises*, pp.117–18.

14. Wilkins, *History*, p.151.

15. V. Schröter, *Die deutsche Industrie auf dem Weltmarkt 1929 bis 1933* (Frankfurt, 1984), p.118.

16. B.P.A. Gales and K.E. Sluyterman, 'Outward Bound: The Rise of Dutch Multinationals', in Jones and Schröter (ed.), *Rise*.

17. J.W. Vaupel and J.P. Curhan, *The Making of Multinational Enterprise* (Cambridge, MA, 1969); idem, *The World's Multinational Enterprise* (Cambridge, MA, 1974).

18. A.D. Chandler, *Scale and Scope* (Cambridge, MA, 1990), pp.157–61.

19. J.M. Stopford, 'The Origins of British-Based Multinational Manufacturing Enterprises' and L.G. Franko, 'The Origins of Multinational Manufacturing by Continental European Firms', *Business History Review*, Vol.48 (1974); Franko, *European Multinationals*.

20. Nicholas, 'British Multinational Investment before 1939'; idem, 'The Expansion of British Multinational Companies: Testing for Managerial Failure', in James Foreman-Peck (ed.), *New Perspectives on the Late Victorian Economy* (Cambridge, 1991).

21. G. Jones, 'Locational Choice, Performance and the Growth of British Multinational Firms: A Comment' and S.J. Nicholas, 'Debating Business History: Location, Performance and Growth of British MNEs', *Business History*, Vol.33 (1991).

22. H.G. Schröter, 'Die Auslandsinvestitionen der deutschen chemischen Industrie 1870 bis 1930', *Zeitschift für Unternehmensgeschichte*, Vol.35 (1990); idem, 'Die Auslandsinvestitionen der deutschen chemischen Industrie 1930 bis 1965' (forthcoming).

23. H.G. Schröter, 'Etablierungs- und Verteilungsmuster der schweizerischen Auslandsproduktion von 1870 bis 1914', in P. Bairoch and M. Körner (eds.), *Die Schweiz in der Weltwirtschaft (15–20 Jh.)* (Zurich, 1990).

24. H.G. Schröter, 'Multinationale Unternehmen aus kleinen Staaten 1870 bis 1914' (Berlin, 1991).

25. Gales and Sluyterman, 'Outward Bound', p.65.

26. On the history of Japanese trading companies, see S. Yonekawa and H. Yoshihara (eds.), *Business History of General Trading Companies* (Tokyo, 1987) and S. Yonekawa (ed.), *General Trading Companies: A Comparative and Historical Study* (Tokyo, 1990). Recent studies on the history of multinational banking include D. Merrett, *ANZ Bank* (Sydney, 1985); F.H.H. King, *The History of the Hongkong and Shanghai Banking Corporation*, 4 vols. (Cambridge, 1987–91); M. Meuleau, *Des pionniers en Extrême-Orient* (Paris, 1990); G. Jones (ed.), *Banks as Multinationals* (1990); R. Cameron and V.I. Bovykin (eds.), *International Banking, 1870–1914* (New York, 1991); Eric Bussière, *Paribas, 1872–1992* (Antwerp, 1992); G. Jones, *British*

16 THE MAKING OF GLOBAL ENTERPRISE

Multinational Banking, 1830–1990 (Oxford, 1993). The history of Canadian FDI in utility businesses has been explored in D. McDowall, *The Light: Brazilian Traction, Light and Power Company Limited, 1899–1945* (Toronto, 1988) and C. Armstrong and H.V. Nelles, *Southern Exposure: Canadian Promoters in Latin America and the Caribbean, 1896–1930* (Toronto, 1988).

27. Important literature on the history of extractives include M.C. Eakin, *British Enterprise in Brazil* (Durham, NC, 1989); C. Harvey and J. Press, 'The City and International Mining, 1870–1914', *Business History* Vol.32 (1990); T.F. O'Brien, 'Rich Beyond the Dreams of Avarice: The Guggenheims in Chile', *Business History Review*, Vol.63 (1989), and C. Schmitz, 'The Rise of Big Business in the World Copper Industry, 1870–1930', *Economic History Review*, Vol.39 (1986). Aspects of the history of Britain's large investment in the world oil industry are examined in G. Jones, *The State and the Emergence of the British Oil Industry* (1981); R.W. Ferrier, *The History of the British Petroleum Company* (Cambridge, 1982) and T.A.B. Corley, *A History of the Burmah Oil Company*, 2 vols. (1983 and 1988).

28. Wilkins, 'European and North American Multinationals'.

29. Two studies of European FDI before 1914 which well illustrate these problems are V.G. Jacob-Wendler, *Deutsche Elektroindustrie in Lateinamerika: Siemens und AEG (1890–1914)* (Stuttgart, 1982) and M. Dumoulin, *Les relations économiques italo-belges (1861–1914)* (Brussels, 1990).

30. For a selection of literature on this subject, see G. Jones (ed.), *Coalitions and Collaboration in International Business* (Aldershot, 1993). There is also important information in A. Kudo and T. Hara (eds.), *International Cartels in Business History* (Tokyo, 1992.)

31. Stopford, 'Origins', p.162.

32. M. Wilkins, 'The Free-Standing Company, 1870–1914: An Important Type of British Foreign Direct Investment', *Economic History Review*, Vol.61 (1988).

33. F.A. Southard, *American Industry in Europe* (Boston, MA, 1931); C.F. Remer, *Foreign Investment in China* (New York, 1933).

34. This literature can be approached through S. Lall (ed.), *Transnational Corporations and Economic Development* (1993), a selection of critical writings on the subject which includes a helpful introduction and literature review.

35. D.K. Fieldhouse, *Unilever Overseas* (Beckenham, 1978); S. Cochran, *Big Business in China* (Cambridge, MA, 1980); F. Carstensen, *American Enterprise in Foreign Markets: Singer and International Harvester in Imperial Russia* (Chapel Hill, NC, 1984); and R.L. Tignor, *Egyptian Textiles and British Capital, 1930–1956* (Cairo, 1989).

36. C. Harvey and P. Taylor, 'Mineral Wealth and Economic Development: Foreign Direct Investment in Spain, 1851–1913', *Economic History Review*, Vol.XL (1987); J.C. Brown, 'Domestic Politics and Foreign Investment: British Development of Mexican Petroleum, 1899–1911', *Business History Review*, Vol.61 (1987); idem, 'Why Foreign Oil Companies Shifted their Production from Mexico to Venezuela during the 1920s', *American Historical Review*, Vol.90 (1985); idem, *Oil and Revolution in Mexico* (Berkeley, 1993); G. Jones, *Banking and Empire in Iran* (Cambridge, 1986); idem, 'The Imperial Bank of Iran and Iranian Economic Development, 1890–1952', *Business and Economic History*, Vol.16 (1987).

37. P. Shepherd, 'Transnational Corporations and the Denationalization of the Latin American Cigarette Industry', in A. Teichova et al. (eds.), *Historical Studies in International Corporate Business*; and H. Shapiro, 'State Intervention and Industrialization: The Origins of the Brazilian Automotive Industry', *Business and Economic History*, Vol.18 (1989).

38. T. Yuzawa and M. Udagawa (eds.), *Foreign Business in Japan before World War II* (Tokyo, 1990); M. Mason, 'Foreign Direct Investment and Japanese Economic Development, 1899–1931', *Business and Economic History*, Vol.16 (1987); idem, *American Multinationals and Japan* (Cambridge, MA 1992).

39. J.H. Dunning, *American Investment in British Manufacturing Industry* (1958); D.T.

Brash, *American Investment in Australian Industry* (Canberra, 1966); D.J.C. Forsyth, *US Investment in Scotland* (New York, 1972); Y.S. Hu, *The Impact of US Investment in Europe: A Case Study of the Automotive and Computer Industries* (New York, 1973).
40. Wilkins, *Foreign Investment*.
41. P. Hertner, *Il capitale tedesco in Italia dall'unità alla prima guerra mondiale* (Bologna, 1984); Special Issue on 'Industria elettrica e movimenti di capitale in Europ', *Studi Storici*, Vol.28 (1987).
42. F. Blaich, *Amerikanische Firmen in Deutschland 1890–1914* (Wiesbaden, 1984). There is also a study of the impact of foreign companies by nationality in Germany in H. Pohl (ed.), *Der Einfluss ausländischer Unternehmen auf die deutsche Wirtschaft vom Spätmittelalter bis zur Gegenwart* (Stuttgart, 1992). The literature on Britain is reviewed in the article by Bostock and Jones in this collection.
43. M. Wilkins, 'The Role of Private Business in the International Diffusion of Technology', *Journal of Economic History*, Vol.34 (1974).
44. This paragraph draws heavily on Lall (ed.), *Transnational Corporations*, pp.11–16. There is a good review of the issues and a survey of the empirical literature in Dunning, *Multinational Enterprises*, Ch. 11.
45. Mason, *American Multinationals*; D. Encarnation, *Rivals Beyond Trade: America versus Japan in Global Competition* (Ithaca, 1992); Robert Z. Lawrence, 'Japan's Low Levels of Inward Investment: The Role of Inhibitions on Acquisitions', *Transnational Corporations*, Vol.1 (1992).

Comparative Hosts

MIRA WILKINS

Florida International University

I

Since the late nineteenth century, many multinational enterprises have crossed borders and had substantial economic impact on the domestic activities as well as on the international relations of the countries abroad in which they did and do business (such recipient countries are in the present article called host nations, or more simply hosts).[1] Yet, some years ago, when I tried to locate an article that compared the hosts of multinational corporations, I failed to find an essay that included both industrial and less developed hosts and had an historical approach.[2] Accordingly, for a conference in Munich in August 1992, I prepared a lengthy study, entitled 'Hosts to Transnational Investments – A Comparative Analysis'.[3] My present paper draws on the findings therein and expands the analysis. Like its predecessor, this paper is tentative, more suggestive than conclusive.

Even though no single historical work exists that compares all hosts to multinationals, there does exist an immense literature, both historical and contemporary, that deals with multinational enterprise behaviour in host countries.[4] Authors, however, tend to specialise. Many are knowledgeable on a nation, a region, or perhaps developing countries. Even so, whether they have dealt with less developed or developed hosts, they have considered a common topic – the presence of multinational enterprise.[5] From an historical perspective, how can one compare the host countries? What, for example, might the historical experience with multinational corporations of Japan share with that of Brazil? How did the impacts differ? Are there significant insights that can be gained by comparing the many different hosts of multinationals?

II

Five general problems surfaced in my efforts to set up a basis for comparison. The first relates to the definition of a multinational enterprise, which I defined in traditional terms: a firm headquartered in one country (or less frequently more than one country) that extends its operations to do business in at least one country abroad.[6] My definition is not confined to companies that manufacture; service sector multi-nationals (trading firms, banks, shipping companies) are included as long as they have a direct investment abroad, however small. Because in their extension abroad multinational enterprises make foreign direct investments (FDIs), often in the literature there is the assumption that multinational enterprises and FDIs are identical, an assumption that creates confusion. I am interested in multinational enterprises rather than in FDIs *per se*. This essay is on the firm that undertakes FDIs *and* also serves as a conduit for trade, product information, methods of production, general know-how, financial acumen, marketing expertise and, most important, management. The provision of capital is only *one* part of the 'package' of multinational enterprise activities.

A second general problem is the formidable number of host countries. When one studies homes to multinationals, the problem does not arise; historically, there were roughly two handfuls of truly significant homes. Even today the number is not much larger. With hosts, the world is our oyster. Host countries abound. This was true historically and has become ever more true in the post-Second World War years. Today, Asea Brown Boveri, a Swedish–Swiss multinational enterprise, for example, has affiliates in 140 nations.[7] Although there is concentration in particular host countries, nonetheless through time there have been, without question, many more hosts to significant multinational enterprise operations than there have been key homes. This fact of life complicates the process of analysis.

A third problem is how to proceed in making legitimate, systematic comparisons. How does one rank the many hosts? I started by following the lead of John Dunning, trying to sort by level of, by size of, foreign direct investments through time.[8] Tables 1 to 4 reflect these rankings. While I imitated Dunning's method, the tables are original. In their preparation, I faced major obstacles based on lack of available information; the rankings are rough, the data fragile. The 1914 table has no dollar amounts, because my personal uncertainty is so great that I do not wish to sanctify such numbers.[9] Table 4 reveals some of the reasons for vulnerability: (1) such tables even in recent times have to be constructed from disparate materials, since there has never been uniform international monitoring of the levels of FDI;[10] (2) what is included in the statistics varies by country;[11] and (3) in periods of exchange rate variations, the stock estimates (translated into dollars) will alter depending on the value of the dollar. But far more important, the ranking of the stock of FDIs at particular points in time does not tell us much about the *impact* of multinationals on the economy of a host nation, because as stated earlier the presence of multinationals is *more* than FDI.

TABLE 1

INWARD STOCK OF FOREIGN DIRECT INVESTMENT IN 1914: RANKING OF HOSTS

Country
1. United States
2. Russia
3. Canada
4. Argentina
5. Brazil
6. South Africa
7. Austria-Hungary
Unranked next tier (8-9)
India
China
Unranked next tier (10-12)
Egypt
Mexico
United Kingdom

Source: M. Wilkins, 'Hosts to Transnational Investments', forthcoming in a volume edited by Hans Pohl and to be published in a supplement to the *Zeitschrift für Unternehmensgeschichte*, Table 1.

Was the exercise in preparing Tables 1–4 for naught? Do these tables have no value? Despite the provisional nature of the FDI numbers and their limited use, the trial ranking of key hosts to FDI does suggest (1) that developed nations have been consistently the most important hosts (measured by size of inward direct investment) and (2) that the very high place of the United States and Canada (both prosperous developed countries) throughout the twentieth century is of note. Can this be interpreted to mean that the stress in the literature on Third World hosts is without merit? I do not believe that to be true. Yet perhaps the traditional emphasis does require modification.

TABLE 2

INWARD STOCK OF FOREIGN DIRECT INVESTMENT IN 1929: RANKING OF HOSTS

Country	Amount
	$2.4 billion - $1.4 billion
1. Canada	
2. United States	
	$1.2 billion - $800 million
3. India	
4. Cuba	
5. Mexico	
	$800 million - $500 million
6. Argentina	
7. Chile	
8. Great Britain	
9. Malaya	
	$500 million - $350 million
10. Venezuela	
11. Brazil	
12. Australia	
13. South Africa	
14. Netherlands East Indies	
15. Egypt	
16. China	
	$350 million - $200 million
17. Germany	
18. Spain	

Source: M. Wilkins, 'Hosts to Transnational Investments', forthcoming in a volume edited by Hans Pohl and to be published in a supplement to the *Zeitschrift für Unternehmensgeschichte*, Table 2.

These absolute FDI measures (even were we able to write them in a more precise, reliable rendition) seem only a first step in our search for bases for comparison. They are clearly inadequate to the task at hand – that of considering the impact of multinationals on host countries. Figures on the size of, the level of, inward direct investment give only part of the story.[12] As a recent United Nations report put it, direct

TABLE 3

INWARD STOCK OF FOREIGN DIRECT INVESTMENT IN 1982
(SELECTED COUNTRIES: AMOUNTS IN BILLION US DOLLARS)

	Country	Amount	Rank in 1975
1.	United States	124.7	2
2.	Canada	56.3	1
3.	United Kingdom	51.3	3
4.	Germany, Federal Republic	32.1	4
5.	Brazil	21.6	9
6.	Netherlands	18.0	5
7.	South Africa	15.9	na
8.	Australia	15.6	7
9.	France	14.8	6
10.	Mexico	14.4	11
11.	Saudi Arabia	13.2	na
12.	Belgium	9.8	12
13.	Italy	7.4	na
14.	Malaysia	6.8	na
15.	Argentina	6.8	na
16.	Venezuela	6.6	13
17.	Panama	5.4	10
18.	Indonesia	4.6	16
19.	Spain	4.5	15
20.	Hong Kong	4.3	22
21.	Japan	4.1	20
22.	Nigeria	3.5	8
23.	Norway	3.5	19
24.	Egypt	3.4	na
.25.	Trinidad and Tobago	3.4	na
26.	Ireland	3.4	14
27.	Austria	3.0	na
28.	Peru	2.7	na
29.	New Zealand	2.3	na
30.	Singapore	2.2	18
31.	Colombia	2.1	24
32.	Zimbabwe	2.0	na
33.	Philippines	1.9	na
34.	Chile	1.9	na
35.	Zaire	1.8	na
36.	China	1.8	na
37.	Denmark	1.7	na
38.	Sweden	1.5	na
39.	Papua New Guinea	1.4	na
40.	Thailand	1.3	na
41.	South Korea	1.2	na
42.	Gabon	1.0	na
43.	Ivory Coast	1.0	na

Source: J. Dunning and J. Cantwell, *IRM Directory of Statistics of International Investment and Production* (New York, 1987), pp. 797–801 and M. Wilkins, 'Hosts to Transnational Investments', forthcoming in a volume edited by Hans Pohl and to be published in a supplement to the *Zeitschrift für Unternehmensgeschichte*, Table 4.

COMPARATIVE HOSTS 23

TABLE 4
INWARD STOCK OF FOREIGN DIRECT INVESTMENT IN MID-1980S
(SELECTED COUNTRIES: AMOUNTS IN BILLION US DOLLARS)

Country (date)	Amount	Comments
United States (1988)	329	Unrevised book value at historical cost
Canada (1984)	60	*Rate of Exchange $1.00 = C$1.30
United Kingdom (1984)	49	*Rate of Exchange £1 = $1.34
Germany, Fed.Rep. of (1985)	28	*Rate of Exchange $1.00 = DM 2.94
Brazil (1985)	26	Based on approvals
Australia (1984)	20	*Rate of Exchange $1.00 = A$.87
Netherlands (1984)	15	*Rate of Exchange $1.00 = £3.21
Egypt (1984)	15	Projects established under Investment and Free Zone Law, cumulative 1974-84
Mexico (1981)	14	
Indonesia (1986)	11	Based on approvals
Japan (1988)	10	Excludes reinvested profits
Singapore (1981)	8	
Taiwan (1986)	6	Based on approvals
Hong Kong (1981)	4	
Nigeria (1982)	4	
Argentina (1985)	3	Cumulative approved FDI since 3 January 1977
Colombia (1986)	3	Excluding oil
Malaysia (1984)	3	Equity shares held by foreign residents Malaysian companies 12 December 1984 (paid-up value)
Venezuela (1986)	2	
Korea (1986)	2	
Chile (1983)	2	
Philippines (1983)	2	
Thailand (1985)	2	Cumulative flows since 1971
Zimbabwe (1982)	2	
Ecuador (1986)	1	Excluding oil
Peru (1986)	1	

Note: No country is included in the table that had less than $1 billion of FDI (this would include Bolivia, Morocco, Panama, Paraguay, Bangladesh, Sri Lanka, where comparative data exist). I have no comparative Indian or Chinese data.

source: Mira Wilkins, 'Hosts to Transnational Investments', forthcoming in a volume edited by Hans Pohl and to be published in a supplement to the Zeitschrift für Unternehmensgeschichte, Table 5. The data are from World Investment Report 1991, p. 32 (United States; Japan); United Nations Centre on Transnational Corporations, Transnational Corporations in World Development (New York: United Nations, 1988), pp. 512–5 (Canada, united Kingdom, West Germany, Netherlands, Australia –* Wilkins translated into US dollars; Indonesia); ibid., pp. 380–1 (Argentina, Brazil, Chile, Colombia, Ecuador, Mexico, Peru, Venezuela, Hong Kong, Korea, Malaysia, Philippines, Singapore, Taiwan, Thailand, Egypt, Nigeria, and Zimbabwe). The approval numbers seem far larger than the book value ones, so the former should be reduced for comparability. Where no exchange rate is given, the source gave US dollars.

'investment flows are an underestimating measure of the activities' of multinational corporations in host countries, because they neglect technology transfers, and, I would add, many more transfers from the multinational enterprise as well. I would extend the United Nations' commentary to include the superior 'direct investment stock' measures as well as the flow figures.[13] Other yardsticks, if available, would be more appropriate. Later in this article, I will discuss possible alternatives.

A fourth general problem relates to 'impact' as such. What seems clear is that impacts differ – through time and circumstances. And at any point in time, impacts need not be uniform. The impacts are generally economic ones, affecting growth and development; they are also often social and cultural ones – which ultimately affect economic growth and development. They may be political. Our interest is in the broad economic impact. It is very important, however, that the perceived impacts (and accordingly host governments' policy response) may diverge from real economic impacts. Our goal is to look at the impacts, real and perceived.[14] Too often, macro-economic indicators obscure profound, real sectoral consequences. Moreover, multinationals have *two* closely interrelated but distinguishable impacts on hosts: one is associated with *domestic* economic and social change and the second specifically with the host's contacts with the rest of the world. Since by definition a multinational extends over borders, the second impact must precede the first and it becomes the basis for *both* subsequent impacts. I will explore this important distinction as this article progresses.

This brings me to the fifth general concern, what I call the 'truncation problem'. This problem, which I identified as I sought to make comparisons, involves the cutting into the fabric of a firm's international business. When one considers multinationals in a host nation, the topic is the firm (as defined earlier), that is a conduit. If one looks exclusively at a single host, one rips into an existing organisational structure. There is a tear, a distortion.[15] Recognition of the truncation problem casts important light on the study of comparative hosts. Most economists think about movements over borders as a transfer from country A to country B. Trade consists of goods going from one country to another. Capital travels in a similar fashion, as does technology. Yet a multinational enterprise does *not* leave nation A for nation B. It extends over the homeland border, remaining in the headquarters country as it spreads into numerous host nations. What stretches over the political boundaries (of home and host) is the management of, the governance of, the organisational capability of, the package offered by the firm.[16] Trade within a multinational enterprise is not a one shot, arms-length transaction between buyer and seller but a continuing process. Likewise, the capital that goes over borders remains under control from headquarters. Technology is not abruptly shipped abroad; it is monitored and adjusted as it evolves at home and abroad.[17] The multinational enterprise establishes, acquires, and administers a network of interrelated businesses. It engages in a collection of associated transactions, not just individual ones.[18] Multinationals penetrate within the host nation economy; their activities are not merely external phenomena. When we study the multinational enterprise in a particular host country, we splinter the story of the firm. I am not implying that it is illegitimate to do country studies. Instead, I argue that national inquiries truncate the firm and that they are accordingly greatly enriched through an understanding of where an individual host fits into the overall strategies of a growing and/or contracting enterprise, as well as by how the multinational affects the unique economy of the host nation.

To eliminate the truncation problem and to accomplish my prescribed goal – to deal with comparisons between and among host countries – it seemed both appropriate and essential to begin with the multinational firm and ask what exactly have been its influences world-wide. To determine these influences (and the rationale behind the firm's very presence in host nations), it is vital to explore the nature of corporate choices. Thus I begin with what is common to host countries, that is, the participation of multinationals, and probe into the wherewithal behind their presence.

III

Based on my own studies of multinationals and the now vast literature on them, I find five sets of considerations (what I call parameters) relate to multinational enterprise decision-making.[19] While the five may be a little too schematic, they seem to capture the way multinationals make choices. Some apply equally to domestic and international firms, while others are confined to the latter. The parameters are not ranked in importance. Some are far more crucial in one period and in one situation than in another.[20] All are pertinent to the understanding of multinational enterprise and its role in any individual host nation.

The first relates basically to economic decision making. I call it the *opportunity parameter*: what are the prospects for markets, raw materials, or other openings? This is straightforward, and could apply to the resource allocation choices of domestic as well as multinational firms. The second is the *political parameter*. Domestic firms are influenced by state, provincial, and local government policies, but fundamentally the operations under diverse national political structures separate the multinational enterprise from a purely domestic business. The political parameter focuses on what kinds of government policies exist within a host nation. Is there political stability? Since multinational firms expand over national boundaries, political conditions in host states affect the behaviour, amount of involvement, and duration of the presence of multinationals. The political parameter is only one of five parameters. My view is balanced. I do not think this parameter (as some have insisted) is pre-eminent, nor do I think it can be neglected as is sometimes the case in the economics literature on multinationals.[21] Frequently, public policy measures not specifically targeted at multinationals have consequences that alter multinational enterprise strategies. Every student of multinationals knows, for example, that barriers to trade (and threatened ones) – from tariffs to voluntary export restraints – have impact on the decision-making of multinational managers *vis-à-vis* investments in manufacturing abroad to sell in host nation markets. Yet in June 1992, at a conference in Fontainebleau, a prominent European Community official discussed unanticipated outcomes of trade policies; evidently the man (and apparently EC policy-makers) knew nothing at all of the large literature on multinational corporations.[22] One critic of my parameters – as presented in my earlier article – suggested that the history of nationalism and national sensitivity should be included.[23] My 'political parameter' is broad enough to encompass this. In any case, many types of political considerations are relevant to multinational enterprise activities.

My third parameter is the *familiarity* one. The more familiar conditions, the lower the transaction costs, the more likely multinationals are to invest. Familiarity involves geography, culture, language, imperial reach, and so forth. It relates to domestic firm behaviour, but is far more significant in the international context. Uncertainties have cost. Costs increase as uncertainty rises.[24]

The fourth parameter affecting corporate decision-making is the *third country* (or *countries*) one. I have found that multinationals not only consider a particular host nation, but will often view third-country conditions. These can serve to encourage or discourage investment. There are some multinational enterprise stakes that cannot be explained without this parameter. Take the case of Standard Oil Company of New Jersey's refinery in Aruba, built by a predecessor company in 1927–29. Why Aruba? Because of opportunity and political stability, certainly. Yet the island's proximity to Venezuela was crucial. More recently, as trade has become freer within the European Community, the configuration of a firm's existing plants frequently determines where subsequent ones are located within the Community. While this implies 'pathways' that establish next steps, more to the point, at least in my view, it is *not* considerations germane to the country of the parent, or to a particular host, but often to a third country (or countries) that *most* influence the choice.

Finally, there is the *corporate parameter*. How might factors distinctive to a particular enterprise shape choices? Here the learning process, the individual firm's experiences, and corporate style are paramount. Included under this rubric are the gives and takes, the bargaining relationships, internal to an enterprise. This parameter has clear domestic counterparts and is in no way special to international business.[25]

All these parameters vary in importance through time. Nothing in my analysis is static. The parameters are broad enough to incorporate change, and, as one traces the history of multinational enterprise, change is, of course, the norm. In my earlier article, 'Hosts to Transnational Investments', I divided the data into three arbitrary periods of roughly equal time span: 1870–1914 (44 years); 1914–50 (36 years); and 1950–92 (42 years). In each period, I tried to apply the paradigms – showing the impact of multinationals. It was in that context that I developed Tables 1–4 (see above). The five parameters seemed to hold up well as aids to interpret (to explain) the rankings on those tables. The temporal dimension showed, moreover, that countries once not significant hosts could become significant ones, and also important hosts might stop being hosts, normally because of political changes. Russia, for example, is in second place on Table 1, but does not appear on Tables 2–4; Cuba is in fourth place on Table 2, but absent from Tables 1, 3, and 4.

IV

What emerged from Tables 1–4 above, as indicated earlier, was that if we used as a criterion the level of FDI, developed countries ranked high as hosts and the consistently high rank of the United States and Canada was particularly notable. Yet, as I noted before, perhaps alternative yardsticks might be more appropriate in evaluating the general impact of multinationals on host nations. In considering suitable measures, I want to ponder the changing extent of multinational enterprise involvement and the assumption prevalent in the general literature, which is that today multinationals have more impact than in times past. I am uncomfortable with that conclusion, and the general problems discussed in the introduction to this essay compound the uncertainties.[26]

Based on long research on multinationals, I believe that the influence of multinationals on host nations has ebbed and flowed since the late nineteenth century, that there has been no simple linear progression to a status of 'more today', that different types of impacts – of varying importance – have been evident over the decades, and that the same companies have had divergent influences in different countries in different periods, and, most important, that we need a disciplined discussion of comparative hosts so as to rethink our overall appraisals of the dramatic developments in the world economy in the modern era. We need systematic, consistent means of comparing the role of companies that have made choices *vis-à-vis* different host countries. In short, we need to ask what measures are fitting for our task of understanding.[27]

As I have sought such bases for comparison through time, I become increasingly convinced that it is necessary to look at both the impact on domestic activities and on international integration. They are not the same. By definition, as a multinational plants itself in the soil of a host country, it would seem to be contributing to international integration. At the very least it is making a direct investment over borders and I argue that it is a conduit for the firm's package of attributes.

What it does subsequently *may* lead a host nation to become involved in greater, or possibly less, international trade; if the multinational firm participates in import substitution, it may well contribute to less international integration as defined by trade. If it finances operations within the host country, it reduces capital movements over borders. It may have influence on the domestic economy through its role in the international economy and/or through its domestic activities within the host economy. These distinctions are unique to the multinational enterprise. They do not exist when economists typically have discussions of the movement of products, capital and people over borders.

In discussing impact, my first, and rather obvious, insight is that depending on the size of the population of the host nation, the impact of the same amount of inward FDI will be different. The *World Development Report* ranks countries by gross domestic product per capita, not by gross domestic product. Were we to list countries by per capita FDI for 1914, 1929, and more recent years, the ranking would differ from that shown in Tables 1–4. But would such a measure greatly improve our understanding of the impact? I doubt it. To repeat, when one deals with multinationals, this is not identical with a discussion of FDIs, in flow, position, or – we can now add – per capita terms, since multinationals provide more than capital, more than simply FDI.[28]

Yet, fettered to tradition, I hesitated (at least not without more commentary) to drop the FDI criterion. Instead of viewing the global picture, perhaps a better approach would be to consider the level of inward FDI in each country as a percentage of that individual country's national wealth (both figures would be kept in the same currency, which would eliminate any foreign exchange distortions). However, since *both* available inward FDI stock figures (even those denominated in national currencies) and national wealth figures are terrible, such an exercise might end up being a waste of time. This is especially true when we deal with historical data. Suppose we could determine the level of inward FDI (denominated in a national currency) and look at it as a percentage of gross national product (or gross domestic product) through time and between countries, would this be preferable? While on a national basis this results in comparing apples and oranges (stock and flow data), it is not a bad idea – since it does give a sense of the overall size of the investment stake and for many countries gross national product (or gross domestic product) figures are reasonably good. The rankings in Table 5 are based on recent data calculations from the United Nations. Note the lofty rank of Singapore, and compare this with Table 4. On the other hand, the developed country, Canada, is still very high on the list – at least in 1970 and 1980. The United Nations has also calculated national ratios of FDI flows to gross domestic capital formation (GDCF), for five-year periods, during 1971 to 1989.[29] Based on these data, Table 6 provides a list of the top five nations in terms of the ratio of FDI flows to GDCF. No First World country is included in the top five countries in Table 6 in any one of the five-year periods. (Note, however, that comparisons between Tables 5 and 6 are flawed by the absence of data on certain countries.[30]) These two approaches to the study of the impact of multinational enterprise (availability of data notwithstanding) are, in my view, in the final analysis unsatisfactory (with Table 6 particularly inadequate), because the approaches still place the emphasis on the FDI measure and, as we have insisted, multinationals are conduits for more than capital.

Sometimes a way of showing contemporary impact has been to rank by sales, or assets, or market value, or employment, the largest companies within a particular host economy and count how many of these firms were foreign controlled. This can have merit. Analogous historical research by host countries might be able to identify the host countries' ten biggest firms. One could also, from an historical standpoint, rank at various periods a nation's ten most technologically advanced companies, and determine how many were foreign owned.

Still better, many students of multinationals have recently adopted another ranking hierarchy that also does not deal with inward FDI, but rather more specifically and with more focus it considers 'foreign owned firms'. It seeks to establish their shares of domestic sales and domestic

TABLE 5

INWARD FOREIGN DIRECT INVESTMENT STOCK AS A PERCENTAGE OF
GROSS DOMESTIC PRODUCT (SELECTED COUNTRIES)

(1)	(2)	(3)
1970*	1980*	1987/1988/1989
Country (%)	Country (%)	Country (%)
Canada (34.0)	Singapore 53.5)	1. Singapore (91.7)[a]
Singapore (30.9)	Canada (24.1)	2. Zimbabwe (58.3)[b]
	Netherlands (12.1)	3. Oman (45.6)[c]
	Australia (8.0)	4. Papua New Guinea (38.6)[a]
	Hong Kong (6.5)	5. Saudi Arabia (29.8)[c]
		6. Costa Rica (28.2)[b]
		7. Malaysia (27.7)[c]
		8. Fiji (26.2)[a]
		9. Botswana (22.9)[b]
		10. Netherlands (22.2)[a]
		11. Australia (22.2)[a]
		12. Hong Kong (22.2)[a]
		13. Canada (20.5)[a]

Note: (a) 1989; (b) 1988; (c) 1987.
Figures not available for any of the other 13 countries listed in column 3. Column 3
contains only those countries where inward foreign direct investment stock as a
proportion of gross domestic product was greater than 20 per cent.
Source: Adapted from *World Investment Report 1992*, pp. 326–30.

employment, exports and imports, and provision of government revenues. (In doing this, it must of course ascertain the size of host country
sales, host country employment, and so on.[31]) Sometimes, such data
home in on particular leading sector industries. When this is done, for
each measure, and for each selected year, it is possible (assuming
available data) to develop different rankings of countries – different
from (1) the standings by size of inward FDI, surely different from (2)
the order by inward FDI per capita or (3) inward FDI as a share of
national wealth (were we to have such measures), or from (4) inward
foreign investment as a percentage of gross national product or (5)
inward foreign investment flows as a percentage of gross domestic
capital formation, and moreover, the rankings within these new categories differ from one another! Tables 7 and 8 indicate some late
1970s–1980s shares of foreign affiliates in exports from host countries
and in employment in host countries.[32]

TABLE 6

INWARD FOREIGN DIRECT INVESTMENT STOCK AS A PERCENTAGE OF GROSS
DOMESTIC CAPITAL FORMATION (ONLY TOP FIVE COUNTRIES LISTED)

(1)	(2)	(3)	(4)
1971-5	1976-80	1981-85	1986-89
Country (%)	Country (%)	Country (%)	Country (%)
1. Liberia (37.3)	Botswana (24.1)	Seychelles (25.2)	Seychelles (39.1)
2. Congo (31.6)	Seychelles (20.1)	Singapore (17.4)	Singapore (35.2)
3. Trinidad & Tobago (22.3)	Swaziland (18.8)	Botswana (16.1)	Swaziland (30.3)
4. Barbados (20.4)	Liberia (18.7)	Papua New Guinea (15.1)	Botswana (25.7)
5. Swaziland (16.1)	Singapore (16.6)	Malaysia (10.8)	Hong Kong (19.1)

Note: The Congo, listed in column 1, is the People's Republic of the Congo (once a French colony); the former Belgian Congo has had the name Zaire since 1971.

Source: Adapted from *World Investment Report 1992*, pp. 322–5.

In the text to follow, I will provide added share data. As might be anticipated, the role of multinationals in Third World countries rises in importance when we use such percentage measures, albeit the high rank of the United Kingdom in Table 7 is impressive; and Canada, which is not included in Table 7 because of lack of information, ranks third in Table 8 and also third on a roster for the mid-1980s that listed foreign affiliates' percentage of sales in manufacturing.[33]

The variations in the rankings, depending on the yardstick, are striking. The figures compel the researcher, however, to study more carefully the historical and contemporary activities of multinational enterprise and to refine the answers to the fundamental question of whether the impacts of multinationals have increased over the late nineteenth and twentieth centuries – and, more important, just how the impacts have changed through time. As noted, the assumption by most present day writers is that the increase has been enormous. But the United Nations' newly developed measures cover only the 1970s and 1980s; in most cases *where* we have data, they seem to show increases. Yet, for recent decades, there are two outstanding exceptions: Canada and Nigeria. The relative decline in inward FDI stock as a percentage of gross domestic product in the case of Canada is apparent in the figures

TABLE 7

HOST COUNTRIES RANKED BY FOREIGN AFFILIATES' SHARE OF NATION'S
EXPORTS, 1985-90

Host Country (Year)	Foreign Affiliates' Percentage of Exports
Singapore (1988)	86.1[a]
Malaysia (1988)	45.7
United Kingdom (1988)	38.0
Argentina (1990)	37.3
Fiji (1985)	35.6
Philippines (1987)	34.7
France (1985)	32.0
Korea (1986)	29.0
Brazil (1987)	26.7[a]
Sri Lanka (1987)	26.2
Peru (1988)	25.3[b]
Germany, Federal Republic of (1986)	24.0
United States (1986)	23.0
Colombia (1987)	22.8
Paraguay (1988)	20.1
Pakistan (1988)	6.0
Japan (1984)	2.0

Notes: (a) Secondary sector only.
         (b) Primary sector only.

Sources: World Investment Report 1992, pp. 330–32; D. Julius, *Foreign Direct Investment*
         (Washington, DC, 1991), p. 10 (for France, the United States, West Germany
         and Japan). Data are not available for most host countries.

given on table 5 above. In Nigeria these percentages dropped from 12.1
in 1970 to 7.9 in 1988.[34] More will follow on the longer historical span –
and on our notion of ebbs and flows of influence.[35]

V

Is it possible to adopt any of these recent approaches and survey, in a
systematic manner, the historical impact of multinationals? Which
measures are best and why? Generally, it depends on the questions we
are asking. All of the above measures deal with economic impacts, none
with social and cultural impacts. The latter appear less amenable to

TABLE 8

HOST COUNTRIES RANKED BY FOREIGN AFFILIATES' SHARE OF
NATION'S EMPLOYMENT, 1976-88

Host Coutry (Year)	Foreign Affiliates' Percentage of Employment
Mauritius (1984)	65.4
Spain (1977)	46.6
Canada (1976)	41.0
Malaysia (1988)	32.2
Singapore (1988)	32.0
Argentina (1984)	26.8a
Fiji (1985)	25.0
Belgium/Luxembourg (1985)	18.0
Brazil (1987)	16.2
Chile (1979)	15.0
Austria (1985)	13.5
United Kingdom (1987)	13.0a
France (1984)	12.0
Italy (1985)	11.8
Germany, Federal Republic of (1982)	8.3
Portugal (1984)	8.2
Peru (1988)	6.5a
United States (1987)	3.7
Korea (1986)	2.7
Japan (1986)	0.4

Sources: World Investment Report 1992, pp. 330–2; D. Julius, *Foreign Direct Investment* (Washington, DC, 1991), p. 10 (for United Kingdom). J. Dunning, *Multinational Enterprises and the Global Economy* (Wokingham, 1993), p. 354 (for Canada, Singapore, France and Chile). Data are not available for many host countries.

quantitative treatment. As noted, multinationals have had two closely related impacts: (1) they influence the domestic host economy (penetrating within national borders) and (2) they influence that host economy's relationship with the outside world. Both are crucial, albeit separable.

Robert Reich has suggested that jobs are important and that it matters not whether they are furnished by domestic or by foreign-owned firms.[36] Indeed, if we study companies with long histories within a host country – Ford in Britain or Shell in the United States, for instance – these foreign-owned businesses have become integral parts of the domestic host economy. That these firms have foreign parents may be irrelevant in *certain* discussions (such as those on how many jobs they provide), while it is very relevant when we ask specific questions about the general impact of multinationals on the domestic host economy.[37] By contrast, that these affiliates have foreign parents is always important when we inquire about how multinationals influence the host economy's relationship with the outside world – *vis-à-vis* trade patterns, balance of payments considerations, technology inputs, organisational capabilities, competitive vigour, and the share of resources obtained at any given point in time – for instance.[38]

Let us take another two examples based on my research on the history of foreign investment in the United States. In the late nineteenth century, foreign-owned companies played a major role in the founding of the iron and steel industry in the southern United States. These companies' activities were not profitable, not long lasting, and the firms never exported, but they did contribute importantly to the establishment of a new industry. They did *not* in any way, except at origin (with the management, capital, technology transfers, and the demonstration of modern methods) integrate the US south into the world economy. In another sector, banking, in the late nineteenth and early twentieth century, foreign banks were crucial in America's *international* finance: in short-term trade financing as well as long-term capital transfers. Sometimes foreign banks extended into the US to carry on these functions. Yet, in that period, foreign banks were insignificant in US *domestic* banking. The foreign banks had, in sum, a major impact on America's relations with the outside world while virtually none on the structure of domestic banking institutions. In short, in two industries (iron and steel, banking) the impact of foreign multinationals was very diverse.[39]

Many of the traditional 'enclave' economies set up in the oil industry in Third World countries have altered host economies in dramatic fashions – and this is true whether we are talking about Venezuela or Saudi Arabia, for example. In each case, oil – initially developed solely by foreign multinationals – has generated high incomes, educated personnel, and a strong basis for growth.[40]

In short, in different sectors the roles of multinationals can vary, both over time and at any particular time. The impacts (however measured) have altered as the years have passed. Sometimes the linkage effects have been substantial and positive – and a company involved only in the external economic relationships serves to transform the host country's domestic economic institutions. At other times this has not been the case. The degree to which foreign multinationals' various offerings are absorbed to the benefit of the host nation is far from uniform. The nature of and the mix of the benefits (and costs) is dissimilar in different cases. Our measures of impacts must be narrow as well as broad, and we must look not only at the extent but also the quality of the impact.

In addition, there are short- and long-run impacts. A short-run impact may be more amenable to measurement by percentages at a particular point in time than the long-run consequences. The long-run impact on the host country deals with both the degree to which a nation is transformed (changed, recast) and the degree to which the nation is able (or unable) to benefit from the entry of multinationals. Regrettably, the percentage figures seem to provide only a starting point in evaluating the long-run impacts. The same individual multinational enterprise's expansion into two countries can have extremely diverse long-run impacts – depending on the circumstances in the host nation. And, it is on this matter that the specialist on the particular host nation makes his or her important contribution. Indeed, the specialist on the host country may throw the greatest light on questions of why the variations after the student of multinationals has determined the same presence in different countries. Also, despite my eagerness to rank countries, while the extent of many economic impacts is amenable to quantification (that is percentage of domestic employment provided by foreign-owned firms, percentage of national revenue generated by activities of foreign-owned firms, percentage of national savings held by affiliates of foreign banks), other economic influences are far less concrete. Thus, an impact that involved technology transfer can be measured in the number of patents registered, yet this has not been found to be a very effective measure in certain industries (it is better, for instance, in the chemical than in the automobile industry).[41] I know no one who has ranked the top technologically advanced firms in a nation over intervals and asked how many were foreign (a procedure suggested above as possible and one that might serve to identify the extent of the most far-reaching technological transfers). Also, what of the often profound influence of the multinational that is characterised by a demonstration effect, a learning experience, a building by nationals within the host country on the framework established by the foreign-owned firm. Such activities may be more consequential in the long run than the ones that show up in any of the numerical renditions. I do not hold to the view that if you cannot quantify it, it must not be important. Nonetheless, at a very minimum, when we can produce (as is possible) measures that reveal shares that are say 20, 30, 50, or 90 per cent in some key aspect of the economic life of a host country, we must accept significance on its face value and analyse the role of multinationals.

VI

In the late 1880s, nine-tenths of Japan's external trade was handled by foreign trading companies and carried on foreign ships. By 1914, the Japanese had taken over from the foreign multinationals much of the trade. In the late 1880s, foreign ships carried the largest part of US exports; this was still true in 1914.[42] In both situations trade had increased greatly. Why the difference?

In the Japanese case, overseas trade was far more vital to the economy; the substitution of control by the Japanese was of greater consequence to the economic growth of that nation. In the United States, with the formidable domestic market, resources were allocated differently. In both instances, foreign multinationals had impact, but conditions within the host country affected the longevity of the significant influence of the outsiders.[43]

It is possible to look at how trading companies moved basic commodities, cotton, grain, copper, and silk. In each commodity, multinational trading companies created the basis for international integration.[44] They were no less significant for US and Japanese exports than for the trade in Cuban sugar or Brazilian coffee. Yet, it seems that American and Japanese traders more quickly shared in the transactions related to international trade in commodities than did Cubans or Brazilians in providing conduits for their export trade.[45] Why was this the case? In all four instances the developments in foreign trade had impacts on the domestic economies.

Traders provided a market for commodities, which in turn stimulated domestic production – sometimes by the buyer and sometimes by host nation nationals. Henequen (sisal) growing in the Yucatan responded to the growth in external demand, yet buyers, which did manufacturing (twine making) in the United States, did not integrate backward into growing the crop.[46] By contrast, British capital developed the jute industry in India. An Indian historian writes

> Even when Indian merchant capital . . . actively invaded the jute industry during and after World War I, it still remained, for reasons that are not clear, much more dependent on Europeans than it ever was in the cotton textile industry.[47]

A student of the history of multinational enterprise should be able to explain the differential impact, based on the nature of British multinationals in the two industries (and in complementary activities).[48] British multinationals had impact on both cotton and jute, but a very different impact.

In 1914, six British managing agencies 'controlled' in India 51 per cent of the rupee capital invested in tea, 57 per cent in jute, and 52 per cent in coal.[49] It is not altogether clear what this means in terms of impact of multinationals – but the percentages are impressive.[50]

In certain commodities that moved into foreign trade, multinationals integrated their operations into growing. In sugar in Cuba and the Dominican Republic (in particular), in bananas throughout Central America and the Caribbean, in rubber in Malaya, the Dutch East Indies, and Liberia, foreign companies played a vital role in encouraging new agricultural exports.

So, too, many of the richest mineral deposits in the world were opened to commercial use in the late nineteenth and throughout the twentieth century by foreign-owned firms. Often, as these multinationals developed the resources, large companies with substantial impact on the host country took on the major role. In 1928, fully 43 per cent of the oil produced in Latin America in 1928, was by two multinational enterprises – Royal Dutch Shell and Standard Oil of New Jersey.[51] In 1937, 88 per cent of the oil in the Netherlands East Indies was produced by these same two companies.[52]

For decades, foreign multinationals provided the overwhelming portion (far more than 50 per cent) of many countries' export revenues. This was true for many years for all the key (and some of the lesser) oil producing and exporting countries (Iran, Iraq, Saudi Arabia, Kuwait, Libya, Venezuela, the Dutch East Indies/Indonesia, Trinidad, for example), for the copper producers (Chile, Northern Rhodesia/Zambia, the Belgian Congo/Zaire), for the bauxite ones (Guyana, Surinam, Jamaica, Guinea), and for those in tin (Malaya in particular). These activities transformed national economies, integrating them into the world economy as never before.

Lest one think that multinationals were only crucial in primary sector activities, we can consider a country such as Canada where the impact of the multinational was both in the primary and secondary sectors (but not in the tertiary one). Here the impact was from the start not confined to international relations. Foreign multinationals created new *domestic* industries (designed to serve Canadian domestic markets). Canada ranks at or near the top on most of the lists of host countries both in absolute terms and in percentages – and over a long period of time (see Tables 1, 2, 3, and 4). It also has a very high standing over time when using certain share criteria. In 1926, American ownership and control accounted for 32 per cent of Canadian mining and smelting and 30 per cent of Canadian manufacturing; by 1962, these figures were respectively 51 and 45 per cent. By 1979, foreign-owned firms (US and others) accounted for 75 per cent of petroleum and natural gas production in Canada, 50 per cent of Canada's mining and smelting, and 60 per cent of the nation's total manufacturing. In particular industrial sectors, the figures were far more dramatic: in 1979, foreign multinationals undertook 86 per cent of Canada's chemical and pharmaceutical, 90 per cent of its rubber and electrical, and 96 per cent of its automotive production.[53] As presented, these micro-economic data would suggest an increase in multinational influence over the years, yet using other more macro-economic measures (see Table 5 herein) there seems evidence of a substantial decline in the extent of the impact in the period 1970–89.[54] If we consider Great Britain and look, as Geoffrey Jones has done, at the size of FDI in 1914 in Britain, the country seems to rank relatively low in the world-wide picture of hosts to multinationals. Moreover, if we focus on the forces that integrated Britain into the world community (trade, capital flows, and so on), one does not perceive of Britain as a host nation. By contrast, if our spotlight is on manufacturing *within* the country and more particularly on the leading modern sectors, we encounter a dramatic change in our perspective. Here the demonstration and linkage effects that came from the multinationals were formidable, for by 1914, in all the 'new features' of British life, the telephone, the portable camera, the phonograph, the electric street car, the automobile, the typewriter, and the elevator, American multinationals were 'supreme'.[55] Even more difficult to appraise are the linkage effects, stemming from foreign multinationals, in Japanese economic growth. There is substantial evidence that US automobile and electrical companies, for example, had major consequences in the early stages of the development of Japanese industry. Yet, our standard broad measures in no way reflect this impact.[56]

It is not only in First World countries that multinationals have provided the basis for the development of significant manufacturing. The sequencing in time was in the main later, but the pattern was not dissimilar. Take the case of the Brazilian automobile industry. Multinationals have created a totally new manufacturing industry.[57] And what of Singapore? Note its prominent rank in Tables 5 to 8 above. Has its experience historical precedent? The World Bank now includes Singapore as a high-income country.[58] Whether dealing with First World or Third World (or former Third World) nations, when we focus our attention on particular, specified leading industrial sectors, the readings on the impact of multinationals are much stronger.[59]

The influence of multinationals in the tertiary sector requires far more study. We have included above something on the historical impact of trading and shipping companies. Geoffrey Jones' new work on British

overseas banking shows that in certain host countries British overseas
banks provided the foundation for *domestic* banking services.[60] And, in
1990, affiliates of foreign banks held fully 21.4 per cent of all US banking
assets; this is a far cry from the late nineteenth and early twentieth
century when, as noted, foreign banks had little impact on US *domestic*
banking, but a major impact on America's international financial
relationships.[61]

VII

Hopefully, the cursory survey given above has been adequate to suggest
to the reader that over the years there has been an important impact by
foreign multinationals on host nations at various stages of development
and that depending on the particular yardstick we can arrive at different
rankings of hosts and indeed, different conclusions. An exploration of
the variety in measures enriches our analysis on the extent of the
impact. I have tried to show – thus far – the problems with different
measures, and how they tell us about different facets of the economic
impact.

But measurements of the extent of the impact fail to tell us much
about the 'quality' of the impact. We have seen that already as we
considered the inadequacies of broad quantitative measures (those on
the amount of investment) in relation to the historical impact of multinationals on the Japanese economy. We have not, however, dealt
(except in passing) with the really fundamental question of whether the
impact has positive, negative, or indifferent consequences. It is not
enough to establish that there was an impact; the next set of questions
on the effects must follow: are they pro, con, or neutral, on economic
growth and development? Can we measure – or at least weigh – with any
degree of objectivity the gains and losses? *Perceived* impacts have often
formed the basis of public policy. Whether after 1917 in Russia or in
many Third World countries in the 1960s and especially in the 1970s,
because of perceived impacts, because of economic ideology, substantial multinational enterprise activity came to a conclusion. It is crucial to
separate the rhetoric on from the realities of past as well as present
impacts of multinationals in host nations.

On the impact of multinationals, the specialist literature (that on
individual hosts, on host regions, on economic development) has had an
immense amount to say, with conclusions that cover a wide range. Too
much of the vast literature on this subject (especially that dealing with
Third World countries) is so narrow and so ignorant of multinational
enterprise behaviour that it is tainted from the start. Yet, there are

perceptive commentators on Third World as well as First World host countries.[62] The specialist literature also considers the non-economic consequences of multinationals, which are very relevant in host country policy-making. Non-economic effects include those on national security, national independence, cultural identity, and so forth. Often these issues are today and have been in earlier years *more important* in public policy-making than the strictly economic ones.[63]

The range of multinational enterprises' economic impact issues go from the general to the particular. The most general, of course, are: does the presence of foreign multinationals add to national income? what are the benefits and costs in relation to national income that come through the type of integration into the world economy that results from the operations of foreign multinationals?[64] how do foreign multinationals affect the distribution of income? do they cause 'immiserising growth'? Most economists are ready to grant that multinationals contribute to efficiency; many are less certain that they add to equity.

More specifically, what is the effect on national saving and investment, on job creation, on the bargaining power of labour, on tax revenues, on the balance of payments, on the balance of trade, on exports, on the gains from trade, on the terms of trade, on national competitiveness, and on national entrepreneurship and small business enterprise? Does the participation of multinational enterprise result in the 'appropriate' (the best) allocation of domestic resources, or does it in some manner bias the process?[65] How does the presence of multinational enterprise affect government fiscal, monetary, and industrial policies? And, what is the effect on the course of technological innovation within the host country? What is the influence on the skill-level, the nature and training of human capital?

In dealing with these many impacts, both direct and 'spill-over' effects have to be considered.[66] Many economists attempt to study these questions in a static rather than dynamic manner. Yet, if the role of multinationals is to be evaluated, the economic historian argues it must be seen over time. Short-term impacts often diverge from those in the long term. It is, accordingly, legitimate to inquire into the extent to which multinationals create the basis for new economic activities, by generating commercially valuable resources. If there is no conduit for the exploration, development, and marketing of oil, for instance, the resource has no commercial value. Often, the economic contributions of multinationals relate to the transmission of the managerial capabilities to develop not only primary, but secondary and tertiary sectors within the host economy, which over time have immense positive impact on economic development. These activities add to national income; however conventional appraisals of how national income grows often neglect them (students of multinationals may be left with Edward Denison's 'residual').

A difficulty in addressing these and many other questions on the positive and negative aspects of the impact lies in the problem of the counterfactual, the assumptions. For each host country, to determine the gain or losses from multinationals, we must assume the absence of such entities. We know that in the absence *ceteris paribus* does not apply, so we must probe more deeply, asking what happens with the multinational's presence. Often our evaluations get caught in the complexity.[67] Although economic growth is a complex process, it is possible to analyse this process in a systematic manner, taking into account the activities of multinational enterprise. The United Nations' *World Investment Report 1992* considers multinationals as 'engines of growth' and looks at the particulars on that 'engine's' performance.[68]

Economic historians must go back in time and evaluate the nature as well as the extent of the long-run impacts. We need to do this from the perspective of the multinational enterprise as an institution, not merely focusing on its investment aspects. We are back to our introductory proposition – multinational enterprise and FDI are not the same; multinationals make FDIs, but more fundamental they transfer over borders an entire business package that includes products, processes, experience, reputation, knowledge of where and how to find financing, marketing know-how and networks, trade marks, technology, research and development background, information, managerial expertise, and so on. This package is what is transmitted, not solely the financing of an affiliate. It is the entire package that continues to be managed within a multinational enterprise structure that must be judged as an evaluation is made on the role the firm plays in the economy of any individual host nation and in the latter's relations with the outside world. Perhaps we should not be too absorbed in impossible-to-obtain precise measures of costs and benefits, and instead should look more closely at the overall performance of multinationals in economic growth and development, considering with more care the quality of and the general long-run consequences of their presence.

In doing so, we will have to ask what is distinctive within each host that influences and alters the gains and losses and the absorption process. Why in some economies have there been sizeable and sustained linkage effects, while in others the long-run impact has been less impressive? Here, for the student of the history of the international economy, we get into a truly exciting subject. Why is it that the same company in different environs, carrying on the same types of activities may have in the long run a totally different impact?[69] What is the role of host government policies in shaping the impact of the multinational enterprise? In determining this, I am not certain that any single policy solution (open versus closed policies) explains the *qualitative* impact of multinationals – especially those impacts in the arena of demonstration and linkage effects, short or long term.

Once we verify the extent of the presence in the twentieth century of multinational enterprise, once we know why the multinational has spread in which direction and when, once we have a framework to inquire on economic impacts, then the next set of queries must concentrate on comparisons and contrasts related to the interactions within each individual host nation, for, to repeat, multinational enterprises not only affect the host's external economic relationships but its *domestic* economy as well. This interpenetration and the resulting interactions within the host economy are absolutely fundamental to an understanding of the costs and benefits. The responses to and behaviour *vis-à-vis* multinationals within a host country – including both private and public sector (government policy) responses and behaviour – are essential in considering economic growth. It is both the behaviour of the outsider, the multinationals, *and* conditions within the host nation that explain impacts over time.

VIII

Both less developed and developed countries have been affected as hosts by the spread of multinational corporations. From the late nineteenth century to the present there have been impacts by multinationals on a large number of different host nations. There has, however, been little systematic *comparative* historical study of these impacts on both developed and Third World hosts. Multinational enterprises can have many kinds of impacts; measures of the level of FDI while of interest are insufficient, in and of themselves, when we consider the impacts. Rather what we should be looking at more closely is the entire multinational firm as it moves internationally and its varieties of effects on the development of host nations over long periods.

Depending on the measures used and the period for which we make the measurement, rankings of countries by importance as hosts vary dramatically. Nonetheless, it seems possible to conclude that if we study gross figures *and* linkages and demonstration effects, First World countries emerge as key recipients – and not only Canada. With gross figures the United States ranks high. But Japan, over the years a relatively small recipient of FDI, nevertheless incorporated many contributions of multinationals (which becomes evident when we study linkages and demonstration effects). By contrast, if our focus is on shares (percentage measures), less developed countries take on a much more important rank. Thus, in 'share figures', the United States – because of its giant economy – does not rank very high historically as a recipient of FDI, while in absolute terms, as shown in Tables 1–4, it was near the top. However, if we narrow our focus to shares in particular specified activities, then it is an admixture of both developed and less developed countries that take on great prominence in the rankings as hosts.

The paper provides figures and information that suggest that in developed as well as less developed countries the extent of the impacts was often sizeable – sometimes persistent and sometimes not. Thus, as noted, Russia, near the top of the list provided in Table 1, is on no other list. The figures given above on foreign investors' control over certain facets of Indian industry in the early twentieth century have no counterpart in 1993. The paper should push us to study changing and various impacts.

It should, moreover, prompt us to recognise that the size, the extent of the impact, may be very separate from the qualitative aspects (pros and cons) of the impact. Determining that the extent was great merely makes us recognise that this is a topic worthy of study. The extent of the impact, by itself, tells us very little about the long-run effects on growth. The next step must be to evaluate the consequences, the economic costs and benefits of the multinational enterprise on the individual host nation's development. This paper argues that the analysis must be holistic and complex and not simply deal with one impact facet (such as balance of payments or exports or contribution to capital accumulation) to the exclusion of others. It must examine *both* the effects in relation to international integration *and* other effects that are normally considered when discussing a host country's domestic economy.

We need to view the multinational enterprise as a conduit not only of capital, but also, far more important, of new technology, new ways of doing things, and as a means by which global integration of various sorts went forward. Then we need to appraise the role of multinationals in providing for (or some – not the present author – would argue, holding back) host nation economic growth, welfare, and competitiveness.

It would seem appropriate to blend our discussion into the general literature on the growth of the world economy. We must depart from the complete transfer notions of goods, people, capital, technology *movements*, and consider instead the distinctive role of the multinational enterprise as it integrates the world economy through managerial co-ordination. This paper, in trying to compare hosts over time, high-lights this issue. The firm, making choices shaped by the parameters outlined earlier in this paper, penetrates within the borders of nations. As economic and business historians, I believe, we should not let students of economic development or sociology capture what is our subject. The scattered statistics in this paper show that in historical terms multinationals mattered to the economies of many host nations at different levels of development – in different periods. How they mattered was extremely uneven – and how long they mattered even more uneven.

Most important, to repeat, the extent of the impact does not deal with the quality of the impact; what requires more inter-country research is how host nations were (or were not) able to absorb what the multi-national enterprise introduced – how they responded to the multi-nationals' activities. The impacts of multinational enterprise on the development of particular host economies were frequently divergent.

In sum, my argument is that students of economic growth and devel-opment should consider the role of multinationals in the economic progress of nations. In doing so, they should concentrate less (than in the past) on the investment aspects *per se*, but rather more broadly on the overall part played by multinational enterprise. In doing this, we may need to revise our standard thinking about the history of the world economy in the late nineteenth and twentieth centuries. We need to go beyond the extent-of-impact criteria and provide more substance to the positive and negative, general and specific, impacts of multinationals on economic change. Hopefully, using the above framework, some of the comparative questions can be better specified and better answered – in a global context.

NOTES

This paper has been greatly enriched by suggestions from Alfred Chandler, Lou Wells, Geoffrey Jones, Mark Mason, Edward Graham, Tony Corley, John Dunning, Knut Borchardt, Harm Schröter, Hans Pohl, Joe Tulchin, Mary Yeager, and two anonymous referees; as always I have learned from (and incorporated) the ideas of Raymond Vernon, Jean-François Hennart, and Mark Casson.

1. It is now generally accepted that multinational enterprises have had a long history and that the modern multinational enterprise dates from the late nineteenth century. On the early history, see M. Wilkins, *The Emergence of Multinational Enterprise: American Business Abroad from the Colonial Era to 1914* (Cambridge, MA, 1970); idem, 'Japanese Multinational Enterprise before 1914', *Business History Review*, Vol.60 (Spring 1986), pp.199–231; idem, 'European and North American Multinationals, 1870–1914', *Business History*, Vol.30 (Jan. 1988), pp.8–45.
2. The search was for an article to include in M. Wilkins (ed.), *The Growth of Multinationals* (Aldershot, 1991). There was not only no article but no book on the subject.
3. 'Hosts to Transnational Investments: A Comparative Analysis', forthcoming in a volume

edited by Hans Pohl and to be published in a supplement to the *Zeitschrift für Unternehmensgeschichte*.
4. Such historical studies include F.V. Carstensen, *American Enterprise in Foreign Markets: Studies of Singer and International Harvester in Imperial Russia* (Chapel Hill, NC, 1984); M. Mason, *American Multinationals and Japan* (Cambridge, MA, 1992); G. Jones, 'Foreign Multinationals and British Industry before 1945', *Economic History Review*, 2nd series, Vol.41 (Aug. 1988), pp.429–53; R. Tignor, *Egyptian Textiles and British Capital* (Cairo, 1989); S. Cochran, *Big Business in China: Sino-Foreign Rivalry in the Cigarette Industry, 1890–1930* (Cambridge, MA, 1980); H. Shapiro, 'Determinants of Firm Entry into the Brazilian Automobile Manufacturing Industry, 1956–1968', *Business History Review*, Vol.65 (Winter 1991), pp.876–947; C. Jones, 'Commercial Banks and Mortgage Companies', in D.C.M. Platt (ed.), *Business Imperialism, 1840–1930: An Inquiry Based on British Experience in Latin America* (Oxford, 1977), pp.17–52. See also the notes to Wilkins, 'Hosts to Transnational Investments'.
5. Contemporary appraisals of multinationals in Third World countries are abundant. By the 1990s, practically every development economics text on a contemporary basis compares less developed country hosts to multinationals. L.T. Wells, 'Foreign Investor Relations with Third-World Countries' (unpublished article, 1992) provides an excellent bibliography on multinationals in Third World countries. I have found particularly useful J.M. Stopford and S. Strange, *Rival States, Rival Firms* (Cambridge, 1991) for contemporary comparative data on Third World hosts; the book's title notwithstanding, it is almost exclusively on Third World hosts. Likewise, the *World Investment Report, 1992*, published by the United Nations, has fine materials on contemporary impacts. Two books that do compare – with an historical perspective – certain developed country hosts are G. Laxer, *Open for Business* (Toronto, 1989), which compares Canada and Sweden, and S. Reich, *The Fruits of Fascism* (Ithaca, NY, 1990), which compares Germany and Britain as hosts to automobile multinationals. K. Levitt, *Silent Surrender* (Toronto, 1970) compares Canada and Third World nations as hosts.
6. By traditional, I mean that this is now a commonly accepted definition. See, however, Wilkins, 'Hosts to Transnational Investments', for a long discussion of the variations in definitions that have and continue to muddy the waters of both historical and contemporary analysis.
7. *World Investment Report, 1992*, p.254.
8. John Dunning has been the pioneer in trying to do this, although most of his rankings were by region rather than by country. His most recent historical rankings by host nation and region are in J.H. Dunning, *Multinational Enterprises and the Global Economy* (Wokingham, 1993), pp.20, 118.
9. Geoffrey Jones has suggested to me that his current research would indicate that European developed countries as hosts have been neglected in the various statistical tabulations and further research might well place some of them far higher on the rosters than is indicated on my tables.
10. There is, for example, no table in the *World Development Report* that presents the stock of inward foreign direct investments. The International Monetary Fund has since 1945 sought to develop uniform methods of balance of payments accounting, but the numbers prepared for such purposes are inadequate for a comparative study of host nations' stock of FDIs. If we had good outward stock figures by country, we could, of course, develop inward ones. Yet see the frustrations Geoffrey Jones and Harm Schröter encountered as they attempted to develop such data for their excellent new book, G. Jones and H. Schröter (eds.), *The Rise of Multinationals in Continental Europe* (Aldershot, 1993), pp.10–11.
11. Lou Wells, after reviewing Table 4, noted that in Indonesia approvals would not include investments in the oil industry! I tried with Tables 1 and 2 to include and to exclude according to my own set definition. When I got to 1980s material this sort of detailed statistical work cannot be done by a single individual with other competing obligations.
12. Nonetheless, I would still like to have – should some graduate student tackle the problem – a set of figures through time that did reveal the total level of FDI world-wide at certain specified dates and then the share of this world-wide total by host nation. In M. Wilkins,

The History of Foreign Investment in the United States to 1914 (Cambridge, MA, 1989), p.145, I calculated worldwide stock of foreign investment and from those figures, it was simple to determine that the United States, which was the world's largest host, attracted 15.8 per cent of the world-wide foreign investment. This, however, was for foreign investment, *not* FDI. There is considerable evidence that a nation's rank as a recipient of foreign investment and of FDI may not coincide.

13. *World Investment Report, 1992.*
14. I am indebted to a very perceptive anonymous reader for this point.
15. I am not using the word, truncation, as do mathematicians or statisticians, nor am I adopting the usage of game theorists. Whereas the game theorist 'truncates' (stops the process) when the outcome is established, in my usage truncation occurs when the scholar breaks into an existing whole and looks solely at one part in isolation, neglecting the uncertainties inherent in the overall behaviour of the firm. The whole, the fabric to which I refer is what R.E. Caves, in *Multinational Enterprise and Economic Analysis* (Cambridge, 1982), p.3, calls the 'transactional advantages' of placing plants under common ownership. The intangible assets that create the basis for the enterprise as a whole are the warp and weft of this fabric. Indeed, the fabric is the very nature of the firm itself. I am indebted to Monty Graham and Ronald Harstad for explaining the divergence in my concept of 'truncation' from that of others' usages.
16. The phrase 'organisational capability' is Alfred D. Chandler's.
17. A sizeable literature exists on the public goods characteristics of technology transfer within multinational enterprise: the consumption of the good by one consuming unit (that is, an affiliate in the host country) does not exhaust its availability to the parent or other consuming units. For a start see C. Kindleberger, 'International Public Goods without International Government', *American Economic Review*, Vol.76 (March 1986), p.2.
18. Chandler made an important point – applicable to multinationals as well as domestic firms – when he wrote recently that in studying the evolution of the firm he differed from Oliver Williamson in that for the latter the transaction is the unit of analysis, whereas for Chandler the firm is fundamental. A.D. Chandler, 'Organisational Capabilities and the Economic History of the Industrial Enterprise', *Journal of Economic Perspectives*, Vol.6 (Summer 1992), p.85. I could not agree more.
19. These five are included and explained in far more detail in Wilkins, 'Hosts to Transnational Investments'.
20. Despite the urging of one colleague, I refuse to rank these parameters; all of these considerations are important, but the importance (the rank) varies sharply in different times and situations.
21. J.N. Bhagwati, E. Dinopoulos and K.-Y. Wong, 'Quid Pro Quo Foreign Investment', *American Economic Review*, Vol.82 (May 1992), p.189, refer to the 'conventional politics-free approaches' to the theory of multinationals. My work does not fall into that category.
22. Peter Buckley, an expert on multinational enterprise, and I were taken aback at how a literature that we both knew well could have so little general visibility.
23. This point was made by Joe Tulchin. Of course he is right; this is an important consideration and fits under the political parameter.
24. My original findings were that over time *more* areas became familiar as the experience of an individual firm grew. In the 1980s, however, studies have determined that the 'clustering of FDI had become more pronounced, with host countries tending to be clustered around a single triad member [the United States, the European Community, or Japan] located in the same geographical region'. *World Investment Report, 1992*, pp.32, 318–19. The implication is that familiarity reinforces familiarity. The familiarity parameter is especially helpful in explaining why firms of different nationalities (in the same industry) will often make dissimilar country choices in their investment patterns.
25. I have already heard major criticisms of these five parameters. Most of the criticisms have related to their conformity to or lack of conformity with the existing theoretical literature. On conformity, as noted in the text, I am deeply indebted to and influenced by others; the formulation is based on my own and others' research. The discussion of the parameters (and the praise and battering they encountered) at a Munich meeting in August 1992

confirmed in my own mind their validity. One critic objected to the absence of discussion of defensive investments (but see Wilkins, 'Hosts to Transnational Investments', note 29, and material therein on the political parameter). Another objection was that 'rivalries' between firms, follow-my-leader investments, were omitted; I would put such motives under the 'opportunities' and 'corporate' parameters (firm 1 perceives opportunities; firm 2 assumes opportunities because of firm 1's choices). A different critic suggested that competitive conditions (which differed by industry) should be added; I felt once more that these were incorporated under the 'opportunities' and the 'corporate' perceptions of opportunities parameters. Another critic noted that in dealing with 'experience' of individual corporations as a determinant of choices, in my 'Hosts to Transnational Investments', I should have cited the work of William H. Davidson. While my ideas did not come directly from Davidson, they may well have emerged from conversations with and readings of those who did obtain their ideas from Davidson; accordingly, he certainly should have been cited (my apologies). Yet another critic believed I should have more than five parameters; after much debate, I thought that each of his additions could be conveniently housed within one of my five categories. Accordingly, this paper repeats the five parameters given in Wilkins, 'Hosts to Transnational Investments'.

26. The opening statement in the *World Investment Report, 1992*, p.1, surely typifies the general literature of today: 'Transnational corporations have been central organisers of economic activities in an increasingly integrated world economy'.

27. Outstanding books on the history of the world economy – see for example R. Cameron, *A Concise Economic History of the World* (New York, 1989) – do not deal with the role of multinationals. The splendid A.G. Kenwood and A.L. Lougheed, *The Growth of the International Economy, 1820–1990* (3rd edn. 1992) does consider FDI but usually in the context of capital flows.

28. For technical reasons too complicated to explain in a short article, I am absolutely convinced that using *flow* data on FDI is not an appropriate way of measuring FDI much less the impact of such stakes. I am thus using the superior stock measures throughout my discussion.

29. *World Investment Report, 1992*, pp.322–30 (these percentages are in many cases broken down by primary, secondary, and tertiary sectors). By all the share measures in the 1980s, Singapore ranks very high, in the top one or two world-wide, but it is not even in the top ten when measured by absolute amount of inward FDI. The inward FDI flows as a percentage of gross domestic capital are in the United Nations data compared with the ratio of gross domestic capital formation to gross domestic product.

30. The data in *World Investment Report, 1992*, pp.322–5, on inward FDI flows as a percentage of gross domestic capital formation, do, however, include developed countries; Canada (for example) ranks way down on the list in all of these four sets of years and indeed in the 1981–85 set, there is a negative percentage (i.e. an outflow).

31. The US Department of Commerce and the United Nations, as well as many other tabulators, are using such measures, with the share of government revenue measure the one least used.

32. In Wilkins, 'Hosts to Transnational Investments', Tables 6 and 7, I gave other rankings of host countries: by foreign affiliates' percentage of sales in the manufacturing sector and percentage of employment in the manufacturing sector.

33. In Canada in 1986 foreign affiliates accounted for 49 per cent of the sales in the manufacturing sector (Wilkins, 'Hosts to Transnational Investments', Table 6).

34. *World Investment Report, 1992*, p.327–8. In the case of India, FDI stock as a percentage of gross domestic product was merely one per cent in 1970, whereas it was down to 0.9 per cent in 1985. It had gone up to slightly over one per cent in 1975 and 1980, so there really was not a significant trend line for the last decades. Other measures would suggest, however, a far more significant role of multinationals in India in the years before the 1960s than in the years after the 1970s.

35. A colleague suggested that the gross measures (even adjusted for inflation) would grow larger over time; but with expropriations and political changes, it seems evident that both the share and the gross measures ebb and flow.

48   THE MAKING OF GLOBAL ENTERPRISE

36. R. Reich, *Work of Nations* (New York, 1991), p.285.
37. Similarly, when the US Food and Drug Administration makes a determination that a drug is safe and effective, it is irrelevant to that decision whether the medicine was produced in the United States by a domestically owned or foreign owned company. See *New York Times*, 20 March 1993, on approval of Betaseron, a new drug to treat multiple sclerosis (made in the United States by Chiron Corporation and by Berlex Labs, a subsidiary of Schering, AG). That a known reliable foreign affiliate was involved was not a consideration in the deliberations on approvals.
38. By share of resources obtained at any particular time, I am assuming that multinationals' accumulated choices over the years serve to allocate resources and that a corporate decision made to build, to buy, or to operate a plant in one country *rather* than another influences 'share' of resources obtained at any point in time (this is different from arguing a zero sum game, for over time, the choice of one host country certainly does not preclude another). Indeed, far from all corporate decisions involve choices between countries, but some clearly do – as for example the decision on which particular nation in the European Community might be an appropriate site for a new plant to serve that market.
39. Wilkins, *History of Foreign Investment in the United States to 1914*, pp.246–52 (iron and steel); Ch.13 (banking); also, idem, 'Foreign Banks and Foreign Investment in the United States', in R. Cameron and V.I. Bovykin (eds.), *International Banking, 1870–1914* (New York, 1991), pp.233–52.
40. In M. Wilkins, *The Maturing of Multinational Enterprise: American Business Abroad from 1914 to 1970* (Cambridge, MA, 1974), pp.399–400, I documented the beginnings of the breakdown of enclave economies; the process has greatly accelerated in recent years.
41. Graham Taylor, in the present publication, discusses technology transfers by parent companies to their affiliates in Canada. Implicitly, he is dealing with impacts and yet he offers no, nor does he find a, satisfactory measure to answer the questions of how much impact. Indeed, he separates his work from the literature that is too (?) oriented toward measuring the results of technology transfer rather than the process and its consequences.
42. M. Wilkins, 'Japanese Multinationals in the United States: Continuity and Change, 1879–1990', *Business History Review* Vol.64 (Winter 1990), p.594; S.G. Sturmey, *British Shipping and World Competition* (1962), p.130, and Wilkins, *History of Foreign Investment in the United States to 1914*, pp.517–19.
43. Americans during the First World War gained control of their shipping, albeit only temporarily. In 1913, only 14 per cent of the shipping in American trades was American (by place of registration); in 1920 it was 50.8 per cent, but by 1929 it was down to 37.6 per cent (Sturmey, *British Shipping*, p.130). There was no comparable fluctuation in the Japanese control over Japanese shipping. Once achieved, it was maintained.
44. As indicated in my text, my definition of multinationals includes service firms that operate over borders.
45. I found very stimulating a session that dealt with commodity exports at the American Historical Association meeting, Washington, DC, December 1992, organised by Steven Topik of the University of California, Irvine.
46. At least in the Yucatan. See A. Wells, 'Henequen and the Hard Fibers Market', forthcoming, and F. Carstensen and D. Roazen, 'Foreign Market, Domestic Initiative, and the Emergence of a Monocrop Economy: The Yucatecan Experience, 1825–1903', *Hispanic American Historical Review* Vol.62 (Nov. 1992), pp.555–92.
47. M.D. Morris, 'Indian Industry and Business in the Age of Laissez Faire', in R.K. Ray (ed.), *Entrepreneurship and Industry in India, 1800–1947* (Delhi, 1992), p.209.
48. There were few traditionally defined European multinationals in basic cotton textiles, although trading companies handled raw cotton imports, cotton goods exports, and machinery exports. There were a number of 'free standing companies' in cotton textile production in India. See M. Wilkins, 'Efficiency and Management: A Comment on Gregory Clark's "Why Isn't the Whole World Developed?" ', *Journal of Economic History*, Vol.47 (Dec. 1987), pp.981–3; see also idem, 'The Free-Standing Company, 1870–1914: An Important Type of British Direct Investment', *Economic History Review*, 2nd series, Vol.LXI (May 1988), pp.259–82. On this subject, S. Chapman, *Merchant*

Enterprise in Britain (Cambridge, 1992), is very useful.
49. R.K. Ray, 'Introduction', in idem (ed.), *Entrepreneurship*, p.37.
50. Students of multinationals, once they have eliminated the top tier of ownership (the individual shareholders), have defined the multinational firm (with its cluster of affiliates) in terms of an equation of ownership and control. Yet, in the case of India, often the ownership aspect was negligible but the control (through the managing agency) might be substantial. On some of the problems of ownership and control, see M. Wilkins, 'Defining a Firm: History and Theory', in P. Hertner and G. Jones (eds.), *Multinationals: Theory and History* (Aldershot, 1986), pp.80–95. In the Indian context more needs to be done on this topic: managing agencies should be re-examined, taking into account the research on the history of multinational enterprise.
51. Based on data in 'Report of the Group on 'American Petroleum Interests in Foreign Countries', 15 Oct. 1945, in US Senate, Special Committee Investigating Petroleum Resources, *American Petroleum Interests in Foreign Countries*, Hearings, 79th Cong., 1st sess. (1945), pp.354–7 and J. Brown, 'Latin America and Foreign Oil Companies', forthcoming paper. These are my own calculations and were presented in comments prepared for the American Historical Association meeting, December 1992.
52. W.N. Medlicott, *The Economic Blockade*, Vol.1 (1952), p.384.
53. See sources for these figures in Wilkins, 'Hosts to Transnational Investments'.
54. We are back to the problem of valid measures, how we use these measures, and choices of benchmark dates.
55. Jones, 'Foreign Multinationals and British Industry before 1945'; Wilkins, *Emergence of Multinational Enterprise*, pp.215–7.
56. On the impact of US business on the Japanese automobile and telephone industries, see, for example, M. Wilkins, 'The Contribution of Foreign Enterprises to Japanese Economic Development', and M. Mason, 'With Reservations: Prewar Japan as Host to Western Electric and ITT', in T. Yuzawa and M. Udagawa (eds.), *Foreign Business in Japan before World War II* (Tokyo, 1990), pp.42–9, 176–85. More narrow measures provide the basis for better analysis: thus, Ford and General Motors appear to have supplied in excess of 90 per cent of the Japanese automobile market from the mid-1920s to the mid-1930s. Wilkins, 'The Contribution', pp.43–5.
57. See Shapiro, 'Determinants'. While in both Japan and Brazil, foreign multinationals were instrumental in the emergence of the industry, in Japan the manufacturing industry came of age under the control of Japanese owned firms, while in Brazil, the development was under the control of foreign multinational enterprises.
58. *World Development Report, 1992*, p.219.
59. Multinationals do not invest evenly in manufacturing in any host country. Often multinationals invest in the most advanced sectors, where they have advantage. If one looks at individual industrial sectors, the concentration shows up in the percentage figures. This is evident, for example, in Jones, 'Foreign Multinationals and British Industry before 1945'.
60. G. Jones, *British Multinational Banking, 1830–1990* (Oxford, 1993).
61. E.M. Graham and P.R. Krugman, *Foreign Direct Investment in the United States* (Washington, DC, 2nd edn., 1991), p.30.
62. There is often now in the Third World host country literature a tendency to see today's multinationals as 'good' (or at least not terrible), while the ones of yesteryear remain the 'bad giants'. On some of the best contributions by specialists, see the works cited in notes 4 and 5 above.
63. Conceptually, the economic and non-economic issues can be separated. At times, there is a convergence since we live in a world of nations and it makes economic sense for national policy makers to carry out certain strategies under certain known political conditions. A colleague, Tony Villamil, recently complained that US trade policy was not formed by economists but by the State Department (and a range of other bureaucrats), and was more a facet of foreign policy than of national economic welfare. His statement is germane to the topic of host nation policies toward inward investments by foreign multinationals. Often, political, and social, rather than economic considerations are and have been paramount in policy making.

64. The *World Investment Report, 1992*, p.106, discusses (as do Graham and Krugman, *Foreign Direct Investment in the United States*, p.57) the possibility of extending the conventional 'gains from trade' approach to a 'gains from direct investment' (or gains from multinational enterprise) approach. See note 67 below.

65. The 'best', the optimum, is often difficult to determine. There may be the matter of what is best for the international economy (i.e. global economic welfare) is not best for the individual host economy. Some critics have maintained, for example, that multinationals by centralising research and development in their home countries are 'depriving' host countries of the benefits of such activities. Is this misallocation of resources from the host nation's standpoint? The complaint assumes that in the absence of the multinational there would be the research and development. It also assumes that the host nation benefits more from home research and development than sharing in world-wide research and development. Those who argue 'immiserising growth' are similarly claiming misallocation of resources, imports of capital-intensive goods as the terms of trade turn adverse. There has long been the argument that there is misallocation because multinationals use capital-intensive rather than labour-intensive methods in Third World countries. However, 'bias' could conceivably have social benefits rather than costs; economists include positive externalities as distortions.

66. Spill-over effects include the development of supplier and dealer networks that provide a vast range of business and employment opportunities that are not internalised within the multinational enterprise. Other spill-over effects include the training of employees that leave the multinational enterprise to go to other firms – thus, disseminating skills. A spill-over effect occurs when new products are introduced; domestic businesses see possibilities in copying and producing the same products; and the demonstration effect creates new domestic entries in the industry. In many Third World countries within 'enclaves' workers got their first cash wages; the spill-over effect was that they had purchasing power (however small); businesses arose to meet their newly created demands.

67. Graham and Krugman, *Foreign Direct Investment in the United States*, pp.58–9, in discussing the contemporary economic impact of multinationals in the United States write: 'The bottom line is that FDI may be expected to bring gains from integration that are qualitatively similar to the conventional gains from trade, but the magnitude of these gains is anyone's guess'. And, in discussing the gains from spill-overs, they write that these are 'even less measurable than the gains from integration'.

68. *World Investment Report, 1992*, passim.

69. The spill-over effects, in particular, vary sharply by country. Sometimes it is argued, for example, that multinationals keep the best jobs for nationals of the home country, thus minimising the managerial training of host country personnel. Yet, this varies substantially by host country and time. It seems, moreover, to be in the long-run highly dependent on whether there are within the host country qualified individuals and thus is a function of conditions specific to the particular host nation, which conditions change as development occurs.

International Financial Capital Transfers: A Transaction Cost Framework

JEAN-FRANÇOIS HENNART
University of Illinois at Urbana-Champaign

I

Until the seminal work of John Dunning and Stephen Hymer, the expansion abroad of multinational enterprises (MNEs) was seen as the consequence of the international export of financial capital, and was assumed to depend on international differences in interest rates.[1] Dunning's empirical study of American foreign direct investment (FDI) in the UK noted that US investments had involved very little financial capital imports. Hymer proposed an alternative theory of FDI. Both authors changed radically the way we look at FDI, moving the discussion from the field of international finance to that of international industrial organisation. Since then the popular view has seen MNEs as internalising firm-specific advantages, mostly proprietary technology.[2]

The switch in focus from the 1960 view of MNEs as conduits for the transfer of financial capital to the present one of MNEs as transferors of firm-specific advantages has been so complete that finance has been relegated to a subsidiary position. Yet although the present theory explains well today's dominant MNE, a large firm with a clean structure of wholly-owned subsidiaries exploiting internally generated advantages overseas, the theory lacks generality. Business historians keep uncovering various types of direct investments which do not fit the model.[3] Free-standing firms, for example, the dominant type of European FDI before 1914, maintained a small head office in the major capital-exporting countries of the time, but all of their productive assets were located overseas. These multinational firms cannot readily be explained by the internalisation of knowledge advantages, since they had no domestic manufacturing activities from which to transfer these advantages.[4] Neither can they be considered portfolio investments, as stockholders often took direct control of the firm's (foreign) activities.[5]

Here I argue that a number of non-conventional types of FDIs – such as the free-standing company – that fit awkwardly in a model where multinational firms arise to exploit abroad their firm-specific advantages, can be explained by looking at the role of these institutions in the international transfer of financial capital. A full theory of why any of these forms exist must specify the necessary and sufficient conditions for their existence. This paper is a first step towards such a theory. The starting point is the premise that financial capital is an intermediate factor like knowledge, goodwill, raw materials, or distribution services. It is an intermediate factor in the sense that obtaining financial capital is one of the tasks necessary to deliver a product or a service to the customer. In this paper we are interested in the way financial capital is transferred across countries to fund the activities of firms. To each type of international financial transfer corresponds a particular institution. Hence, to explain why a particular institution emerges, one needs to look at all the alternative ways in which capital is transferred internationally, and specify under which circumstances one form (for example free-standing firms) is more efficient than another in transferring financial capital across countries.

There are two main dimensions that can be used to describe and categorise how financial capital is transferred across national boundaries (see Figure 1). One is whether the transfer takes place through price or hierarchical means. Bonds and loans are price modes of transfer, while equity is the hierarchical mode. The distinction between 'price' and 'hierarchical' transfer of financial capital is crucial to students of the MNE because it defines whether we are dealing with a multinational firm or not. In the absence of other internalised inputs, a multinational firm exists when the behaviour of savers and borrowers located in different countries is co-ordinated through hierarchical control, but not when it is organised through a loan contract.

The second dimension is whether savers deal directly with investors, or whether the process is intermediated. These two dimensions yield four cells, into which all potential forms taken by the international transfer of financial capital can be arranged. For example, free-standing companies are in cell 2, as they effect hierarchical but non-intermediated international transfers of financial capital.

The paper develops a theory of why a particular form of transfer will be used, based on the determinants of the choice between price and hierarchical transfer on one hand, and intermediated versus non-intermediated transfer on the other. The choice between hierarchical and price modes of transfer is shown to hinge on information and enforcement costs in the market for investible funds, with equity chosen when those costs are high. Intermediation, it is argued, will take place when there is considerable asymmetry between savers and investors. Hence free-standing firms are shown to arise to finance highly risky foreign projects offering no collateral (hence a need for equity) but when the scale of the investment is low and the technology relatively well known (hence no pay-off from intermediation). By contrast, the

Intermediation

	No	Yes
Contract (loan)	1. Foreigners sell bonds to the public	3. Banks make loans to foreigners
Hierarchy (equity)	2. Foreigners sell stocks to the public	4. Firms take equity in foreign firms

model predicts that international bank lending will be used to finance large-scale, complex projects (hence the need for intermediation) which offer good collateral, thus making co-ordination through price methods (loans) efficient. As shown by the above example, a full classification of international financial institutions requires simultaneous consideration of both internalisation and intermediation.

Section III looks at the empirical evidence and shows it to be consistent with the hypotheses. The conclusion summarises the contribution of the present work and makes some suggestions for future research.

II

Because of international differences in savings rates, in risk aversion, in access to information, and/or because of the desire to diversify portfolios, the transfer of financial capital from one country to another is often profitable. One can think of four main methods by which funds can be transferred from savers to borrowers. An entity located in capital-poor country A can obtain finance from capital-rich country B through:

(1) bonds directly subscribed by individuals in country B;
(2) stocks directly subscribed by individuals in country B;
(3) loans obtained from institutions (for example banks) located in country B – these institutions in turn take deposits (loans) from the public in B;
(4) equity contributions from firms based in B – these institutions in turn obtain finance from residents of country B by floating bonds and stock to the public or borrowing from banks in B.

There are two main dimensions in the preceding list. The first one is whether the transfer of funds is intermediated, that is whether firms in A contract or not with some intervening institution which collects the funds in B. (As argued below, the definition of intermediation used here requires that the intermediaries do more than just pass through the funds. They must make possible a pattern of investments that differs from – and is superior to – that which savers could make on their own.) Solutions (1) and (2) do not involve intermediation while (3) and (4) do. Intermediation thus determines the structure of the international transfer of financial capital. For example, international banks will play a major role when intermediation is efficient, but internalisation of markets for financial capital is not. The second dimension is whether the transfer of funds between A and B is effected by price or hierarchical processes. This dimension describes the nature of the relationship between savers and investors. For example, when efficiency requires intermediation, multinational firms will play a major role in the international capital flows if it is more efficient to effect the transfer of financial capital through hierarchical processes than through market means. Multinational banks will take front stage in situations when internalisation is not efficient.

Taken together, these two dimensions allow us to specify the conditions that are necessary and sufficient for the emergence of each type of international financial transfer. For example, as will be argued later, free-standing firms will arise whenever cross-border hierarchical co-ordination is efficient, but intermediation is not. Naturally, most projects are financed from a mix of debt and equity, and from both intermediated and non-intermediated sources. Nevertheless, it is useful to examine the four categories separately. The actual complex financing methods used by firms can best be grasped from an understanding of the individual components.

Internalisation

What determines whether the international transfer of financial capital will take the form of loans or of equity? Williamson's pathbreaking 1988 *Journal of Finance* article argues that debt and equity can be seen as alternative governance structures, and the discussion here follows his approach. Bank loans and corporate bonds can be distinguished from equity (stocks, shares) by the fact that they do not give the lender any right to the residual value of the venture, that is they do not remunerate the provider of funds through a share of the profits. Lenders also do not have a *general* and *discretionary* right to direct the behaviour of borrowers (although specific rights are generally specified in loan contracts). In contrast, holders of equity receive in exchange for their supply of finance a share of the profits of the venture, and they are given the right to control directly the use of funds, or to nominate delegates charged with that task.[6]

The parallel with the supply of other inputs is clear. The principal difference between co-ordination through hierarchy and co-ordination through prices is that hierarchy uses behaviour constraints: in other words, the behaviour of agents is co-ordinated by one agent directly controlling the behaviour – and hence indirectly controlling the output – of others through an employment relationship. By contrast, co-ordination through prices is effected by having one agent directly specifying outputs, but letting the other agent free to choose the behaviour to bring forth this output. In the well-known case of the international transfer of technological knowledge, the 'price' solution is licensing: the licensee is left free to maximise his profits, subject to payment of the licence fee (an output constraint). By contrast, the hierarchical solution is FDI, where the local manager is given specific instructions on how to operate (behaviour constraints).[7] In the case of the international transfer of financial capital, the hierarchical solution is when one agent provides funds and tells the other agent where and how to invest, and this corresponds to equity. The market solution (lending) is when one agent contracts with another how much will be paid back, but leaves the user of funds free to behave as needed to reimburse the principal with interest.

As in the case of any other intermediate factor of production, the hierarchical solution will be chosen when market transactions are subject to significant transaction costs, so that the cost of market exchange is raised over that of hierarchical co-ordination. Transaction costs are the costs of informing the parties about potential trades, of enforcing the contracts, and of curbing bargaining.[8]

There are two aspects of loan transactions that lead to significant enforcement costs. First, in a loan transaction, the lender makes funds available today to the borrower, to be repaid later with interest. This non-simultaneity between the two sides of the transaction increases enforcement costs. Second, incentives in a loan transaction are not symmetrical: because the returns to lenders are contractually fixed, lenders do not share in the gains if the venture is more profitable than expected, while they lose everything if the venture fails. The borrower, on the other hand, stands to capture the entire gain if the venture is successful, but will only lose his equity in the venture if the project fails. Hence the borrower will be incited to undertake projects which are overly risky if his equity in the project is small compared to the loans taken.

Four scenarios are possible: (1) the borrower repays in full and with interest; (2) the borrower is not able to repay because he has used the money for other purposes (such as consumption); (3) the borrower has invested the funds, but is unable to repay with interest, because he has undertaken overly risky projects which have failed; (4) the borrower is unable to fulfil his obligation because, while the project was sound and well managed, unforeseen circumstances beyond his control have reduced its profitability.

With perfect information, the lender would avoid default by refusing to lend to dishonest individuals or to overly risky ventures. With perfect enforcement, the penalties for default would be so predictable as to persuade borrowers to be honest and prudent. In the real world, where neither information nor enforcement are perfect, scenarios (2), (3) and (4) will be common.

Lenders will use a number of strategies to protect themselves against the likelihood of default. The first strategy consists in asking the borrower to pledge a collateral to be forfeited in case of non-repayment of the loan. Entrepreneurs who come from moneyed families may provide collateral from their own fortune. Others may have to pledge the assets financed through the loan. Projects vary greatly in the degree to which they can provide collateral. Good collateral for a lender are assets which are not specialised to one use and have good resale value. As I will show, the value of collateral, and hence the transaction cost of lending, varies systematically across projects. For example, lenders will hesitate to lend to mining firms and to small high-technology outfits because of their lack of collateral.

A second strategy available to lenders is to screen projects and applicants, and to lend only to borrowers known to be both honest and capable, and to sound projects. Lending will be restricted to individuals who are personally known to the lender, and who have good verifiable track records.

A third way to reduce default is to monitor the use of funds. The use of this method by lenders is limited by the fact that they have no legal right to interfere in the day-to-day management of the business. They can, however, screen projects *ex-ante* and earmark funds for specific investments. Here again, projects are likely to differ greatly in the extent to which they can be effectively monitored. New businesses operate in more uncertain environments and require more major decisions than ongoing enterprises. The range of activities undertaken may differ across projects. It is, for example, smaller for an utility than for an agricultural enterprise, and hence outside monitoring is easier for the former than for the latter.[9]

As in the case of other intermediate inputs, one solution to high transaction costs of lending is to internalise the market for loanable funds. Internalising the market for funds means in this context that the transfer of funds between saver and investor will be organised through hierarchical directives. The saver will now be the investor, or will direct the behaviour of the investor. Hierarchical co-ordination has two main advantages: first, an equity owner usually has much greater control over the use of funds than a lender. Equity owners are granted the power to determine the firm's activities and to be involved in its day-to-day management. Second, the incentives to default are eliminated because borrowers are now also lenders, and they are paid from the profits of the venture. This applies even if the providers of finance are not directly involved in the management of the firm, but instead hire professional managers to act on their behalf. Employment contracts give equity owners the power to direct behaviour and to discipline employees. These employees have less incentive to misrepresent projects since they no longer have title to the residual, but are paid a fixed amount to obey managerial directives.[10] On the other hand, breaking the connection between project-specific earnings and rewards encourages shirking by managers, either in the form of on-the-job consumption, or in the form of overly conservative investment policies.

Intermediation

The other dimension of the transfer of financial capital is intermediation. Intermediated transfers are those in which a third party, a bank, a trading company, or a manufacturing concern, stands in between lenders and borrowers. Intermediated transfer is more efficient than direct transfer in two main cases: (1) when there are significant mismatches between the average size and time-structure of savings and investments; (2) when the process of transforming savings into investments is characterised by a minimum efficient scale that is much larger than that which is economical for savers to undertake (one particular aspect of this case is when collecting information and linking savers and investors is subject to large economies of scale). Additionally, history may be relevant. For example, intermediation may dominate in countries where merchant banks became established before capital markets, and *vice versa*.

Case (1) is well known, and does not justify further comments, but it may be worthwhile to expand on (2). Intermediators centralise the transfer of information between savers and borrowers. When information is complex and rapidly changing, the minimum amount of necessary information to make wise investment decisions may be large. Because information is a public good, this may make centralised information collection by an intermediator economical. As a result, individual investors may find it efficient to lend or to take equity in an intermediator who will specialise in screening projects.

Note that underwriting of bonds and stocks by banks or other intermediaries is not considered intermediation here. In this paper, intermediation takes place when individuals or businesses raise funds in their own name and transfer them to other entities.

Internalisation and intermediation are separate concepts. The transfer of financial capital can be internalised both when it is intermediated and when it is not. The former case corresponds to a conglomerate multinational firm collecting funds from stock-holders and allocating them to be invested by various divisions or subsidiaries. A case where the transfer of financial capital is internalised but not intermediated is that of free-standing firms, where each firm was basically set up to invest in a single project. Inversely, intermediation can exist both in firms and in markets. Intermediation characterises the transfer of financial capital effected by multinational firms (internalised) as well as that undertaken by US multinational banks (not internalised).

A Typology of Financial Capital Flows

Combining the two dimensions of intermediation and internalisation yields four categories of transactions which together account for all types of international transfer of financial capital (Figure 1). Quadrant 1 describes non-intermediated, non-equity international financial capital transfers. Such transfers take place when citizens of the capital-exporting country make loans to borrowers in the capital-poor country. An example would be the sale of US railroad and government bonds to European investors in the nineteenth century.[11]

In quadrant 2, the export of financial capital is not intermediated, and takes the form of equity. One example of such transaction would be the direct selling of stock by entities of capital-poor countries (or by entities of capital-rich countries investing in capital-poor countries) on the stock markets of capital-rich countries. The best example of this latter type of transfer is the free-standing company, an important type of FDI between 1870 and 1914.[12] These companies were registered in the main capital-exporting countries of the time – the United Kingdom, France, Belgium, and the Netherlands. They floated stock on the UK and, to a lesser extent, continental European stock markets, and used the proceeds to finance enterprises located exclusively in foreign countries. Hence they internalised the international transfer of financial capital.[13] Yet, they did not have any domestic operations, and therefore were not exploiting abroad some technological or marketing advantage gained at home.

Quadrant 3 corresponds to transactions which are intermediated, but which take the form of loans. An example would be loans by banks, trading, or manufacturing firms located in capital-rich countries to borrowers in capital-poor countries.

In quadrant 4, intermediated equity, financial capital is transferred from capital-rich to capital-poor countries by intermediators taking equity positions in foreign firms. The best example of such transactions is the MNE. In this form of transfer, investors in capital-rich countries take equity in firms which in turn take (often full) equity in a variety of foreign ventures.

III

The preceding analysis can predict the conditions under which international financial capital transfers will take one of these four forms. In the following pages, I focus mostly on the form taken by financial capital transfers in the nineteenth century, a period that saw the emergence of many of the least well explained forms of international business involvement. Nevertheless, much of the discussion is applicable to today's institutions as well.

Loans or Equity?

As argued above, international financial capital transfers will be undertaken through equity in the following circumstances:

(1) the activity to be financed offers little collateral;
(2) the activity to be financed is new and untested, and requires rapid, non-standard decisions;
(3) there are few personal links between lenders and investors.

There is a fair amount of evidence that both intermediated and non-intermediated equity transfers have been used to finance activities that meet those criteria. For example, British free-standing firms were disproportionately involved in colonial plantations and mining. This striking concentration in a limited number of sectors can be explained in terms of our model.

As Michie notes, these sectors were seen at the time as highly speculative.[14] Mining is an extremely risky industry, which offers little collateral as much of the investment is in diggings. As a result, new mining ventures are, and have always been, financed through equity.[15] As Mikesell and Whitney note, 'debt financing from commercial sources is almost impossible to obtain'.[16]

Initial exploration and development of mines are typically financed by the personal capital of the owner of mining claims, his friends and relatives, or by syndicates of affluent individuals. Once the deposit has been proved, one way to obtain the funds needed for development is through public stock offerings on stock markets. This was the pattern in the nineteenth century, when much of the international investment in mining was undertaken by free-standing firms floating shares on European capital markets. This pattern of equity financing of new mines continues today. Small mines in North America have been financed by stocks floated on the penny stocks markets of Spokane, Denver, and Vancouver.

Another way by which new mines obtain financing is when established mining companies, suppliers, or customers, take an equity ownership in the project. These intermediators, because they are larger and well established, have available funds from reinvested profits or can more easily obtain equity or loan financing. They also have privileged information on the prospects of the borrower. Much of the financing for the development of open-pit porphyry copper orebodies in the late nineteenth century thus came from existing copper mines in northern Michigan, from the owners of successful gold and silver mines, and from the exporters of American copper to Europe.[17] After the first World War a substantial percentage of mining projects in developing countries was financed by multinational mining firms. Until the wave of nationalisation of the 1960s equity financed 90 per cent of the total capital requirements of mining projects in developing countries.[18]

Similarly, international equity financing has been prevalent for some types of agricultural investments. The main collateral for agricultural investments is land. When land has little value for alternative crops it provides limited security for a loan and lending becomes difficult. Managerial decisions are also difficult for an outside lender to monitor. Hence we would expect speculative endeavours, such as new export market crops, to be shunned by lenders and to have to rely mostly on equity financing, in either its intermediated or non-intermediated forms.

The evidence on the financing of rubber plantations and tea gardens is broadly consistent with our hypothesis. As predicted, rubber planting was financed by equity, both non-intermediated (free-standing firms) and intermediated (rubber manufacturers and trading companies). Rubber planting was a risky business when it was introduced to the Far East in the 1890s. There were no settled techniques of cultivation and great uncertainty as to the size of the market. The land which rubber planters were using had been previously uncultivated, and hence had little value for alternative uses.[19] Rubber investments are also long term, as it takes seven years before *heveas* yield marketable rubber.[20]

Ramachandran's study of the methods of financing rubber and tea estates in Ceylon is supportive.[21] It shows that the ordinary share was the only type of security used by rubber companies to raise initial funds. In contrast, Ceylon's tea companies made greater use of debentures when they were established in the 1890s. Ramachandran explains the difference by the fact that by then the tea industry had been firmly established. Debentures could then be secured by the value of estates.[22]

A third type of activity which we would expect to be shut off from loan financing is research and development. R & D-intensive activities are by definition speculative, and provide little collateral. Commercial banks have always been very unsympathetic to the requests of managers of small high-technology start-ups.[23] Consequently, R & D projects have traditionally been financed by equity. Initially, the project is financed with funds from the inventor, his friends, relatives, and acquaintances. Once the potential has been proved, the project is further developed by floating on the stock market or by sale to an established firm.

This pattern was as true in nineteenth-century England as it is today.[24] Today, the initial development of US high-technology firms is financed to a large extent by venture-capital firms (intermediated equity, in our classification). These firms collect funds from pension funds, endowments and foundations, affluent individuals, US and foreign corporations, and US insurance companies. Venture-capital firms invest for ten years or so in exchange for an equity stake, and realise their return when the company makes a public stock offering or is acquired by another company.[25]

Michie notes that another source of intermediated equity for the high-technology start-ups of nineteenth-century England was established British companies in fields not far removed from the new ventures. The same pattern applies today. 3M, for example, had $85 million invested in 1989 in 37 venture-capital funds, but made also 20–30 direct equity investments of $2–3 million each. Lately, Japanese foreign direct investors have played the same role, providing funds to cash-starved US firms in exchange for a share of the equity.[26]

The model predicts that, by contrast, loans (intermediated or not) will be used for investments which provide collateral, and in which the performance of management is relatively easy to monitor. A cursory look at international capital flows in the nineteenth century shows the following pattern:

1. in general, banks provided only short-term lending, mostly on receivables;
2. long-term lending took the form of bonds and debentures, mostly government bonds, railway bonds, and mortgages.

One striking feature of long-term financial capital flows in the nineteenth century is the very limited role played by banks. Lending by banks was overwhelmingly short term. Banks provided short-term advances of working capital, and they financed the international movement of commodities, but they did not lend long-term.[27] Long-term lending was through bonds, mostly issued by governments and railways, and for mortgages, three situations under which lending has relatively low transaction costs. As is well known, the default risk of lending to governments is reduced by the fact that governments have taxing powers, and can therefore raise taxes to repay loans. Land was also a good collateral in a number of fast growing nineteenth century countries, and so it is not surprising to read that considerable sums of European (mostly British and Scottish) money were lent as mortgages to farmers in North America, Australia, and Argentina.[28]

Railways are another interesting case. In Europe and Russia, the construction of railroads in the nineteenth century was financed through the emission of state-guaranteed bonds.[29] American railroads obtained most of their funds from Europe in the form of mortgage bonds.[30] There are two reasons why US railroads were generally financed by loans and not by equity. First, the land owned by the railroads provided good collateral.[31] Second, railroads were the first regulated enterprises in the United States, and were early users of cost accounting. In 1909, the US Interstate Commerce Commission prescribed a standard balance sheet for all railroads, at a time when few of the firms quoted on the New York Stock Exchange published annual reports.[32] Hence the risk of default for railroads was much lower than for other firms, and this made financing through loans possible.

Intermediated or Not?

We have argued earlier that financial intermediation will take place (1) when there are large differences between the average size and term structure of savings and investment and (2) when there are such information asymmetries between savers and investors that centralisation of information collection and processing makes sense. There is a good deal of evidence to support this argument. Take the case of the financing of new, risky projects.

As we have seen earlier, the general pattern of financing of such projects is that it is very difficult to obtain any type of large financing (loans or equity) at very early stages of development when the viability of the project is not established. Hence the flow of initial capital for such development is generally not procured from the public at large, but comes from the reinvested profits of existing concerns (manufacturers, traders) or from the savings of the initiator of the project, his friends and acquaintances. As initial development is completed, additional financing is obtained either from existing concerns or by equity financing obtained by floating the project as a separate entity.

There are three main patterns. The first is full intermediation, in which the project is developed within an existing concern. This pattern is that of today's 'textbook' multinationals which raise funds from investors in their home countries (and increasingly elsewhere) and invest these funds in a portfolio of projects, some of which are located abroad. The second pattern is zero intermediation, in which the new project is floated as a separate entity whose shares are directly offered to the public. This flotation may be facilitated by a specialist agency, such as a promotor or a merchant bank, but once floated the new firm is basically independent. This is the way many free-standing firms were established. Venture-capital firms also proceed in this manner. Finally, the most interesting cases are intermediate cases, where the new projects remain connected to their sponsors.

One such intermediate case is the mining finance house, a characteristic feature of gold mining in South Africa. The first South African gold mines were outcrop mines. The initial development of these mines did not require large investments, and they therefore could be financed by syndicates of wealthy individuals. In the 1890s the action moved to the Witwatersrand underground mines (deep levels). The development of these mines required an unprecedented volume of financial capital, much greater than that which syndicates of wealthy individuals could provide.[33] The solution was the development of mining finance houses.

Mining finance houses were created by diamond merchants who used their good name to raise money in Europe for the initial development of deep levels. When these could be shown to the public to be promising, they were floated as separate companies, but the mining finance house kept a controlling minority share. The mining finance houses had centralised management and prospecting divisions which provided managerial, secretarial, and administrative services to the firms which were members of the group.[34] Some of these houses are still active today in basically the same form.

Another interesting case is that of trading companies. British trading companies in the nineteenth century helped float companies which were or could become their customers. For example, British companies trading in Malaya provided working capital to estates switching to rubber plantations, helped float them in London as limited liability companies, and retained an equity ownership in them. Trading companies handled the imports and exports of the estates in which they had ownership and supervised the work of the local estate managers, all in exchange for a commission, a system known as the 'agency house' system.[35] This system by which a trading company helps float a concern and keeps a share of the floated companies leads to the creation of what Chapman has called 'investment groups'. Companies that were part of these groups were active in a variety of industries in all parts of the world (from jute mills and tea estates in India to flour mills in Argentina).[36]

These examples show that the extent of intermediation seems to hinge on three factors, the size of the investment, the degree of information asymmetry, and the presence of sale economies. The greater the size of the investment, the more difficult it was for an isolated promoter to obtain the necessary finance to bring the project to the point where its shares could be sold to the general public, and the greater the need to finance the development from the earnings of existing operations – whether in the same or in different fields. Hence the shift from individual free-standing companies to mining finance houses in South Africa coincided with the shift from outcrop to deep-level mines.

The same pattern is clear in tin mining in Malaya. Up until 1910, the dominant mining technique for alluvial ores in Southeast Asia was gravel pumping, a relatively simple, low-cost, labour-intensive method. Between 1910 and 1930 gravel pumps were replaced by dredges, a method much more technologically sophisticated and 30 times more capital intensive. Interestingly, while gravel pump companies were all floated as free-standing firms, the 1920s saw the rise of mining finance houses, such as Anglo-Oriental, which invested in a portfolio of mines in Thailand, Burma, Malaya, and Nigeria.[37]

The second factor seems to be the extent of information asymmetry between the promoter and the public. For example, the role of agency houses in floating rubber planting companies declined as the industry became better established.[38] Similarly, the Witwatersrand gold deposits were quite different from other known deposits at the time, and this may explain the comparative advantage of established and well-known diamond merchants over local mining entrepreneurs in raising financial capital for their development. Lastly, the reason why companies stayed in groups is linked in part to the provision of common services subject to scale economies, such as shipping, group buying and selling, and management and technical services.

IV

In spite of its recent vintage, transaction cost theory has proved to be remarkably useful in explaining the main features of MNEs.[39] Yet in the last two decades historians of the MNE, and especially of its non-American incarnations, have uncovered a number of types of FDI, such as free-standing firms and investment groups, which are quite different from the traditional MNE described and explained by mainstream transaction cost theory. The forms taken by many of these investments were in fact so different from the typical MNE that for long they were not recognised as belonging to the genus, and not included on statistical compilations of FDI.[40] This has led some economic historians such as Fieldhouse to question the ability of transaction cost theory to account for the wide variety of forms and motives of FDI.[41]

To an international business theorist, the curious forms taken by some non-American FDIs present an interesting challenge. The goal of this paper has been to show that transaction cost theory can be extended to meet that challenge. There are two important steps in this extension. The first step is the abandonment of the view that MNEs arise when firms internalise the exploitation abroad of firm-specific advantages. This commonly held view tends to focus attention on R & D-intensive firms expanding abroad from a home base. Such a focus makes it difficult to explain the international expansion of firms which do not enjoy any technological home-based advantages, such as free-standing firms, trading, or holding companies.

In reality, firms do not internalise advantages, they internalise markets for intermediate inputs, including, but not exclusively, markets for what are called 'advantages'.[42] R & D intensive firms do not internalise their technological advantages, they internalise the market for their technological advantages. Understanding this makes it possible to explore cases where MNEs internalise markets for other inputs.

In this paper, I look at financial capital as an intermediate input. I identify all possible ways in which capital can be transferred internationally. Two of the main dimensions of this transfer are its governance mode (price or hierarchy) and the degree of intermediation. The governance mode depends on the level of transaction costs. This in turn will vary with the type of activities funded. Specifically, transaction costs of lending will be high for activities which provide poor collateral. When lending fails, a way to reduce transaction costs is to have the lender and the borrower joined by equity links. Hence the theory developed in this paper offers clear predictions as to the type of activity that is likely to be financed through lending and through equity.[43]

Another important dimension of financial markets is the extent of intermediation, that is the extent to which it pays for institutions to act as brokers in the relationship between suppliers and demanders of credit. Intermediation is efficient when there are large differences between the average size and term-structure of savings and investments and large information asymmetries between savers and investors. Combining these two dimensions gives us a typology of international financial capital transfers and of the corresponding financial institutions.

Although some of the hypotheses presented here are quite speculative, they seem at least superficially consistent with some of the historical evidence, which shows that some activities offering little collateral, such as mining, some types of agriculture, and the manufacture of new science-based products have always been financed through equity. Inversely, international lending has historically been extended to a limited set of borrowers offering good collateral, including railroads, land-owners, and governments. The evidence on intermediation is also supportive, with intermediation observed when the minimum efficient size of the investment is large and there is considerable information asymmetry between savers and investors. The model suggests that we should see free-standing firms used to finance projects offering little collateral, but of relatively small size and using fairly standard technology. Mining finance houses and other types of intermediated equity (such as venture capital and investment groups) will be used to finance investments with little collateral, but of greater minimum efficient size and more complex technology. This seems to have some empirical support.

Naturally, internalisation of capital markets was only one of the motives leading to the creation of these institutions. In many cases, other intermediate inputs were internalised as well. However, financial capital played a major role, and the characteristics of many of these unconventional FDI forms cannot be understood without consideration of their role in the international transfer of financial capital.

The model is unconventional in two ways: first, debt and equity are seen as governance structures.[44] Debt is the market method of co-ordinating savers and investors, equity is the hierarchical one. Second, intermediation is seen as a feature of both markets and firms. The model provides a general theory of the forms taken by international financial flows, and of the corresponding institutions. It provides a rationale for a number of institutional forms which have not fitted well into existing theories. It also suggests similarities between a number of previously poorly understood forms.

The approach taken here is 'comparative institutional', in the sense that the various ways in which financial capital can be transferred are examined simultaneously. This way of looking at financial capital transfer may save us from the temptation of comparing real-life institutions with absolute standards which do not take into account transaction costs. Seen in this light, the negative views of some business historians towards free-standing firms and agency houses need to be re-evaluated.[45]

NOTES

I acknowledge the useful comments of Robert Grosse, Bruce Kogut, Adrian Tschoegl, and Mira Wilkins on the many previous incarnations of this paper, and of Charles Harvey, Tom Roehl, Geoffrey Jones and two anonymous referees on the present one.

1. J. Dunning, *American Investments in British Manufacturing Industry* (1958); S.H. Hymer, *The International Operations of National Firms: A Study of Direct Foreign Investment* (unpublished Ph.D. dissertation, MIT, 1960, later published by MIT Press in 1976).
2. This view of MNEs as internalising firm-specific advantages contrasts with the view that MNEs internalise markets for intermediate factors, including goodwill, marketing services, and raw materials and components. For the latter view, see for example J.-F. Hennart, *A Theory of Multinational Enterprise* (Ann Arbor, MI, 1982) and M. Casson, *The Firm and the Market* (Cambridge, MA, 1987). For a recent survey, see J.-F. Hennart, 'The Transaction Cost Theory of the Multinational Enterprise', in C. Pitelis and R. Sugden (eds.), *The Nature of the Transnational Firm* (1991).
3. M. Wilkins, 'European Multinationals in the United States, 1875–1914', in A. Teichova, M. Levy-Leboyer, and H. Nussbaum (eds.), *Multinational Enterprise in Historical Perspective* (1986); M. Wilkins, 'The Free Standing Company 1870–1914', *Economic History Review*, 2nd series, Vol.61 (1988), pp.259–82; S.D. Chapman, 'British-Based Investment Groups Before 1914', *Economic History Review*, 2nd series, Vol.38 (1985), pp.230–51.
4. J.-F. Hennart, 'Internalization in Practice: Foreign Direct Investment in Malaysian Tin Mining', *Journal of International Business Studies*, Vol.17 (1986), pp.131–43.
5. Wilkins, 'Free Standing Company'; Hennart, 'Transaction Cost Theory'.
6. O. Williamson, 'Corporate Finance and Corporate Governance', *Journal of Finance*, Vol.63 (1988), pp.569–98. In general, the two dimensions are aligned, i.e. owners of residual claims also have control rights. In practice, there are some anomalies that would deserve further study: it is possible for equity shares to have no voting rights and for debenture shares to carry votes. I am grateful to an anonymous referee for this point.
7. In practice, both firms and markets make use of a mix of price and behaviour constraints. See J.F. Hennart, 'Explaining the Swollen Middle: Why Most Transactions are a Mix of "Market" and "Hierarchy" ', *Organization Science*, Vol.4, No.4 (1993).
8. Hennart, *Theory of Multinational Enterprise*.
9. The three techniques are to some extent substitutes. Collateral is a substitute to screening borrowers and projects, as shown in pawnbroking, where the identity of the borrower and the uses to which the borrowed funds will be put are unknown to the lender.
10. M. Jensen and W. Meckling, 'Theory of the Firm: Managerial Behavior, Agency Costs, and Capital Structure', *Journal of Financial Economics*, Vol.3 (1976), pp.305–60.
11. Those bonds were often placed by foreign banks, but without changing their characteristics. Hence I do not consider this to be intermediation.
12. According to the US Federal Trade Commission, there were more than 2,500 British free-standing companies operating outside the US and Canada in 1916. The Bancroft Library of the University of California, Berkeley, lists 1,600 British companies as having invested in the American and Canadian west between 1870 and 1914. See A. Ostrye, *Foreign Investments in the American and Canadian West, 1870–1914: An Annotated Bibliography* (Metuchen, NJ, 1986). To this must be added the numerous French and Belgian free-standing companies that invested in central Europe and Russia. See John McKay, *Pioneers for Profit* (Chicago, 1970).
13. Wilkins, 'Free Standing Company'.
14. R. Michie, *Money, Mania, and Markets* (Edinburgh, 1981).

15. One exception to the rule is the recent development of project finance. This development, which is due to the increased risk of nationalisation of mining projects by host countries, mixes debt financing by an international banking consortium to finance construction, supplier credits for the equipment, and company equity to finance exploration and the feasibility study. The security of the loan usually consists of contracts for the output of the mine, but the mining parent does not assume the liability for the indebtedness of the project. The record of this type of financing has been mixed. See R. Mikesell, 'Materials Industries: Financing' in M. Bever, (ed), *Encyclopedia of Materials Science and Engineering*, Vol.8 (Oxford, 1986).
16. R. Mikesell and J. Whitney, *The World Mining Industry* (Boston, 1987), p.41.
17. The capitalists who backed Anaconda and Bingham Canyon were owners of gold and silver mines who invested their profits in copper. The Montana Copper Company of Butte got its backing from the Lewisohn trading firm. The Phelps-Dodge trading firm backed Morenci and Bisbee, while the Guggenheim trading firm invested in South America and the Hochschilds in Northern Rhodesia. See T. Navin, *Copper Mining and Management* (Tucson, 1978), p.113.
18. M. Radetzki and S. Zorn, *Financing Mining Projects in Developing Countries* (London, 1979).
19. N. Ramachandran, *Foreign Plantation Investment in Ceylon, 1889-1958* (Colombo, 1963), p.27.
20. R. Stillson, 'The Financing of Malayan Rubber, 1905-1923', *Economic History Review*, Vol.24 (1971), p.589.
21. Ramachandran, *Foreign Plantation Investment*.
22. Ibid., pp.26-7.
23. E. Carlson, 'Japanese Bankroll Small U.S. Firms', *Wall Street Journal*, 2 Nov. 1989, B1.
24. R. Michie, 'Options, Concessions, Syndicates, and the Provision of Venture Capital, 1880-1913', *Business History*, Vol.23 (1981), pp.147-64.
25. As we would expect, venture capital investments are very speculative, with a very small number of stakes returning ten to 290 times the invested capital, while the majority earns little or nothing. See A. Pollack, 'Venture Capital Loses its Vigor', *New York* Times, 8 Oct. 1989.
26. In mining, plantations, and high tech, initial funding takes the form of equity. As firms become more established, they make greater use of debt. See 'Little needs Large', *Economist* 11 Nov. 1989, p.100; Carlson, 'Japanese Bankroll'.
27. R. Cameron, 'Conclusions', in Cameron and Bovykin (eds.), *International Banking: 1870-1914* (New York and Oxford, 1991).
28. M. Wilkins, *The History of Foreign Investments in the United States to 1914* (Cambridge MA, 1989).
29. Cameron, 'Conclusions', p.530.
30. It is estimated that 90 per cent of the $4 billion of US railroad securities held in Europe in 1914 were in the form of bonds, and ten per cent in shares (*Bradstreet's*, 31 Oct. 1914, p.690, quoted in Wilkins, *History of Foreign Investments*, p.725 footnote 11).
31. In 1913, 90 per cent of the $11.2 billion of US railroad debt was backed by some forms of mortgage. See J. Baskin, 'The Development of Corporate Financial Markets in Britain and the United States, 1600-1914: Overcoming Asymmetric Information', *Business History Review*, Vol.62 (1988), pp.199-237.
32. Baskin, 'Corporate Financial Markets', p.228.
33. The estimated cost of sinking a deep-level shaft to 5,000 feet was £0.5 million sterling. See R. Turrell and J.-J. Van Helten, 'The Rothschilds, the Exploration Company, and Mining Finance', *Business History* (1986), pp.181-205.
34. Turrell and Van Helten, 'Rothschilds', p.188.
35. J.H. Drabble, *Rubber in Malaya 1876-1922* (Kuala Lumpur, 1973).
36. Chapman, 'British-Based Investment Groups'.
37. Yip Yat Hoong, *The Development of the Tin Industry in Malaya* (Kuala Lumpur,

1969).
38. Drabble, *Rubber in Malaya*, p.85.
39. Hennart, 'Transaction Cost Theory'.
40. J. Stopford, 'The Origins of British-based Multinational Manufacturing Enterprises', *Business History Review*, Vol.48 (1974), pp.303–35.
41. D.K. Fieldhouse, 'The Multinational: A Critique of a Concept', in A. Teichova, M. Levy-Leboyer, and H. Nussbaum (eds.), *Multinational Enterprise in Historical Perspective* (1986), pp.9–29.
42. The point is implicit in Hennart, *A Theory of Multinational Enterprise*. For an explicit statement, see M. Casson, 'General Theories of the Multinational Enterprise: Their Relevance to Business History', in P. Hertner and G. Jones (eds.), *Multinationals: Theory and History* (Aldershot, 1986).
43. One might argue that free-standing firms were internalising an ownership advantage, consisting of preferential access to financial capital. One danger of this formulation is that it assumes that the impetus for free-standing firms must necessarily come from firms in capital-rich countries. The 'internalising of markets' approach, on the other hand, suggests that the initiative for internalisation may come from either firms in capital-rich or in capital-poor countries, and the historical record supports that intuition. One Bolivian entrepreneur, F.A. Aramayo, for example, floated a free-standing firm in London in 1906 to obtain financial capital to develop its Bolivian tin properties. See J. Hillman, 'The Emergence of the Tin Industry in Bolivia', *Journal of Latin American Studies*, Vol. 16 (1986), p.429.
44. This is in contrast to finance theory, which argues that the choice between debt and equity financing depends on taxes, earnings volatility, growth opportunities, and industry structure. See S. Balakrishnan and I. Fox, 'Asset Specificity, Firm Heterogeneity, and Capital Structure', *Strategic Management Journal*, Vol.14 (1993), pp.3–16.
45. For such negative views, see, for example, C. Spence, *Mining Investments and the American Mining Frontier, 1860–1901* (Ithaca, 1958).

Britain's Overseas Investments in 1914 Revisited

T.A.B. CORLEY

University of Reading

Despite a considerable amount of research, the anatomy of the pre-1914 British economy has not yet been completely laid bare. A recent useful approach was via the topic of comparative, or competitive, advantage. Nicholas Crafts and Mark Thomas related this concept to Britain's manufacturing overseas trade between 1910 and 1935. They found that the country's comparative advantage in manufactures had, ever since 1870, rested in unskilled-labour-intensive, capital-neutral and human-capital-scarce commodities. The sectors which they identified in the UK's 'revealed comparative advantage' for 1913 were the staple industries of textiles and iron and steel, and also railways and ships, spirits and tobacco; a corresponding disadvantage was to be found in technologically advanced industries. They stressed Britain's relatively low labour productivity in manufacturing, associated with a dearth of trained skills, 'an essential input to the technologically progressive product-cycle industries that dominated the Second Industrial Revolution'. Hence Britain's manufacturing exports tended to comprise goods principally made by unskilled and low-wage labour.[1]

These findings broadly accord with those of Alfred Chandler, that by about 1900 the largest and most successful enterprises in Britain were those making branded consumer goods, including foodstuffs, cigarettes and tobacco products, drinks, and consumer chemicals such as soap, starch, cosmetics, paints and pills.[2] To be sure, not all such manufacturers were necessarily large exporters. Some products were earmarked for domestic customers, and others may not have appealed to overseas markets. For others again, entry into foreign countries was impeded by high tariffs or other barriers to trade. Even so, Britain was an open economy, with visible imports equivalent to nearly 33 per cent of its net national product in 1913, and visible exports to almost 29 per cent. To that extent, the question of comparative advantage was linked with the UK's involvement overseas.

Another form of international involvement by British firms was that of foreign direct investment (FDI). Firms acquired assets overseas which they planned to control themselves; FDI was thereby

distinguished from foreign portfolio investment, by individuals and
sometimes firms, where no control was entailed and the investors merely sought interest and dividends. As John Dunning has shown, decisions to undertake FDI and to create multinational enterprises
resulted from competitive advantage. Entrepreneurs tended to undertake production overseas, to the extent that they enjoyed ownership,
location and internalisation advantages over rivals. Dunning stressed
that his 'OLI' framework or paradigm related to firms in general, from
which a 'representative firm' could be selected for each group; he also
further identified country-, industry- and firm-specific factors which
affected advantage. He was aware that, while some entrepreneurs
would actively exploit the advantages which they had perceived, others
with equal awareness of such advantages failed to do so through inertia
or risk-aversion. Like Crafts and Thomas, he identified trends, showing
that entrepreneurial perceptions of advantage in Britain were sufficient-
ly widespread to generate considerable quantities of both exports and
foreign investment.[3]

The present article sets out to examine data of Britain's FDI during
the years before 1914, in the context of the country's overall foreign
investment record. Since the procedure for constructing such data may
not be too familiar, Section II contains a general 'scope and method'
discussion. Section III then tackles the practicalities of estimating the
relevant quantities for this period. Section IV concludes by attempting
to assess how far this study has enhanced our understanding of this part
of the UK economy's anatomy.

II

This section outlines the principles behind an investigation into Britain's
overseas assets in the period shortly before 1914. As the size of the
country's investment stock was then closely related to its balance of
payments position, the latter forms a starting point of the present
discussion.

Since Britain earned a current account surplus on its balance of
payments in all but a handful of years between 1816 and 1914, by the
latter year it had built up what Albert Imlah has termed a substantial
'accumulating credit abroad'.[4] British citizens and companies held a
negligible amount (less than five per cent in 1913) of this surplus in the
form of gold and silver, and devoted some to short-term lending overseas. However, the bulk was spent on long-term foreign investment.[5] As
shown above, this took two forms, depending on the presence or
absence of control, namely portfolio and direct investment.

As to portfolio investment, individuals or corporate investors held securities of overseas-based companies in their portfolios. Their holdings in each represented too small a proportion of the whole for them to be able to influence its strategy, even had they wished to do so. Hence no control was involved.

In the 'direct' case, however, joint-stock or unincorporated companies carried out overseas investment with the specific purpose of obtaining control. That entailed either creating enterprises from scratch in the host countries or purchasing existing productive units. They therefore owned all or a substantial part of the assets in which they had invested.

Confusion has arisen in the literature because the concept of FDI has been understood in two different senses. Before 1914, it was defined as private-sector capital invested overseas other than through a stock exchange. This definition has relevance as long as attention was focused mainly on the channels for securing the funds required. However, it became less useful in practice once economists, and later economic and business historians, from the 1960s onwards began to study the theory and conduct of the multinational enterprise, being heavily influenced by the pioneering work of Stephen Hymer.[6] Dunning's researches into FDI, for example, concentrated on questions of control rather than on the sources of funds.

However, as some scholars have – at least until recently – continued to use the old definition, there is a strong argument for adopting a fresh name for FDI which unequivocally reflects the criterion of control. Hal Lary's term of 'entrepreneurial investment' fully satisfies such a requirement, and it will be used below when this criterion needs to be emphasised.[7]

Outward British FDI, at least of the manufacturing kind, has been undertaken by two distinct kinds of firm, namely those which mainly produced at home, for the domestic and export markets, but then established one or more branches abroad, and those formed for the purpose of operating wholly or mainly overseas.

The largest firm in the former (mainly domestic) category by 1914 was probably J. & P. Coats Ltd, cotton thread manufacturer of Glasgow, which set up a US branch during 1869. In part this operated through the locally formed Conant Thread Co. Samuel Courtauld & Co. Ltd i 1910 established a US subsidiary for rayon manufacture, the American Viscose Co. Not all such investing firms were incorporated. In 1890 Thomas Beecham of St Helens began manufacturing his partnership's pills in New York, the branch remaining the personal property of successive Beechams until the 1920s. This type of individual ownership of overseas ventures, held alongside domestic corporate assets, was by no means unique. Although Lipton Ltd was registered in 1898, Sir Thomas Lipton kept as his personal fiefdom the Lipton companies in the US and Canada and tea plantations in Ceylon; Lipton Ltd did not acquire them until after his death. Such privately owned overseas units were no less adequately controlled than if they had been integrated into the main enterprises.

To set up branches from scratch or to purchase an existing local company, the finance normally came out of the investing company's undistributed profits. Occasionally, subsidiary companies were registered in Britain, such as those for America and Russia of the petfood makers Spratts, and an American and Continental 'Sanitas' Company Ltd, by the British chemical firm of that name, both in the 1880s. Funds were not often raised in the host country.

In the second case, overseas companies were established in Britain specifically to operate abroad. If not abortive, new issues of funds were made on their behalf. An example, taken at random, is that of the Argentine Timber & Estates Co. Ltd of 1909, which after registration acquired property in Argentina for both ranching and the manufacture of railway sleepers and of tanning extract.

Two basic questions arise about overseas companies. The first is why many or most of these companies were in the past regarded as portfolio investments rather than, as here, allocated to the direct (entrepreneurial) category. The second is how far they can be identified as free-standing companies, where control from Britain was weak or non-existent.

As to the first question, it was shown above that because the earlier definition of FDI was concerned only with the channel of financing, and because the bulk of overseas companies' initial funds came via Britain's stock exchanges, these companies were assumed to be the result of portfolio investment. Thus successive authors have reckoned UK total overseas investments by 1914 to have been overwhelmingly portfolio and only ten (or no higher than 20) per cent direct. As will be explained in Section III, Houston and Dunning in 1976 were the first to estimate that Britain's FDI stock for 1913, defined according to the control criterion, had comprised above 34½ per cent of its aggregate overseas capital. Partial studies of 1977–78, for Latin America and for Third World recipient countries in 1914 by Irving Stone and Peter Svedberg respectively, confirmed that this proportion was not unreasonable, having been about 40 per cent for British investments in Latin America and at least 44–60 per cent for those in the Third World.[8]

What now becomes clear is that overseas companies of that era were developed by a two-stage process. In the initial stage, wealthy individuals – and sometimes companies, including investment trusts – bought shares and debentures, and thus 'invested', in such enterprises. Those scholars who approached this subject from the macro-economic and institutional viewpoints, have interestingly discussed such aspects as the marked preference of 'investors' for safe overseas securities, with low variance of returns, at the expense of domestic outlets for their funds. Here, however, the micro-economic approach requires the second stage in overseas companies' operations to be investigated as well, namely their carrying out of direct (entrepreneurial) investment, as the Argentine Timber & Estates Co. did in order to purchase and ship out, or buy locally, the necessary equipment for ranching and its various manufacturing operations.

One area where the proportions of portfolio and direct investment are difficult to disentangle is that of railways. A number of British domestic companies, as well as private 'investors', held spare cash in, say, American railroad securities as being both good earners and readily marketable. Fortunately for enquirers into this issue, the Inland Revenue reports for these years gave annual figures of income from 'railways abroad which are owned and worked by British companies with the seat of management in the United Kingdom': a precise definition of the control exercised as a result of direct (entrepreneurial) investment. The numbers of such incorporated companies are given as 104 in 1907, rising to 142 in 1913 and 1914. In Section III, the Inland Revenue data are used to estimate the railway component in aggregate FDI.

The second question about overseas companies is that of identifying the extent to which they were free-standing. The latter concept was first put forward by Mira Wilkins, who defined such companies as those set up to operate wholly or mainly overseas, and as representing an important type of British FDI between 1870 and 1914.[9] According to Wilkins, they were legally and administratively independent units, since the management strategy of each was not subordinated to, nor co-ordinated with, that of a parent operating at home in the same industry. Because they did not grow out of the domestic operations of existing enterprises with headquarters in Britain – as, it should be pointed out, the branches of home companies discussed above did – they differed from what Wilkins has called the 'American model'. In the US, the home-country head office both controlled overseas branch operations and internalised all activities within the whole enterprise, most notably the dissemination of know-how.

By contrast with the rigorous control from home and centralised strategy of US multinationals, then, the typical head office of British free-standing companies was small; in Wilkins' words, it 'normally comprised a corporate secretary and the board of directors (whose members participated in other activities in Britain), and little else'. She therefore characterised many free-standing firms as possessing 'little more than a brass nameplate' somewhere in the City of London. Many confined their operations to one overseas country, as indeed the Argentine Timber & Estates Co. did, and they tended to fall into clusters which comprised 'numerous overlapping circles of individuals and enterprises'. These circles included groups of solicitors, accountants and managers of trading companies, while among the industrial groups were mining, brewing and foodstuffs manufacture. It thus emerges that these interlocking areas of enterprise were precisely those in which Britain enjoyed a comparative advantage.

A great deal of further research on the free-standing company is needed before the full value of Wilkins' contribution to our understanding of UK overseas ventures in 1870–1914 can be assessed. Here the point at issue is whether such free-standing companies were so inadequately controlled from Britain that they should be regarded as the fruits of portfolio rather than direct (entrepreneurial) investment. In an article of 1974, John Stopford specifically excluded from the direct category overseas foreign investment where a 'sense of management' was to be found, but no strategic control exercised from Britain. That type he called 'expatriate', and thus separate from the portfolio and direct kinds.[10] As Wilkins pointed out, genuinely expatriate investment has no place in Britain's overseas assets; however, Stopford did include in the expatriate category such firms as the Burmah Oil Co. and the Anglo-Persian Oil Co., later British Petroleum, on the grounds that non-British-based interests were involved. This is a dubious argument, as the pre-1914 archives make clear the stringent and unremitting control exercised from home over both companies' ventures abroad. Thus Wilkins was correct in placing her free-standing companies not in a distinct third category but in the direct class. The debate on the whole issue continues.

To sum up, the present section has comprised an introduction to this topic, with a broad reassessment of the scope of Britain's outward foreign investments before 1914. A detailed presentation of the empirical data is given in Section III.

III

Now that Britain's overseas investment record has been discussed generally in Section II, the present section offers estimates of the actual figures. These are broken down into the portfolio and direct (entrepreneurial) categories in Table 1, while the industrial composition of FDI is set out in Table 2, and – as far as the still sketchy information allows – the recipient countries or areas are listed in Table 3. The most trustworthy method of compiling the data would have been by submitting questionnaires to all firms concerned, both domestic enterprises with branches abroad and overseas companies. However, the US authorities did not introduce this method until 1929 nor those in Britain until the early 1960s. The estimates given here, while less comprehensive, are not thereby rendered useless. Carefully calculated orders of magnitude can help to identify the dimensions of a given issue.

The estimate offered here is based on the three thorough contemporary investigations by (Sir) George Paish, editor of *The Statist*, into Britain's stock of 'capital investments in other lands' for 1907, 1910 and 1913 respectively.[11] His 1907 enquiry is one of the most important privately calculated sources of British economic data for the early decades of the twentieth century, comparable with the enquiries of, say, Arthur Bowley into Britain's capital, income, prices and savings. Paish used Inland Revenue data on income from two of the three forms of outward foreign investment, namely the securities of overseas governments and municipalities, and those of UK-owned and managed railways. As the Inland Revenue did not comprehensively record the income earned by overseas private-sector enterprises, for 1907 he compiled data of capital and income from the published accounts of the 2,172 non-railway overseas companies which he was able to obtain. For 1910 and 1913, he added particulars of the relevant new issues in the intervening years.

From these three sources, Paish estimated both the income and the total value of capital invested by Britons both in long-term loans to public-sector authorities abroad and in overseas enterprises. As the railway companies, which he included, to a considerable extent belonged to the portfolio category (for the reasons explained in Section I), here the Inland Revenue income figures are taken, and multiplied up by the reciprocal of the rate of interest – weighted by the relative amounts of capital – for the Indian, other British empire, American and non-US foreign railways included in Paish's industrial tabulation. The weighted average interest rate came to 4.407 per cent in 1907. As Paish gave no comparable income figures, but only capital, for 1910 and 1913, and as the rate of return is unlikely to have changed materially over three or six years, the 1907 railway multiplier is employed for 1910 and 1913 also.

Table 1 shows the overall figures for these years 1907, 1910 and 1913, and the attached notes specify as fully as possible the basic methods

TABLE 1

ACCUMULATED STOCK OF BRITISH OVERSEAS INVESTMENT, 1907–13 (a)

	1907		1910		1913	
	£m.	% of £2,694m	£m.	% of £3,192m	£m.	% of £3,715m
Direct investment						
Quoted companies operating overseas and directed from Britain: capital(b)	737.3		902.8		1,086.6	
Railways controlled from Britain: estimated capital(c)	277.7		366.0		454.5	
Total 'quoted'	1,015.0		1,268.8		1,541.1	
Deduction for foreign participation(d)	-101.5		-162.4		-231.2	
	913.5	33.9	1,106.4	34.7	1,309.9	35.3
Other (incl. unquoted) companies(e)	269.4	10.0	319.2	10.0	371.5	10.0
Total direct	1,182.9	43.9	1,425.6	44.7	1,681.4	45.3
Portfolio investment(f)	1,510.8	56.1	1,766.2	55.3	2,033.3	54.7
Paish's estimates	2,693.7	100.0	3,191.8	100.0	3,714.7	100.0
Feis's amended estimate(g)					3,763.3	
'Accumulated credit abroad'(h)	2,913.7		3,371.3		3,989.6	
'Accumulated net holdings of overseas assets'(i)	2,889.0		3,355.0		4,165.0	

Notes: (a) Derived from Paish's articles – see text.
  (b) 2,172 companies for 1907; for 1910 and 1913, Paish added on subsequent overseas company formations.
  (c) Data from Inland Revenue reports. Figure of £12,237,423 quoted by Paish in his 1909 article p. 468 for 1906/7, that for 1907/8 being £13,554,511. These and subsequent figures are adjusted to relevant calendar years. Capital estimated by multiplying up with weighted average of 'rate of interest' on Indian, colonial, American and foreign railways (ibid., p. 475) = 4.407 per cent. In the absence of comparable data for later years, the same rate of interest, and hence multiplier, taken for 1910 and 1913.

(d) Paish suggested 10 per cent for 1907 (ibid., p. 490), but made larger deductions for subsequent years e.g. 12.8 per cent for 1910 (Paish's 1911 article p. 171). 15 per cent assumed for 1913.
(e) £500 millions = British capital privately invested in other countries (Paish's 1909 article p. 490) = 18.6 per cent of £2693.7m. Say 10 per cent represents corporate investments, by unquoted companies and others. Ten per cent taken also for 1910 and 1913.
(f) Residual.
(g) H. Feis, *Europe: The World's Banker, 1870–1914* (New Haven, CN, 1930), p. 27. Percentages for 1913 remain unchanged if amended figures are used.
(h) A.H. Imlah, *Economic Elements in the Pax Britannica* (Cambridge, MA, 1958), p. 28.
(i) Estimates of 'accumulated (balance of payments) balance on current account (net)', omitting holdings of gold and silver in C.H. Feinstein and S. Pollard, *Studies in Capital Formation in the United Kingdom, 1750–1920* (Oxford, 1988), pp. 397, 462–3.

used. Since a major object of the present paper is to estimate the accumulated value of foreign direct (entrepreneurial) investment, particular attention is paid here to the capital of the 'quoted' enterprises operating abroad, which includes that of both overseas companies and British-controlled railways.

Holdings by foreigners need to be deducted in order to estimate the purely British share. Using data of the taxable income received by foreigners from overseas investments, Paish estimated for 1907 an average figure of ten per cent for these foreign holdings. On the basis of estimates for the subsequent new issues, his allowance for 1910 was 12.8 per cent; hence it seems fair to give a figure of 15 per cent for 1913. In a critique of the Paish estimates, Christopher Platt judged that higher deductions would be more appropriate, of 15 per cent to 1907 and 20 per cent from 1908 to 1914.[12] He based his judgement on a number of share issues which he analysed. However, these were largely of government and municipal issues, and it seems relevant to suggest that most foreigners would have sought the greater security and marketability of public sector and railway portfolio issues in preference to direct (entrepreneurial) corporate investment outlets.

The allowance for foreign holdings, used here, can be checked by the balance of payments data of accumulated credit abroad, cited at the bottom of Table 1. To the extent that foreigners purchased British overseas company securities, the proceeds increased the current balance of payments surplus, without affecting the data of (purely) British overseas investment. The gaps of £220 million in 1907, £180 million in 1910 and £226 million in 1913 between the two totals suggest possible outer limits of the foreign holding figures; these provide a reasonable fit except for 1907. The 'accumulated net holdings of overseas assets' in the

TABLE 2

QUOTED BRITISH OVERSEAS COMPANIES – INDUSTRY GROUPS (a) (%)

	Paish 1907	Paish 1910	Paish 1913	FTC 1915(b)	Houston 1914(c)
Resource-based					
Mining	25.1	21.0	18.5	21.1	24.9
Oil	1.4	1.9	2.6		5.2
Plantations (tea, coffee rubber)	2.6	4.3	4.1	5.2	23.3
Total	29.1	27.2	25.2	26.3	53.4
Market-based					
Food (esp. brewing)	1.7	1.4	1.2		3.3
Metals, incl. motor traction and mfrg.	-	1.7	2.0		4.1
Other	7.6	8.1	9.4		4.5
Total	9.3	11.2	12.6	2.1	11.9
Railways	27.4	28.9	29.5	36.8	10.3
Banking and insurance	5.3	4.8	4.8	4.0	3.5
Utilities and services					
Electric power	0.8	1.1	1.8		4.2
Gas and water	2.2	1.9	1.9		
Tramways	3.5	4.4	5.0		1.4
Telegraphs	3.4	3.1	2.9		1.3
Shipping, docks, etc.	0.6	0.3	0.5		1.6
Land and other	18.4	17.1	15.8		12.4
Total	28.9	27.9	27.9	30.8	20.9
	100.0	100.0	100.0	100.0	100.0
Total estimated FDI of quoted companies(d) (£ m)	1,015.0	1,269.0	1,541.0	1,647.0	above 1,300.0

Notes: (a) For sources, see text.
(b) Excluding assets in US and Canada.
(c) Numbers of companies only.
(d) Gross of any foreign holdings.

TABLE 3

RECIPIENT COUNTRIES OF BRITISH OUTWARD FDI, 1907-14

	Paish 1907(a)		Paish 1910 (a)		Estimates 1914	
	£ m	%	£ m	%	£ m	%
Empire						
Canada			57	6.3	40(b)	3
Australia and New Zealand			113	12.6	90(c)	5
South Africa			227	25.1		
Rest of Africa			21	2.3	105(d)	6
India and Ceylon(d)			47	5.1	135(d)	8
Malaya(d)			14	1.6	30(d)	2
Other			26	2.9	?	?
Total Empire	434	58.9	505	55.9	688(i)	41
Foreign						
United States			97	10.8	140(e)	8
Latin America			148	16.3	546(f)	33
Europe			90	10.0	225(g)	13
China, Japan & Thailand			62	7.0	82(h)	5
Total foreign	303	41.1	398	44.1	993	59
Total	737	100.0	903	100.0	1681	100

Sources: (a) See texι.

(b) D.G. Paterson, *British Direct Investment in Canada, 1890–1914*, (Toronto, 1976), pp. 49, 56.

(c) J.H. Dunning, *Explaining International Production*, (1988), p. 75.

(d) P. Svedberg, 'The Portfolio-Direct Composition of Private Foreign Investment in 1914 Revisited', *Economic Journal*, Vol. 88 (1978), pp. 770–74.

(e) J.H. Dunning, 'United States Foreign Investments and the Technological Gap', in C.P. Kindleberger and A. Shonfield (eds.), *North America and Western European Economic Policies* (1971), p. 370.

(f) I. Stone, 'British Direct and Portfolio Investment in Latin America before 1914', *Journal of Economic History*, Vol. 37 (1977).

(g) Calculated from Dunning, *Explaining*, p. 75.

(h) China and Japan, as (d). Thailand, R.P.T. Davenport-Hines and G. Jones (eds.), *British Business in Asia since 1860* (Cambridge, 1989), p. 123.

(i) Residual.

bottom row of Table 1 accord well with the 'accumulated credit abroad' item immediately above, except for the 1913 figure, which has yet to be explained.

The total for quoted companies of £1,310 million in 1913 needs to be compared with the estimate for the same year by Tom Houston and John Dunning, referred to in Section II.[13] Their estimate, of 'above £1,300 million', equivalent to 34½ per cent of the total overseas investment stock, was calculated from the *Stock Exchange Year-Book* for 1914 and relates entirely to overseas companies. Of the 13,500 enterprises quoted that year on the London Stock Exchange, they identified 3,373 as overseas companies, 2,643 being UK-registered and 730 registered abroad. This £1,300 million, or $6,500 million, figure has been widely quoted. It appears as the British element in Dunning's tabulation, country by country, of both outward and inward accumulated FDI totals for selected years between 1914 and 1978, first published in 1983.[14] However, it does not include any allowance for overseas branches of domestic companies. As the estimate is gross of foreign holdings, its discrepancy with the £1,541 million 'quoted' figure in Table 1 requires some explanation.

For instance, possibly some of the 2,172 'public (non-railway) companies' in Paish's calculations for 1907, if not the subsequent share issues, were not quoted on the stock exchange. Again, the estimates for the capital of the British-controlled railways might have been incorrectly multiplied up from income data by the procedure explained in Section I. A.R. Hall, in his tabulation of companies in 1914, discussed below, identified 112 overseas railway companies that year: somewhat fewer than the 142 noted by the Inland Revenue, but his total overseas railway capital of £466 million was reasonably close to the £454.5 million for 1913 given in Table 1.[15] The discrepancy remains to be resolved.

Hall found that 1,976 of the 5,337 companies registered in England and Scotland and listed in the *Stock Exchange Official Intelligence* for 1914 were operating wholly or very largely overseas, having total share and loan capital of £927 million. This authoritative stock exchange source clearly noted only those companies whose shares and debentures were being actively traded there – which does not by any means suggest that the overseas operations of the remainder were by then defunct. Houston and Dunning's UK-registered companies, it will be recalled, numbered 2,643, and many of the 760 or so firms not common to both lists must have been on the small side: while the average capital of Hall's overseas companies amounted to £469,000, those of Houston and Dunning – including a sizeable number of overseas-registered ones which cannot be separated out – had no more than £385,000 capital on average. Indeed, the latter sum was not far from the £369,000 average capital of Paish's 2,172 non-railway companies.

Also included in Table 1 are the value of unquoted overseas companies and that of home-based companies' branch operations abroad, the latter companies (as explained in Section II) being either quoted, unquoted or unincorporated. For 1907 Paish allocated £500 million for what he called direct (that is non-stock exchange funded) investment, or about 18½ per cent of that year's combined portfolio and direct total. However, a proportion of that £500 million comprised short-term overseas loans by banks and other companies. According to Christopher Platt's calculations, these short-term loans may have amounted to no more than £130 million by 1914.[16] The residual of £370 million was thus roughly equivalent to ten per cent of Paish's overseas investment total in 1913. This ten per cent allocation is therefore used for 1907 and 1910 also.

However, the £500 million just quoted far exceeds the £300 million 'direct' figure later estimated by Paish for 1913. If £130 million were deducted for short-term lending, the remaining £170 million is clearly too small to cover the total value of unquoted overseas companies and of branch activity by domestic companies that year. As to the latter, branch, activities, the corporate secrecy of the day, and the absence of official censuses, make it impossible to provide anything like a reliable estimate of their value, but even a sample list of the companies concerned would be helpful.

In 1974, for instance, Stopford noted the 14 significant pre-1914 British manufacturing overseas investors, from Lever Brothers to Vickers, and the 16 'outpost' foreign production activities.[17] Stephen Nicholas's data on 448 pre-1939 manufacturing multinational enterprises world-wide include over 200 which had been established before 1914.[18] Just three British ventures in the US, by Coats, Courtaulds and Shell, in 1914 had an aggregate book value of above £5 million. Mira Wilkins noted over 100 British manufacturing multinationals in the US by 1914, owning about 255 plants. Even if a third of them had closed down, or passed out of UK ownership by then, those left still represented a substantial direct (entrepreneurial) investment stake in one country.[19]

To sum up on the aggregate figures in Table 1, these show that the proportions of FDI, in relation to all overseas investment, rose from just over 44 per cent in 1907 to above 45 per cent in 1913. These findings are broadly in line with the above-mentioned partial estimates, offered by Stone and Svedberg, and greatly exceed the 10–20 per cent shares widely accepted until the 1970s. Scholars can no longer assert that FDI was a negligible part of Britain's outward foreign investment total.

Table 2 allocates the quoted overseas companies to their industry groups. As no systematic evidence exists on the industrial composition of unquoted firms and on that of mainly home-operating companies with overseas branches, data are given only of the 78 per cent of the FDI total that can be identified. In each case, percentages are given.

Partial checks on Paish's estimates are provided from three sources. First, the US Federal Trade Commission compiled from 'foreign statistical manuals of 1915' a list of 'British organised or controlled companies whose properties are located outside of the United Kingdom, United States and Canada'. Its value for the present purpose is diminished by the omission of British companies operating in North America; moreover, some categories, such as the 70 'industrials' and 386 'trading and various miscellaneous', do not closely overlap with the market-based companies listed by Paish.[20] The second source is Houston's abovementioned tabulation, of 3,373 overseas companies. While all the other estimates are weighted by the relevant forms' actual capital, Houston gave only the number of firms in each category.

A third check is from Hall's figures for 1914. His estimate for 'mines, nitrate, oil, tea, coffee, rubber' came to £258 millions, compared with £388 millions by Paish. The number of 1,346 companies in this category is likewise smaller than the 1,590 specified by Houston and Dunning. The information which Hall furnished on overseas railway companies has already been mentioned. The residual industrial category, given by Hall, is entitled 'financial land and management, operating mainly overseas'. This numbered 518 and had capital of £203 million, and corresponds to Houston and Dunning's service industries, less railways, which totalled 553 enterprises. One service industry, for which corroborative information exists, is that of banking. Geoffrey Jones has identified 31 British multinational banks in 1914, with 1,387 overseas branches and total assets – not capital – of £366 million.[21]

Table 2 confirms the accepted view that Britain's resource-based multinationals were decidedly commoner than market-based ones in this period. The former are shown to have been two or three times as large (in value) and over four times as numerous as the latter. Britain's need for the primary products which it lacked from domestic sources had been acute ever since the 'workshop of the world' era of the 1850s and 1860s; some firms had 'scoured the world' for the raw materials which they needed, and then established overseas branches to ensure supplies.[22] Sometimes efficient markets existed for such inputs, as for cotton and many types of produce. However, organisational skills and the use of technology provided entrepreneurs with the opportunity of

TABLE 4
ADJUSTMENT OF PAISH'S FIGURES OF RECIPIENT COUNTRIES, TO INCLUDE
BRITISH-CONTROLLED RAILWAYS, 1910

	£m	%
Empire		
Paish's total (Table 3)	505	
+ railways	52	
	557	43.9
Foreign		
Paish's total (Table 3)	398	
+ railways	314	
	712	56.1
Global figures of quoted overseas companies (Table 1)	1,269	100.0

Source: See text.

fully appropriating the returns on these corporate efforts, as well as of minimising transaction costs when the market was unable to supply these production requirements.

Evidence on the geographical distribution between countries of British outward FDI in this period is set out in Table 3. Paish provided no data for 1913 and only an 'empire-foreign countries' breakdown for 1907. His detailed figures for 1910 are incomplete because they omit unquoted companies, and also British-controlled railways, the latter accounting for about £366 million that year. To estimate the latter, Table 4 makes some adjustments, partly based on the Federal Trade Commission's list of overseas railways for 1915, to both the 'empire' and the 'foreign' data.

In the 'empire' total, the value of Indian railways under British control is likely to have been small, as by 1910 many networks were under Indian central or state government ownership. There do not seem to have been any British railway interests in Canada. The only other important territory with British-controlled railways, and then not on an extensive scale, was South Africa. Hence £52 million seems a reasonable estimate. As to foreign countries, well before 1914, according to Mira Wilkins, there was little or no controlling interest from abroad in US railroads.[23] Thus the really heavy British railway presence was in Latin America, with £340 million capital according to Stone and £252 million according to Svedberg. Edelstein has argued that, for all British investments in Latin America, the 40 per cent of debentures in the direct category should be treated as portfolio since these debentures were seldom closely held and thus not organised for collective pressure on the companies concerned.[24] If Edelstein's argument is correct in the case of railways, then the Svedberg estimate is probably nearer to the truth. Adding the few overseas railways in Spain and Egypt gives an estimate of £314 million for this category.

Thus the adjusted Paish figures relating to 1910 yields a proportion of 56 per cent for foreign countries and 44 per cent for the empire. As to the right-hand column in Table 3, independent estimates are not easy to find and are then clearly far from reliable. The estimates there, from a variety of sources, highlight the number of problems that remain. For example, the 59 per cent for foreign countries include the large aggregate figure by Stone to cover Latin America, thus neglecting Edelstein's reservations about the debenture component. The 'total empire' figure of £688 million is a residual, leaving a considerable gap of £400 million still to be allocated.

Even so, simply compiling these estimates provides a useful pointer to the kinds of question which need to be looked into. For example, there must be a substantial underrepresentation of the widespread mining interests in South Africa. The geographical findings of Nicholas are of interest here. On the basis of his sample of 200 pre-1914 manufacturing MNEs, he estimated that foreign countries accounted for 66 per cent of British FDI, 43 per cent in Europe and 13 per cent in the US, while territories in the empire accounted for 34 per cent, 28 developed (in the 'white dominions') and six per cent undeveloped.[25]

After this presentation of the quantitative data, some conclusions are offered in Section IV.

IV

The present article began by discussing the anatomy of the British economy before 1914, and most notably the sectors concerned with overseas activities. As was made clear at the outset, the comparative advantage possessed by Britain helped to determine not only the total volume and composition of its exports, but also those of its long-term outward investments abroad. Thus these two forms of overseas involvement should properly be studied more closely together than hitherto, if Britain's still very positive role in the world economy at that time is to be adequately recognised. For instance, exports were the result of entrepreneurial initiatives, but so was FDI. Hence it was crucial here to distinguish the latter from overseas portfolio investment. As long as that portfolio element was believed to make up some 90 per cent of the total, it was all too easy to assume that the wealthy in Britain placed their money abroad because entrepreneurs were not creating the required profitable investment opportunities at home. However, a large proportion of overseas investment can now be seen as having been entrepreneurially generated and thereby adding to the economy's strength rather than representing a source of weakness. While, therefore, Britain's share of world trade fell from 23 to 17 per cent between 1870 and 1914, its FDI stock rose from about £160 million in 1870 to no less than £1,680 million in 1913, an average annual growth rate of 5.3 per cent.[26] The data of the industrial breakdown of this FDI and of its geographical spread in Tables 2 and 3 show the extent to which British entrepreneurs were substituting overseas investment for visible trade. Tariff and other trade barriers imposed by Britain's competitors, in particular the US and continental European countries, gravely hampered much exporting effort by the UK. However, at the same time British entrepreneurs were pursuing national competitive advantage in a range of resource-based, infrastructural and service ventures in most quarters of the globe. This essay has therefore attempted to sketch out the principles of and some quantitative backing to the whole topic, in the hope that it will inspire further systematic research along the lines suggested above.

NOTES

This paper develops some of the themes which are discussed in the author's 'Foreign Direct Investment and British Economic Deceleration 1870–1914', to be published in *Zeitschrift für Unternehmensgeschichte* (1993). Tables 1 and 3 are taken from the same source. I am particularly grateful to Tom Houston, who kindly provided information regarding the data in his and John Dunning's *UK Industry Abroad* (1976) and allowed me to follow the methods of calculation for these tables, which he used in his 'Knowledge as a Factor Input in International Business' (Unpublished D. Phil. thesis, University of Sussex, June 1977). My thanks are also due to Mark Casson, Geoffrey Jones and John Stopford and two referees for their comments.

1. N.F.R. Crafts and M. Thomas, 'Comparative Advantage in UK Manufacturing Trade, 1910–1935', *Economic Journal*, Vol.96 (1986), pp.629–45.
2. A.D. Chandler, *Scale and Scope: The Dynamics of Industrial Capitalism* (Cambridge, MA, 1990), p.262.

3. J.H. Dunning, *Explaining International Production* (1988), esp. pp.1–40; T.A.B. Corley, 'John Dunning's Contribution to International Business Studies', in P.J. Buckley and M. Casson (eds.), *Multinational Enterprises in the World Economy: Essays in Honour of John Dunning* (Aldershot, 1992), pp.1–19.
4. A. Imlah, *Economic Elements in the Pax Britannica: Studies in British Foreign Trade in the Nineteenth Century* (Cambridge, MA, 1958), pp.70–5.
5. C.H. Feinstein and S. Pollard, *Studies in Capital Formation in the United Kingdom, 1750–1920* (Oxford, 1988), pp.395–8.
6. S.H. Hymer, *The International Operations of National Firms: A Study of Direct Investment* (Cambridge, MA, 1976), originally a Ph.D. thesis at MIT, 1960.
7. H. Lary, *The United States in the World Economy* (Washington, DC, 1943), p.100.
8. I. Stone, 'British Direct and Portfolio Investment in Latin America before 1914', *Journal of Economic History*, Vol.37 (1977), pp.690–722; P. Svedberg, 'The Portfolio-Direct Composition of Private Foreign Investment in 1914 Revisited', *Economic Journal*, Vol.88 (1978), pp.763–77.
9. M. Wilkins, 'The Free-Standing Company, 1870–1914: An Important Type of British Foreign Direct Investment', *Economic History Review*, 2nd series, Vol.41 (1988), pp.259–82.
10. J. Stopford, 'The Origins of British-based Multinational Manufacturing Enterprises', *Business History Review*, Vol.48 (1974), pp.303–35.
11. G. Paish, 'Great Britain's Capital Investments in Other Lands', *Journal of the Royal Statistical Society*, Vol.72 (1909), pp.465–95; idem, 'Great Britain's Capital Investments in Individual Colonial and Foreign Countries', ibid., Vol.74 (1911), pp.167–200; idem, 'The Export of Capital and the Cost of Living', *Transactions of the Manchester Statistical Society* (1913/14), pp.63–92.
12. D.C.M. Platt, *Britain's Investment Overseas on the Eve of the First World War* (1986), p.36.
13. T. Houston and J.H. Dunning, *UK Industry Abroad* (1976), p.40. As Dunning explained in the Preface, Houston provided all the tables, including this estimate.
14. J.H. Dunning, 'Changes in the Level and Structure of International Production: The Last 100 Years', in M. Casson (ed.) *The Growth of International Business* (1983), pp.84–139.
15. A.R. Hall, *The London Capital Market and Australia, 1870–1914* (Canberra, 1963), p.201.
16. Platt, *Britain's Investment Overseas*, p.57.
17. Stopford, 'Origins', pp.316–17, 324.
18. S. Nicholas, 'The Expansion of British Multinational Companies: Testing for Managerial Failure', in J. Foreman-Peck (ed.), *New Perspectives on the Late Victorian Economy: Quantitative Economic History, 1860–1914* (Cambridge, 1991), pp.130–34.
19. M. Wilkins, 'European and North American Multinationals, 1870–1914: Comparisons and Contrasts', *Business History*, Vol.30 (1988), p.14.
20. Federal Trade Commission, 'British Investments Abroad', *Report on Cooperation in American Export Trade*, Vol.2 (Washington, DC, 1916).
21. G. Jones, *British Multinational Banking, 1830–1990* (Oxford, 1993), pp.396–7.
22. H.J. Habakkuk, 'Free Trade and Commercial Expansion, 1853–1870', in J. Holland Rose, A.P. Newton and E.A. Benians (eds.) *The Cambridge History of the British Empire*, Vol.2 (Cambridge, 1940), p.773; G. Wilson, *The Old Days of Price's Patent Candle Company* (1876), pp.27–8.
23. M. Wilkins, *The History of Foreign Investment in the United States to 1914* (Cambridge, MA, 1989), p.197.
24. M. Edelstein, *Overseas Investment in the Age of High Imperialism: The United Kingdom, 1850–1914* (1982), pp.34–5.
25. Nicholas, 'Expansion', pp.130–34.
26. T.A.B. Corley, 'Economic Theory and the Evolution of Multinationals before 1870: A UK–US Comparison' (Unpublished MS, 1992).

Foreign Multinationals in British Manufacturing, 1850–1962

FRANCES BOSTOCK AND GEOFFREY JONES
University of Reading

I

This article presents new evidence on the dimensions and characteristics of foreign multinational investment in British manufacturing between 1850 and 1962. Although such investment was considerable, and had a large impact on several British industrial sectors, research on the period before British official statistics began in the early 1960s has remained limited. The study begins with a brief review of the importance of foreign multinationals to the British economy. This is followed by a description of a new database on inward investment. The main part of the article provides an analysis of the flow of foreign multinational investment into Britain between 1850 and 1962, followed by an examination of some of its most important characteristics at benchmark dates.

II

During the 1980s and 1990s, the re-industrialisation by Japanese-owned companies of parts of British industry, notably motor vehicles and consumer electronics, has focused attention on the role of foreign multinationals in the British economy. Not surprisingly, a large literature has developed on the impact of foreign multinationals on the contemporary British economy.[1] In contrast, there remain few studies of the origins and growth of inward FDI into Britain before the 1960s. This reflects the much smaller overall size of foreign multinational activity in Britain compared to the more recent past, as well as the difficulties of researching a period when no official British statistics whatsoever exist. Nevertheless, it is well-established that Britain's position as an important host economy for foreign multinationals goes back to the nineteenth century. It was very often the preferred first location in Europe of the pioneer American multinationals of that era, as it was to be for Japanese companies later. And American – and other European – firms acquired leading positions in certain British manufacturing activities decades before the first Japanese manufacturing multinational began production in Britain in 1969.

By far the most important research to date remains Dunning's path-breaking book on US investment in British manufacturing industry, published in 1958. Dunning surveyed the growth of American FDI in Britain from the first recorded cases in the 1850s, and undertook a detailed analysis of the characteristics of over 200 US-owned subsidiaries active in that country in the early 1950s. The overall conclusion pointed to the positive impact of American FDI, which permitted Britain 'to derive benefits from the competitive and dynamic qualities of the American economy'.[2]

The relative absence of research on this subject since Dunning's book reflects the fact that when business historians began to study the growth of multinationals, they took a home country perspective, examining outward FDI rather than inward FDI. It was not until much later that business historians began systematic research on countries such as Germany, the US and Japan as host economies for foreign multi-nationals.[3] An article by one of the present authors on foreign multi-nationals and British industry before 1945, published in 1988, formed part of this new interest in the evolution of host economies. Using a sample of 125 foreign investments in Britain between 1850 and 1945, this study looked at the timing and characteristics of foreign multi-national entry into Britain, attempted to explain the attractiveness of the UK as a host economy in the period, and tentatively discussed the impact of foreign companies on British industry.[4] This study also con-cluded, as had Dunning earlier, that inward FDI had in general exer-cised a positive impact on Britain.

Foreign-owned companies in Britain are interesting because they have exhibited a number of different characteristics from their indigenous counterparts. It was evident in the 1960s and later that they were particularly concentrated in growth sectors, and in the more technologically advanced parts of manufacturing,[5] and this appears to have been true historically. A series of studies of foreign multinational subsidiaries in Britain have shown their higher productivity and profitability compared to manufacturing industry as a whole. A study of the 1950 to 1974 period, for example, showed that the average rates of return of US affiliates in Britain were consistently much higher than those of leading quoted companies in UK manufacturing. United States affiliates in Britain had considerably higher productivity than British firms, and the greater the capital intensity of the sector, the bigger the differential. Overall the productivity of US subsidiaries was an average 20 per cent higher than their UK competitors. A productivity differential persisted over subsequent decades.[6]

The evidence on the superior performance of foreign multinationals in Britain has to be treated with caution. Research on profitability in the contemporary period generally shows a superior performance for multinational affiliates in all developed countries: there are, however, numerous accounting and other problems in the way of meaningful comparisons. Again, the general experience is for multinationals everywhere to achieve higher productivity in their affiliates than the average achieved by indigenous competitors, though usually less than that achieved in the parent company.[7] Nevertheless, there is sufficient evidence of the superior productivity of foreign affiliates in British manufacturing to suggest clear superiorities in managerial or other entrepreneurial abilities over British firms.

This essay is an exercise in mapping foreign multinational activity in Britain before 1962 rather than explaining its differences with indigenous firms, or its impact on them, although it is hoped that the new data presented here will assist subsequent research on such topics.

III

The analysis which follows is based on a database comprising information on 685 foreign manufacturing companies which undertook FDI in the United Kingdom between 1850 and 1962. Between them, these foreign parents established 927 new manufacturing subsidiaries. In addition, there were 80 transfers of ownership between foreign parents. The database has been compiled from multiple sources, including annual reports of US and other foreign companies, British government files, and corporate histories, as well as the raw material used by Dunning to write his 1958 book. The files of Raymond Vernon's Multinational Enterprise Study project of the 1960s undertaken at Harvard Business School were also examined.[8]

A multinational has been defined simply as a firm with at least one manufacturing, assembling or packaging facility in a foreign country. The hundreds of foreign manufacturing firms which established sales and marketing subsidiaries only in Britain were excluded, as were non-equity licensing agreements between foreign companies and British firms, even though agreements have been vital at times for some British industries, such as chemicals and pharmaceuticals.

While the majority of foreign companies before 1962 established wholly-owned subsidiaries in Britain, a minority used different ownership arrangements. This raises problems about whether investments should be regarded as FDI or portfolio in nature. In addition to 100 per cent ownership, three other types of ownership have been considered. Firstly, there were joint ventures, when a foreign company owned a British subsidiary jointly with another foreign company or a British company. Secondly, there were instances when a foreign company owned the majority of the stock of a British company, with the British public or other non-corporate investors holding the rest. A prominent example of this category was Ford between 1928 and 1961. Both joint ventures and majority-owned subsidiaries have been counted as FDI.

The most problematic ownership category has been that of British companies in which foreign firms owned only a minority of the stock. The question of managerial 'control' has been the critical factor in deciding whether such minority foreign shareholding in a British firm should be counted as FDI. Unfortunately, the proportion of equity in foreign hands provides little guidance as to whether or not foreign 'control' was exercised, which could only be ascertained by an examination of circumstances of each case.[9]

The focus of this study on foreign companies in Britain, rather than foreign individuals, means that firms established by foreigners who resided in Britain have not been counted as FDI. However, there are ambiguous cases here also, such as that of the Weston family. In 1934 Garfield Weston, who controlled a large Canadian biscuit company, George Weston Ltd, purchased a small Scottish biscuit company and opened an Edinburgh factory. Other biscuit factories were also purchased and, following the introduction of Canadian production and sales techniques, Weston rapidly gained market share. At the same time a number of bread plant bakeries were also acquired. The initial acquisitions were made through George Weston Ltd of Canada, although the funds were borrowed from the United States, but by the end of 1935 a British public company, Allied Bakeries, had been formed to acquire the investments. The Weston family controlled a majority of the shares, but Allied Bakeries was never a subsidiary of the Canadian company. Weston himself largely resided in Britain, and was a Conservative MP between 1939 and 1945. In the 1950s Weston acquired the famous London store Fortnum & Mason, and founded the Fine Fare chain of supermarkets. In 1960 the large British baking and milling interests were brought together as Associated British Foods (ABF). The absence of Canadian corporate control over Allied Bakeries and ABF means they cannot be described as subsidiaries of a Canadian multinational, and this study has followed earlier writers in regarding them as British rather than foreign firms, though the initial acquisitions in 1934 are counted as Canadian FDI.[10] Yet it is evident that from the mid-1930s until the present day ultimate control over the Weston interests in Britain has lain in the hands of shadowy family holding companies, which also controlled Weston companies in North America and elsewhere. The Westons were able to transfer the Fine Fare supermarket chain into Canadian hands in 1963 – and then transfer it back to ABF four years later.[11]

The database is considerably larger than the sample studied by Jones in 1988. The present database has 495 foreign-owned manufacturing companies set up in Britain between 1850 and 1939 with around 600 plants, while the earlier study only located 125 manufacturing invest-ments in the 1850–1945 period. The database compares well with Dunning's research. Dunning found 169 US-owned manufacturing units in Britain in 1929, while the database has 200 US parents controlling 262 plants in 1935. Dunning estimated that in 1953 there were 246 US-owned manufacturing enterprises in the UK, and his sample had 205 firms with 306 manufacturing plants.[12] The database for benchmark date 1955 has 270 US parents controlling 433 plants. The first official statistics for inward FDI are contained in the 1963 Census of Production, which shows that 502 foreign-owned enterprises in Britain controlled 1,098 manufacturing establishments. Of these foreign companies, 369 were US-owned, and they controlled a total of 813 establishments.[13] The totals contained in the database for benchmark year 1962 fit quite closely with these numbers. It has 448 parents (of whom 366 were US) controlling 901 plants (of which 718 were American).

There are good grounds for believing, therefore, that the database includes the great majority of foreign companies which manufactured in Britain between 1850 and 1962. It is quite likely that a number of small FDIs have escaped identification, but it is most unlikely that larger investments have been missed. There is certainly room for discussion about whether certain partly foreign-owned firms should have been included or excluded, and about ambiguous cases such as the Westons. Nevertheless, the database can be regarded as offering a good basis for generalisation about the population of foreign firms which invested in British manufacturing.

IV

The first instances of FDI in manufacturing in Britain occurred in the 1850s. Two of the pioneers in this decade were the US firms Colt and J.R. Ford, manufacturers of hand-guns and rubber footwear respect-ively. The Colt factory, established in 1853, was in London, while that of Ford was located in Edinburgh in 1856.[14] The 1860s arrivals included a German firm, Ohlendorff & Co., which manufactured guano fertiliser in London; A. & J. Ettlinger of France, which manufactured fans, also in London; and R. Hoe & Co., an American printing press manufac-turer. The Colt investment was only sustained until 1858, but the others survived longer. J.R. Ford continued in American ownership until 1888, while Ohlendorff continued until the First World War, when it was sequestrated. The two most significant direct investments in this early period were those of Siemens and Singer. The international expansion of the German firm of Siemens & Halske is hard to classify in modern terms because its foreign ventures were managed by family members who resided abroad. However, its first FDI in Britain can probably be regarded as dating from 1858, when William Siemens (who became a naturalised Briton in the following year) set up a 'finishing works' for telegraphic material in the Westminster area of London. This operation continued until 1866, but meanwhile another British subsidiary of the firm, also founded in 1858, began to manufacture sea cables in Woolwich in 1863, having previously purchased them from a British supplier. In 1865 the British interests of the German firm were reorganised as Siemens Brothers.[15] Two years later, Singer, the American company which had grown rapidly in the 1850s through the exploitation of the world's first commercially successful sewing machine, established an assembly plant in Glasgow. This came to manufacture entire machines, and supply them to other markets, and in 1885 Singer opened a new factory, again near Glasgow, which was the largest sewing machine factory in the world.[16]

The chronological pattern of subsequent new foreign entrants to British manufacturing is shown in Table 1. This is analysed by product: the Standard Industrial Classification (SIC) is given in Appendix 1. Both the 1900s and the 1920s were periods when inward investment reached new peaks, but perhaps more surprising is that even war and economic depression did not halt multinational investment. Fourteen new foreign-owned manufacturing subsidiaries were established between 1915 and 1918, mostly by American, Dutch and Swedish firms. More striking still was the large number of new entrants in the 1930s, which contrasts sharply with the evidence on FDI stock levels. The book value of US FDI in British manufacturing grew by only a marginal 2.6 per cent between 1929 and 1940.[17] Yet while the stock level remained nearly constant, this disguised the fact that many foreign firms were investing in Britain, in part at least because of the growth of tariff barriers, while others were divesting. New American entrants in the 1930s included Hoover, whose factory at Perivale began production in 1932; Briggs Bodies, which opened a factory at Dagenham in 1930 to manufacture automobile bodies and stampings; and Coca Cola and Pepsi Cola, which established concentrate manufacturing plants in London in 1935 and 1939 respectively.[18]

TABLE 1

NEW MANUFACTURING FDI IN THE UK PER DECADE BY TWO DIGIT SIC CODE,[1]
1850–1962

Decade	New subsidiaries	11	14	16	22	24	25	26	31	32	33	34	35	36	37	41	42	43	44	45	46	47	48	49
1850-59	3	-	-	-	-	-	-	-	-	1	-	1	-	-	-	-	-	-	-	1	-	-	-	-
1860-69	4	-	-	-	-	-	1	-	-	2	-	-	-	-	-	-	-	-	-	1	-	-	-	-
1870-79	4	-	-	-	-	-	-	-	-	-	-	-	-	1	1	2	-	-	-	-	-	-	-	-
1880-89	8	-	-	-	-	-	3	-	-	1	-	1	-	1	1	1	-	-	-	-	-	-	-	-
1890-99	30	-	1	-	1	1	9	-	1	7	1	3	-	1	1	-	-	-	-	1	1	1	-	1
1900-09	75	5	-	-	7	1	9	1	4	11	-	17	3	2	-	5	5	-	1	-	1	2	-	1
1910-19	56	-	-	-	2	1	10	-	3	11	-	8	2	-	4	7	2	-	-	2	1	-	-	3
1920-29	158	-	3	2	6	3	28	2	17	23	4	21	8	3	5	8	6	-	-	3	2	3	8	3
1930-39	157	-	-	1	7	4	38	1	10	18	1	19	4	-	11	10	14	5	-	6	1	4	2	1
1940-49	68	-	-	-	2	-	13	-	5	14	4	6	1	-	4	2	2	2	1	1	1	4	2	4
1950-59	230	-	-	-	10	7	60	2	12	60	6	20	2	1	10	5	15	1	-	5	-	5	5	4
1960-62	134	-	-	-	5	1	33	1	5	31	1	18	2	1	11	6	6	-	-	-	-	5	5	3
Totals	927	5	4	3	40	18	204	7	57	179	17	114	22	10	48	46	50	8	2	20	7	24	22	20

Note: 1. Main Product Codes on Entry.

Source: Database.

Foreign multinational investment was particularly active in chemicals, mechanical engineering, and electrical and electronic engineering before the First World War. These are represented by SIC codes 25, 32 and 34. In these industries, foreign firms like Siemens, the General Electric Co., Westinghouse Electric, Singer, Hoechst and Ciba dominated British production of certain products. Singer, for example, faced no serious British competitor in the sewing machine market, unlike the situation in Germany – for example – where Pfaff became a vigorous rival.[19] The British subsidiaries of German and Swiss firms became preeminent in British manufacturing of a number of chemical and pharmaceutical products, while the entire heavy plant side of British electrical machinery production was dominated by German and American-owned firms.[20]

In the inter-war years there was also significant new investment in metal goods, motor vehicles, and food and drink products (SIC codes 31, 35, 41 and 42). The latter category included firms such as Mars, which began manufacturing chocolate and pet food in the 1930s, and most of the leading American breakfast cereal manufacturers, including Shredded Wheat, Quaker Oats, and Kellogg. The latter began exporting its famous Corn Flakes and All Bran products to Britain in 1922, followed by Rice Krispies in 1928, and opened a Manchester factory, the largest of its kind outside the United States, in 1938. The inter-war British breakfast cereals market was dominated by such American firms, against whom only a handful of British firms, notably Weetabix, offered even token competition.[21] The Swiss firms Nestlé and Wander were important in milk products. Wander established production facilities at Hemel Hempstead in 1919 to manufacture its malted milk drink Ovaltine. This was the market leader in inter-war Britain, some way ahead of the rival Horlicks drink produced by its main British competitor.[22]

After the hiatus caused by the Second World War and its aftermath, the 1950s witnessed another surge of inward investment. US FDI in British manufacturing rose from $542 million in 1950 to $1,611 million in 1959, and reached $2,521 million in 1962.[23] American business in this latter period assumed (prematurely as it turned out) that Britain would join the newly formed European Community, and was attracted to Britain as a location from which to export to the regional market. Table 1 shows that this period was noteworthy for high levels of inward investment in chemicals and mechanical engineering, and to a lesser extent in electrical and electronic engineering. In the chemical sector, these years saw important investments in British pharmaceuticals by US firms such as G.D. Searle, which opened a High Wycombe factory in

1953; Smith Kline & French, which purchased the British firm of A.J. White in 1956; and E.R. Squibb, which manufactured in Liverpool after 1949 and was a pioneer in new anti-tuberculosis drugs. Other pharmaceutical companies which began manufacturing in Britain post-war included the Upjohn Co., Chas. Pfizer & Co., Armour, and the French companies Roussel and Uclaf, which later merged. Roussel, which began manufacturing in Harrow in the London suburbs in 1948, was Britain's first large-scale producer of cortizone.[24]

Within the wider product groups identified in Table 1, there was also further concentration. The foreign companies in chemicals, for example, were heavily clustered in basic industrial chemicals and pharmaceuticals. In mechanical engineering, FDI was concentrated in machine tools and mechanical equipment. In electrical engineering, foreign firms clustered in telecommunications equipment, electronic capital goods and passive electronic components.

It is important to recognise that this table – and subsequent ones – are based simply on the number of foreign subsidiaries, without regard to their importance in terms of employment, sales and asset size. Table 2 gives the first available official data on these subjects in the 1960s.

A most striking difference between Tables 1 and 2 is the comparative importance of FDI in vehicles. While a comparatively small number of foreign-owned companies entered motor vehicles production before 1962, this dramatically understates their overall importance to the British economy. By 1962 foreign companies accounted for a quarter of total British employment in the vehicle sector, and nearly one-third of the sales, while vehicles accounted for almost one-fifth of total foreign-owned assets in Britain.

These statistics emphasise the point that a few large firms played a dominant part in the economic activity of foreign companies in British manufacturing. In 1973 around a quarter of total US affiliates in British manufacturing had assets over £5 million, but this accounted for 87 per cent of total US assets in British manufacturing. Well over a half of the US affiliates employed less than 500 people: the largest 12 per cent of affiliates employed 65 per cent of total workers in US affiliates.[25] In 1962 three US companies, Ford, Standard Telephone & Cables (STC) and Vauxhall, employed around one-fifth of the workforce employed by foreign-owned companies in British manufacturing, with 61,000, 32,000 and 24,879 workers respectively. Four more US affiliates accounted for another 40,000 workers: Kodak (11,000); Singer (10,150); Hoover (10,000) and Goodyear (9,000).

Throughout the entire period from 1850 to 1962, the large dominant foreign-owned companies in Britain were overwhelmingly American,

TABLE 2

EMPLOYMENT, SALES AND ASSETS OF FOREIGN-CONTROLLED MANUFACTURING
COMPANIES IN THE UK, 1963 AND 1965

Industry Group	Foreign Employment (1963)		Sales (1963)		Foreign-Owned[1] Assets (1965)
	No (000)	% UK	£m	% UK	£m
Food, drink and tobacco	40.9	5.4	278.9	5.4	187
Chemicals	48.3	12.2	287.2	13.1	227
Metal manufacturing	27.0	4.7	162.0	6.2	154
Mechanical engineering	116.1	6.8	361.7	8.7	337
Electrical engineering	100.9	13.1	270.7	14.5	185
Vehicles	110.7	25.6	647.1	31.1	304
Other Manufacturers	96.4	2.9	518.1	5.3	249
Total Manufacturing	540.3	6.8	2525.7	9.0	1,643

Note: 1. Book values of net assets attributable to overseas investors at year end.

Source: M.D. Steuer et al., The Impact of Foreign Direct Investment on the United
Kingdom (1973), pp. 195–6.

though non-US firms were important in particular products. In 1907
three of the largest ten foreign employers which can be identified were
non-American: Siemens (1,533 workers) Mannesmann (1,500), and the
Danish firm Otto Mønsted (750), but all three were dwarfed by Singer's
7,000 workers. In 1935 L.M. Ericsson, with 4,300 workers, was among
the ten largest (identified) foreign employers, while another Swedish
firm, SKF with 5,200 British workers, was the only non-US company
among the ten largest identifiable employers in 1962.

In contrast to these large firms, quite a number of the inward investments in all periods were on a small scale, and undertaken by 'small'
companies. One example was the Norwegian firm of Mustad & Son,
which built a factory near Bristol in 1911 to manufacture horseshoe
nails. The workforce may have been as small as 50, but the firm had
evident competitive advantages in the British market. By 1928 it had

purchased all eight British competitors, with a particular eye on their trade names, and it became the sole British manufacturer of horseshoe nails. The enterprise diversified into wood screw manufacture in the mid-1930s, and its employment climbed to 220 during the Second World War. The subsidiary continued on a modest scale in the post-war world, finally abandoning horseshoe nail production in 1963, although an upsurge in demand led it to resume their manufacture in the early 1980s.[26] There were subsidiaries on a smaller scale still than Mustad. The pre-1914 British subsidiaries of the German chemical firms Hoechst and BASF, for example, employed a mere 57 and 37 workers respectively at their Liverpool plants.[27] Luminous Processes Inc., one of the new American entrants of the 1950s, began luminising clock faces in Alexandria, Scotland, in 1951 with a workforce of 11. It later moved to a plant at Dumbarton, but still only employed 19 workers in 1957.[28]

Table 3 confirms that the United States was always the single most important home economy for foreign multinationals in Britain. Many of the pioneer pre-1914 US multinational manufacturers identified by Wilkins had built or acquired plants in Britain by the time of the First World War. Examples included, in addition to the firms already mentioned, Kodak (cameras), United Shoe Machinery (boot and shoe machinery) and Ford, which opened a motor car assembly plant in Manchester in 1911.[29]

This American pre-eminence was most closely challenged in the 1900s, when the total number of Continental European FDIs was larger than American. Around 30 per cent of the new manufacturing FDI in that decade came from Germany. The German firms were clustered in the electrical, chemical and pharmaceutical sectors and included subsidiaries of Mannesmann, Hoechst, Bayer and Bosch. The latter began manufacturing in Britain in 1907, and by the eve of the First World War provided between 85 and 95 per cent of the British market for magnetos and spark plugs.[30] German FDI in British manufacturing may have been higher still: Schröter has recently estimated that there were 33 German-owned manufacturing affiliates in the British chemical industry alone by 1914, but it has proved impossible to verify this number.[31] Among the other Continental European investors in Britain was a Danish margarine manufacturer, a Swedish telephone manufacturer, and the Swiss pharmaceuticals and chemicals companies Hoffman La Roche and Ciba. Anglo-Swiss Condensed Milk, which merged with Nestlé in 1905, began production of condensed milk in Chippenham as early as 1872.[32]

The First World War, and its aftermath, resulted in a dramatic fall in German FDI, which did not resume really dynamic growth until the 1970s. This general picture is certainly confirmed in Table 3, yet there

TABLE 3

NEW MANUFACTURING FDI IN THE UK PER DECADE FROM 1850 TO 1962 BY NATIONALITY

Decade	Total Subsidiaries	USA	Canada	CH	Sweden	Germany	France	NL	Other
1850-59	3	2	-	-	-	1	-	-	-
1860-69	4	2	-	-	-	1	1	-	-
1870-79	4	1	-	2	-	-	1	-	-
1880-89	8	4	-	1	-	1	1	-	1
1890-99	30	16	-	-	-	8	4	1	1
1900-09	75	35	1	2	3	22	5	3	4
1910-19	56	31	-	5	8	2	1	5	4
1920-29	158	118	1	2	5	6	7	14	5
1930-39	157	110	8	9	5	12	2	2	9
1940-49	68	53	3	3	2	-	3	2	2
1950-59	230	187	12	4	9	6	2	2	8
1960-62	134	116	1	5	4	3	-	2	3
Totals	927	675	26	33	36	62	27	31	37

Source: Database.

was a minor renaissance of German FDI in Britain in the late 1920s and 1930s partly because of the re-acquisition of former subsidiaries.[33] Between 1926 and 1929 Mannesmann, for example, re-acquired majority control over its former British subsidiary in Wales, which had been sequestrated during the war. There was a series of German joint ventures with British firms, such as that between Bosch and Lucas in 1931 to manufacture fuel injection equipment and electrical products at Acton. I.G. Farben, the giant German chemicals group created in 1925, generally confined its international strategy to market-sharing agreements and FDI in distribution, although major direct investments in manufacturing were made in the United States. In Britain, the German firm had various collaborative arrangements with ICI, which meant that it had neither the incentive nor the opportunity to undertake large-scale manufacture. However, even in Britain I.G. Farben established four small British production subsidiaries in this period, two of them joint ventures with ICI, one with another German firm, and one wholly-owned.[34]

In addition to these German ventures, firms from the smaller European countries were active inward investors in the inter-war years. The Dutch investors included large companies such as Philips, which made a series of direct investments in Britain after 1919, but there were also smaller firms involved. One example was N.V. Hollandia Fabrieken Kattenburg, which started manufacturing raincoats in Manchester in 1927.[35] Important new Swedish entrants included Elektrolux, which started manufacturing vacuum cleaners and refrigerators in Britain in 1926, and dominated that market along with the US-owned Hoover. The inter-war years also saw some significant French investments, including the building of car assembly and manufacturing plants by Citroën and Renault in 1926 and 1927 respectively, and Michelin's establishment of a tyre factory at Stoke-on-Trent in 1927.[36]

Nevertheless, the overall US pre-eminence in new FDI between 1919 and 1962 is striking. The numbers of new US-owned subsidiaries are higher than that calculated by Chandler from the Harvard Multinational Enterprise Study, which gave 42 new US investments in British manufacturing between 1918 and 1929 and 93 between 1930 and 1948, compared to the 119 and 163 shown in Table 3 for comparable periods.[37] The inter-war American entrants were often major US corporations, which made large investments in Britain. Well-known examples include Goodyear and Firestone, which started tyre manufacture in Wolverhampton and London in 1927 and 1928 respectively; and Monsanto, which made its first FDI in Britain in 1920 and manufactured over 80 chemical products by the 1950s. The American investments in the motor industry included not only Ford, which opened its giant new factory at Dagenham in 1931, and General Motors, which acquired the British firm of Vauxhall in 1925, but suppliers such as Briggs Bodies, and the Kelsey-Hayes Wheel Co., which started manufacturing wheels for Ford – and others – at Dagenham in 1931.[38]

Table 3 shows clearly the enormous importance American firms had compared to those of other countries among the post-Second World War inward investors. The many American newcomers included Texas Instruments, which began manufacture of integrated circuits, semiconductors and transistors in Bedford in 1957, and Hewlett-Packard, which began manufacture, also at Bedford, four years later; Campbell Soups, which started manufacturing at King's Lynn in 1959; and the Dictaphone Corporation, which began production of dictating machines in London in 1948. The latter formed part of a cluster of US-owned firms in office equipment manufacture by the mid-1950s, which included Remington Rand, National Cash Register and IBM.[39] IBM had only a modest assembly operation in Britain before the Second World War, because of a licensing agreement dating from 1908 with the British Tabulating Machine Co., which gave that British firm exclusive rights to manufacture and sell tabulating machines in the British Empire outside Canada. Following the termination of this agreement in 1949, IBM rapidly expanded its business in Britain.[40] The 1950s and early 1960s were a high point of American efficiency over their British competitors. The productivity 'gap' and profitability performance between American affiliates and British firms appear at their widest in this period: they subsequently narrowed through the 1960s and 1970s.[41]

Non-American investments between 1950 and 1962 were modest by comparison, although there was significant expansion by firms such as Philips, Geigy, Ciba and Nestlé, which were already established in Britain.[42] A handful of new German direct investments were made after 1952, when the German authorities again permitted FDI under certain circumstances. Examples included the establishment of a record pressing company at Walthamstow by Deutsche Grammophon in 1954, and of a subsidiary to manufacture mining equipment in Wales by Thyssen in the same period.[43] Canadian firms were some of the most active investors. In 1945 Massey-Harris began manufacturing agricultural equipment in Britain, building a large new factory at Kilmarnock, Scotland, three years later. In 1953 the only important British manufacturer of tractors, Ferguson, merged with the Canadian company to create Massey-Ferguson, which was Canadian-controlled.[44] There was also significant Canadian investment in Scotch whisky. Hiram Walker had acquired its first Scottish whisky distillery in 1930, and made further acquisitions later in that decade, and again in the 1950s. In 1949 Seagrams of Canada acquired Chivas Brothers of Aberdeen, blenders and grocers, and used this as a vehicle for the acquisition of distillery interests in the following decade.[45]

Table 4 examines the modality of entry of foreign multinationals into Britain. It includes information on the 80 cases when foreign companies acquired manufacturing firms in Britain which were already owned by another foreign parent. The subject is an important one because it may affect the nature of the impact of inward FDI on Britain: greenfield and acquisitions, for example, are likely to have different effects on concentration ratios and on technology transfer. Greenfield investment was the predominant means of establishing manufacturing in Britain for the whole period 1850 and 1962, but acquisitions comprised a significant number of the new entries from the 1880s onwards. Throughout this period British governments put almost no restriction on foreign takeovers of British companies, and this highly liberal policy stance undoubtedly further increased the attractiveness of Britain as a host economy.[46] When foreign firms 'disguised' their acquisition of British companies – as when Poulenc Frères secretly acquired May & Baker, the fine chemicals company, in 1927 – it was for reasons quite other than fear of hostile British government reactions.[47]

US firms were the most active in acquiring British firms, although acquisition strategies were by no means confined to them. The first acquisition was in 1874, when Anglo-Swiss Condensed Milk purchased the English Condensed Milk Co., and with it two factories in Middlewich and Aylesbury.[48] In the 1880s there were acquisitions by American and German firms. The former – the Edison Electric Light Company – entered British manufacturing in 1883 by merging its pre-existing British sales subsidiary with its British competitor, to form the Edison & Swan United Electric Co., with plants at London and Newcastle. Two years later the Vereinigte Rheinisch-Westphalische Pulverfabriken of Germany acquired the Chilworth gunpowder factory in Surrey.

The inter-war years saw many acquisitions of British companies, some of which had – or developed – considerable significance. Examples included General Motors' acquisition of Vauxhall in 1925, and the Procter & Gamble acquisition of Thomas Hedley, the oldest established Newcastle soap manufacturer, in 1930. The American purchase of Thomas Hedley heralded a major assault on the British soap market. Within three years Procter & Gamble had not only modernised the acquired factory in Newcastle, but built a large new factory in

TABLE 4

MODE OF ENTRY OF MANUFACTURING FDI IN THE UK, 1850-1962

	Total Subsidiaries	Acquisition of foreign-owned company	Total New Subsidiaries	Greenfield	Acquisition	Unknown
1850-59	3	-	3	3	-	-
1860-69	4	-	4	4	-	-
1870-79	4	-	4	3	1	-
1880-89	8	-	8	6	2	-
1890-99	30	-	30	25	5	-
1900-09	77	2	75	46	25	4
1910-19	58	2	56	38	17	1
1920-29	167	9	158	95	61	2
1930-39	170	13	157	113	36	8
1940-49	71	3	68	46	21	1
1950-59	270	40	230	135	85	10
1960-62	145	11	134	54	74	6
Total	1007	80	927	568	327	32

Source: Database.

Manchester. Under American control, the firm launched the first powdered soap detergent on the British market, and achieved an increase in its share of the British soap market from 1.5 per cent in 1930 to 15 per cent in 1935. The recently created Unilever lagged behind Procter & Gamble in the development of detergents, and was, at best, able only to slow down the American gains of market share.[49]

Firms often combined greenfield and acquisition strategies to enter Britain, as well as entering Britain 'accidentally' through the acquisition of other foreign companies which possessed British subsidiaries. The International Telephone & Telegraph Company (ITT), for example, first entered Britain in the mid-1920s when it acquired Western Electric's international business, which included the British subsidiary that became Standard Telephones and Cables. Three years later ITT acquired Creed & Co., a South London manufacturer of teleprinter and data-processing equipment. The new subsidiary, ITT-Creed, extended production of communication equipment to a new site in Wales in 1938. In 1930 ITT also acquired an American company, Kolster Radio Corporation, which had begun manufacturing headphones in Slough in 1924.[50]

There was a considerable expansion in the number of acquisitions after 1950. No official statistics of foreign acquisitions of British firms exist before 1969. The Dunning sample of American manufacturing affiliates active in Britain in the early 1950s showed that only one-fifth had involved a takeover of existing British interests.[51] Table 4 suggests a higher level of acquisition activity.

Firms which were already manufacturing in Britain expanded further through acquisition. United States examples included Monsanto, Union Carbide and ITT. In the food industry, Corn Products Inc., for example, had acquired a British manufacturing company in 1920, and expanded further with the acquisition of Brown & Polson in 1935, securing thereby a virtual monopoly over British starch output. After 1945 the American company made further acquisitions, including a London manufacturer of dextrins in 1948; a London sugar refiner in 1955; and a Surrey adhesives manufacturer in 1961.[52] Acquisitions by American food-processing firms included the purchase of Alfred Bird, the custard producer, by General Foods in 1947.[53] Among the non-American acquirers was Nestlé, which in 1960 purchased the British diversified food products company Crosse & Blackwell, which had six British factories, as well as five foreign plants. This acquisition gave Nestlé the largest fish canning factory in Britain, situated at Peterhead.[54] Many acquisitions in the 1950s were of modestly sized enterprise, although sometimes important in their specialised products. The Diamond National Corporation – to give one example of many – entered Britain in 1956 by acquiring the Hartmann Fibre Co., which had a factory at Great Yarmouth making egg trays for the bulk packaging of eggs in crates. The enterprise was not large, but it was one of the leading producers of such moulded pulp products in Britain.[55]

The fate of foreign-owned companies in Britain is examined in Tables 5 and 6. The first table explores the fate of the 209 of the 927 manufacturing subsidiaries established by foreign firms in Britain which are known to have ceased manufacturing by 1962. A further 89 firms were absorbed into the other British operations of their parents, and the fate of 40 subsidiaries is unknown. The remainder, some 589 firms, continued in existence at the end of 1962. In 26 cases the foreign parent withdrew from British manufacturing by closing down the operation or

TABLE 5

EXIT OF MANUFACTURING FDI BY FATE FROM THE UK, 1850–1962

Decade	Total Exit of Subsidiaries	Fate			
		A	P	S	L
1850-59	1	-	-	-	1
1860-69	-	-	-	-	-
1870-79	-	-	-	-	-
1880-89	1	-	1	-	-
1890-99	4	-	4	-	-
1900-09	7	3	2	-	2
1910-19	50	6	13	30	1
1920-29	28	15	3	-	10
1930-39	43	14	24	-	5
1940-49	34	13	6	14	1
1950-59	27	11	13	-	3
1960-62	14	8	3		3
TOTALS	209	70	69	44	26

Notes: A= Control passed to British corporate interests.
P = Control passed to British public.
S = Sequestrated and sold by British government.
L = Manufacture stopped, either because of liquidation of company, or sales only company retained.
Source: Database.

retaining a sales function only, but in the majority of instances control of the subsidiary passed into British hands. This happened most visibly during the First and Second World Wars, when 44 foreign, all but two German, companies were sequestrated and subsequently sold.

A large number of foreign firms passed into British control through less traumatic means. Some 70 were sold to British companies or else to British partners in joint ventures, for a variety of reasons. Mannesmann, for example, having gained control over its former British subsidiary in 1929, sold it to its British competitor, Stewarts & Lloyds, seven years later.[56] In 1929 American Can acquired a small British container manufacturer Ernest Taylor & Co., in order to challenge Metal Box's position in the British market, but sold it to Metal Box two years later having been defeated in this strategy.[57] On occasion firms passed into and out of British ownership. An example was A.G. Spalding, which established a London subsidiary in 1915 to manufacture sports equipment. In 1937 this subsidiary was sold to BTR Industries, but in 1960 it was reacquired once more by A.G. Spalding.[58]

In other instances, the ownership of foreign-owned subsidiaries passed into public hands through sales of the equity in Britain. In the 1930s a number of US-owned subsidiaries in Britain sold part of their stock to the public, including Ford, American Radiator and Monsanto. In some cases, such as US Rubber in 1934, the whole shareholding was sold off. In other cases, the foreign shareholding slowly faded over time. The Ruberoid Co., for example, had begun to manufacture bituminous roofing materials in Britain in 1909, but over the years the American shareholding slowly declined down to 65 per cent in 1952, when it was sold off altogether to British investors.[59] A more significant example was General Electric's role in Associated Electrical Industries. When this was formed in 1928, it was (secretly) controlled by the American company, with a 54 per cent shareholding. However it began to sell its shares by the mid-1930s. The shareholding fell to 40 per cent by the end of the decade, although AEI was still effectively controlled by the Americans. In 1953, by which time the American shareholding was 25 per cent, GEC disposed of the residual stock.[60]

Many FDIs in British manufacturing proved short-lived, a point which emerges in Table 6. This table excludes the cases of sequestration, whose demise can be regarded as 'artificial', and examines the timing of the other 'exits' shown in Table 5. It should be noted that it only considers the fate of firms before 1962: that is, of the 134 new foreign subsidiaries established between 1960 and 1962, one had ceased operation by 1962. No attempt has been made to measure post-1962 experiences of these firms. Despite such obvious limitations, some interesting points emerge. Between the 1890s and the 1930s, some 10–13 per cent of new entrants disappeared within one decade, and a larger number within two decades. Almost a third of the 1900s cohort disappeared within 20 years. If the analysis is extended to the eight 1900s entrants which were sequestrated during the First World War, then it emerges that 43 per cent of the firms established in this decade were no longer controlled by foreign parents by 1930.

TABLE 6

LONGEVITY OF MANUFACTURING FDI IN THE UK, 1850–1962

Decade of Entry	Years of Operation before Exit					
	0 - 9	10 - 19	20 - 29	30 - 9	40 - 9	50 - 89
1850 - 9	1	-	-	1	-	-
1860 - 9	-	-	-	-	-	1
1870 - 9	-	-	-	1	-	-
1880 - 9	-	2	1	-	-	2
1890 - 9	4	1	-	1	-	-
1900 - 9	10	14	5	2	2	4
1910 - 9	7	8	4	-	3	-
1920 - 9	17	14	6	5	-	-
1930 - 9	16	11	4	-	-	-
1940 - 9	5	1	-	-	-	-
1950 - 9	11	-	-	-	-	-
1960 - 2	1	-	-	-	-	-
Totals	72	51	20	10	5	7

Note: This analysis is confined to the 165 cases of exit by fates A, P and L defined as in Table 5. Sequestrated companies are excluded.

Source: Database.

V

While section IV has examined the flows of FDI in British manufacturing between 1850 and 1962, this section analyses the stock of foreign multinationals in Britain at the benchmark dates of 1885, 1907, 1935, 1955 and 1962. The first date was chosen to offer a snapshot of inward FDI at an early stage in its development, while the last date was selected as the last one before official data was available. The years 1907, 1935 and 1955 have been widely used in studies of the growth of large enterprises in Britain,[61] and it was believed that their use in this analysis would facilitate comparisons between indigenous and foreign firms. The analysis of the stock of inward FDI complements the flow data by picking up, for example, subsidiary and plant expansion by foreign companies already established within Britain.

Table 7 shows the growth over time in the number of foreign parent companies, subsidiaries and foreign-owned plants. There were 17 foreign-owned plants in 1885. Seventy years later the figure was 562. The subsequent growth in the number of foreign parents, subsidiaries and plants between 1955 and 1962 alone is striking. The steady growth in multi-plant operations is observable in Britain over a long period. In 1885 only two foreign companies were multi-plant: Anglo-Swiss Condensed Milk had three plants, while the partly US-owned Edison Electric Light had two plants, in London and Newcastle. Over time the number of multi-plant enterprises grew. In 1935 there were several foreign companies with four or more plants, including Nestlé (eight), General Motors (four), ITT (five) and the United Shoe Machinery (four). By 1962 almost as many plants were part of a multi-plant foreign-owned subsidiary as a single-plant one. Some of the multi-plant operations were considerable. Nestlé, after the acquisition of Crosse & Blackwell two years previously, had 19 plants in all. The US car giants Ford and General Motors had 11 and eight plants respectively. US firms with at least five plants in Britain in 1962 included Corn Products (five), Ekco Products (five), United Shoe Machinery (19), Johnson & Johnson (seven), Hoover (eight), Union Carbide (11), Monsanto (nine) and Sperry Rand (ten). Multi-plant operations by non-US firms were rarer, but the Dutch electricals company Philips had eight plants in 1962, while the Canadian firm of Hiram Walker had eight whisky distilleries and blending plants in Scotland.

The number of foreign-owned companies which were multi-product also grew steadily, as shown in Table 8. This table defines 'product' using a three-digit SIC code grouping rather than the two-digit one adopted in Table 1. In 1907 the handful of foreign companies with multi-product operations were usually producing in very much related areas: examples included United Shoe Machinery, manufacturing boot and shoe machinery and shoemakers' lasts, and the Torrington Co., manufacturing sewing machine needles, bicycle spokes and nipples. By 1962 a number of firms had more diversified product lines. For example, Monsanto's factories in Britain produced chemical products, artificial fibres, and plastics. Johnson & Johnson manufactured surgical dressing products, disposable syringes, brushes and sanitary products. Corn Products manufactured starches, soup powders and stock cubes as well

TABLE 7

FOREIGN PARENTS, SUBSIDIARIES AND PLANTS AT BENCHMARK DATES

	1885	1907	1935	1955	1962
No. of Foreign Parents[1]	14	87	274	340	448
No. of Subsidiaries	14	98	301	403	604
Total No. of Plants	17	110	378	562	901
Single Plants	12	91	264	304	460
Multi-plants	5	19	114	258	441

Note:. 1. Joint parent entries have not been counted twice if they already appear in their own right.

Source: Database.

as adhesives. Michelin manufactured tyres, but its purchase of Citröen in 1935 also gave the firm a British car manufacturing operation until the latter's closure in 1965. Over all, by 1962 some 31 per cent of the US-owned subsidiaries in Britain and 25 per cent of the European-owned ones were 'multi-product' by this calculation. These percentages are lower than those estimated by Dunning for US subsidiaries in his 1958 study, but there are definitional problems in this area. In general, there is no reason to differ from Dunning's opinion that there was, through the 1950s, no marked contrast between the degree of product specialisation practised by the average US-owned firm and British industry as a whole.[62]

The very first foreign companies in British manufacturing quite often established 'branches' of their parent firm rather than locally incorporated companies. This strategy was quickly replaced by one of local incorporation. By 1935, of the 301 subsidaries of foreign companies only 17 were branches. By the 1950s and 1960s it is already known that the British-incorporated subsidiary was overwhelmingly the most favoured organisational form.[63] The vast majority of these ventures took the form of private companies, a form of organisation which provided limited liability, but where the shares were not quoted on the Stock Exchange.

While the majority of foreign-owned firms in Britain were always wholly-owned by their parents, Section III has already discussed the fact

TABLE 8

MULTI-PRODUCT AND SINGLE-PRODUCT COMPANIES AT BENCHMARK DATES[1]

	1885	1907	1935	1955	1962
Foreign Parents	14	87	274	340	448
UK Subsidiaries	14	98	301	403	604
Single Product	13	75	212	272	432
Multi-product	1	23	89	131	172

Note: 1. 3-digit SIC Code Grouping.
Source: Database.

that a spectrum of ownership arrangements existed. This matter is explored more fully in Table 9. This shows that roughly around 60 per cent of subsidiaries were wholly-owned in 1907, 1935, 1955 and 1962. The remainder were a mixture of joint ventures, majority- and minority-owned arrangements. Subsidiaries owned by several foreign parents were always the smallest category. The tiny handful of cases included, before 1914, the small Mersey Chemical Works, established in 1907 by the German 'Dreiburg' group consisting of Bayer, BASF and Agfa,[64] and, in the inter-war years, the Clayton Aniline Co., which was jointly owned by the Swiss chemical companies Ciba, Geigy and Sandoz after 1918.[65]

In contrast with such exceptional cases, it is evident that the strategy of entering the British market through a joint venture with a British company grew in popularity over time. An early example was the joint venture in telephone manufacturing established in 1903 by the Swedish firm L.M. Ericsson and its major British customer, the National Telephone Co. The Swedes had formerly supplied the British market – where there was no domestic telephone industry of importance – with exports, but as it grew in size it was decided that local production was necessary. The joint venture took over a small workshop owned by National Telephone at Beeston, near Nottingham, and telephone production began in 1904. It was agreed that when the National Telephone Co. handed over its business to the General Post Office at the end of 1911, the manufacturing subsidiary would pass entirely into Swedish hands, and this duly happened in 1912.[66] A slightly later example was

TABLE 9
OWNERSHIP STRUCTURE OF BRITISH SUBSIDIARIES OF FOREIGN PARENTS AT
BENCHMARK DATES

	1885	1907	1935	1955	1962
Wholly-Owned	12	60	193	265	393
Majority-Owned	1	17	61	68	78
Minority-Owned	1	5	13	11	11
JV with British Co.	-	5	14	34	78
JV with Foreign Co.	-	2	2	3	6
Unknown	-	9	18	22	38
Total	14	98	301	403	604

Source: Database.

the foundation in 1914 of the Pirelli General Cable Works by Pirelli of Italy and the British-owned General Electric Co.[67] Some of the inter-war joint ventures were very modest affairs: such as a company established in 1932 by Kymeia of Denmark and National Smelting to manufacture wood rot inhibitors at a small factory at Avonmouth.[68]

After the Second World War, American joint ventures with British firms proliferated. The many examples included the establishment by the Scott Paper Corporation and Bowater of Bowater-Scott in 1956, which manufactured facial and toilet tissues, paper towels and other similar products. As in other British–American joint ventures, Scott was able to apply advanced marketing techniques to the operation.[69] Another prominent joint venture of the 1950s was the formation in 1956 of Rank-Xerox as a joint venture by the Haloid Co. (which became the Xerox Corporation in 1960) and the Rank Organisation. This was the vehicle used by the then small American firm to penetrate many eastern hemisphere markets for its office copiers. By 1962 Rank-Xerox had two British factories, 1,500 workers, and widespread international marketing operations. It also had its own joint venture with Fuji Photo Film in

Japan called Fuji Xerox, which had begun manufacture in that country in 1962. In 1969 the American firm took over management control of Rank-Xerox.[70]

Existing information on the spatial pattern of inward FDI in Britain is sparse. There are no official data before the Second World War. The available estimates are by Law for initial foreign manufacturing investment in Britain between 1918 and 1944, and Jones for the location of the first manufacturing plant in Britain of foreign companies between 1850 and 1939.[71] Both studies exclude transfers or expansions of activity by foreign-owned firms already in Britain. The Board of Trade's data for industrial 'movement' between 1945 and 1965 do provide an official source of information on geographical location, but this also only applies to new ventures originating outside Britain. The clear picture emerging from all the existing studies is that the south-east was the main location for inward FDI before 1945, with the north-west of England in second place. Table 10, which counts the 'stock' of foreign-owned plants rather than their flow, confirms the findings of these earlier studies, although it is worth noting that the south-east, though a very important location, only accounted for around half of the foreign-owned plants in 1885, 1907 and 1935. Some of the first inward investments were located in regions which were subsequently to receive comparatively little FDI, such as the north and the south-west.

The vast increase in the number of plants located in the south-east by 1935 indicated the surge of new investment into that region in the inter-war years. American firms in consumer goods, light engineering and motor cars clustered in a few locations on the outskirts of London (especially on the Great West Road and the North Circular Road); and in the surrounding industrial conurbations such as Welwyn Garden City and Slough.[72] Beyond the south-east, the inter-war years saw some industries and nationalities cluster in particular regions. There was a considerable number of foreign-owned plants in heavy machinery around Manchester and Birmingham. There was a group of rubber tyre manufacturers in the West Midlands, including Pirelli at Burton-on-Trent, Michelin in Stoke-on-Trent, and Goodyear at Wolverhampton. Various food products were located in rural regions. Nestlé had three plants in the inter-war years in the south-west; Libby McNeil Libby had an evaporated milk factory in Cumbria, in the north, from 1935.

After the Second World War, there was a remarkable rise in the relative importance of Scotland, and to a lesser extent Wales, as a location for inward investment. The growth of new FDI into Scotland was particularly strong in the immediate post-war years: one estimate is that between 1945 and 1951 two-thirds of the nearly 45,000 jobs created

THE MAKING OF GLOBAL ENTERPRISE

TABLE 10
GEOGRAPHICAL LOCATION IN THE UK OF PLANTS AT BENCHMARK DATES

Regions	1885	1907	1935	1955	1962
South East	9	55	205	262	373
East Anglia	-	1	10	7	15
East Midlands	1	9	21	22	42
West Midlands	-	10	33	33	58
Yorks & Humber	-	1	14	23	39
North	1	3	5	13	17
North West	2	16	46	60	83
South West	1	5	8	13	28
Wales	-	4	10	38	62
Scotland	3	3	13	70	124
Northern Ireland	-	1	-	11	23
Unknown	-	2	13	10	37
Total No. of Plants	17	110	378	562	901

Note: All-Ireland pre-1922.
Source: Database.

by new foreign activities in Britain were in Scotland.[73] Among the American firms establishing Scottish plants at this time were the Burroughs Corporation (in Glasgow), National Cash Register (in Dundee), and IBM, which opened a factory at Greenock in 1951. British regional policy was undoubtedly a very important influence on this geographical pattern. The government used both planning controls – for example, industrialists intending to erect buildings in an area over a certain size needed government approval – and incentives – including the provision of factories at below average costs – to influence both British and foreign firms to locate in the so-called 'Development Areas', or regions suffering from high unemployment. However Scotland's attractiveness did not entirely rest on such factors: Northern Ireland also had Development Area status, but far fewer foreign firms located there. It is evident that foreign firms were also interested in a supply of labour or other favourable environmental factors, which were vigorously publicised by regional development officials, and it is possible that cultural links favoured American FDI in Scotland at this time.[74] This factor may have been even more important in the substantial Canadian investments in Scotland. Examples included, in addition to Seagram and Hiram Walker's whisky investments, Massey-Ferguson's Kilmarnock plant operating in 1949 and a number of very small enterprises, such as Wall Colmonoy (Canada), which opened a small plant at Carfin in 1951 manufacturing insulating board and corrosion resisting alloys, which employed a mere 12 workers three years later.[75]

Wales, another Development Area, played the role of a minor Scotland in the post-war years. Among the notable US investors in the late 1940s and 1950s were ITT, Hoover, and Minnesota Mining & Manufacturing, which established a large plant at Gorseinon and a smaller one at Tredegar to manufacture adhesive tapes. However, Wales received a number of investments from other European countries, including Sweden, Denmark, France and Germany.[76] Northern Ireland, in contrast, was never as successful as Wales in attracting foreign investors, although a number did establish plants in the 1950s and 1960s. In 1959 Camco Inc., for example, established a factory near Belfast to manufacture tools and oilfield equipment, citing as attractive features a government low-rental factory, tax breaks, 'currency advantages for Sterling area products, English-speaking trained labour . . . a stable, conservative government and friendly, co-operative people'.[77]

Between 1955 and 1962 a substantial number of foreign-owned plants were established in the south-east, often quite small ventures located near Heathrow Airport, or in counties like Kent and Sussex. The location of plants given in Table 10 can be compared with the 1963 Census of Production's data for the regional distribution of employment in foreign-owned manufacturing establishments. This showed that there were 540,300 workers, or just under seven per cent of total manufacturing employment in the United Kingdom, in foreign-owned plants. Of this number, 277,900 or 51.4 per cent were located in the south-east. The north-west (13.1 per cent), Scotland and the West Midlands (8.5 per cent), and Wales (4.4 per cent) followed in importance.[78]

Table 11 explores further three characteristics of foreign-owned companies in British manufacturing at the benchmark dates which provide important indicators about the nature of their impact on Britain. These

TABLE 11

CHARACTERISTICS OF FOREIGN-OWNED SUBSIDIARIES IN THE UK AT BENCHMARK
DATES

	1885	1907	1935	1955	1962
British Managing Director					
Yes	1	11	70	118	192
No	5	26	46	51	62
Not Known	8	61	185	234	350
R & D					
Yes	-	1	33	110	138
No	10	60	97	109	134
Not Known	4	37	171	184	332
Exporter:					
Yes	5	32	113	214	293
No	2	5	15	16	25
Not Known	7	61	173	173	286
Total Subsidiary Companies	14	98	301	403	604

Source: Database.

are the employment of British nationals as managing directors; whether the firms exported; and whether they undertook research and development.

The employment of British nationals as MDs provides evidence on both the kind of employment offered by foreign companies, and also perhaps the degree of autonomy from their foreign parents of British subsidiaries. Studies in the mid-1960s showed that three out of four US-owned companies in Britain were headed by a British MD. In 1966 only 793 of the 582,269 employees of majority-owned US manufacturing affiliates in Britain were American: about 2.2 per cent of total managerial personnel.[79] United States companies in Britain, therefore, not only created jobs, but offered British nationals employment at all levels of management.

The employment of British MDs grew over time. In 1885 only one subsidiary – Siemens – has been identified as having a British MD, while other important foreign-owned firms, such as Singer and Anglo-Swiss, did not. By the inter-war years a British MD had become a regular occurrence, including in the largest US affiliates, such as Ford, Vauxhall, and STC. This was evidently even more the case by the 1950s, although the large number of firms for which information cannot be obtained makes the evidence inconclusive.

A foreign MD tended to indicate close supervision by the parent of the British subsidiary.[80] Firms which were closely controlled from the United States, such as Gillette, Goodyear and the Dictaphone Corporation, often had US MDs. However, it also reflected the age of the FDI, as new ventures typically began with nationals from the parent firm in senior positions. American MDs were frequently installed after the acquisition of British firms as part of the process of upgrading their managerial and technological levels to American levels.[81] There were also cases of Americans being appointed as MDs when British managers became too powerful, or even successful, for the taste of their US parents: this was probably the reason for Hoover's removal of its highly successful British MD, who had built up the subsidiary dramatically between 1928 and 1954.[82]

A second notable characteristic of foreign-owned companies in Britain was their exporting activity. It is well established in the literature that foreign affiliates generally have a high propensity to export – as well as to import – and, as a result, tend to tilt the industrial structures of host economies towards internationalisation.[83] In contrast to earlier research which suggested that before 1945 most foreign subsidiaries in Britain manufactured largely for the local market,[84] it is evident that many foreign-owned firms were also exporters in the earlier period. Even in 1885 Singer and Siemens were actively engaged in exporting. An exceptional case was British American Tobacco, established in 1901 as an American-controlled joint venture between American Tobacco and Imperial Tobacco, which exclusively exported from its British factories and did not supply the British market at all.[85] In the inter-war years companies like Ford developed important export businesses.[86]

From the 1920s to the 1950s, British subsidiaries were extensively used by American and other foreign firms to supply empire and sterling area markets. It was only from the late 1950s that many foreign affiliates in Britain began exporting to elsewhere in western Europe, as that market became increasingly attractive. For example, Texas Instrument's British subsidiary exported to the Continent soon after it was established in 1957. Avon Products, which began cosmetics production in Northampton in 1959, began exporting to Germany within three years. Another example was Tampax, which began manufacturing women's tampons in Britain in 1937, and opened a new plant at Havant in 1959. The British subsidiary controlled the Continental subsidiary which sold Tampax products elsewhere in western Europe.[87]

Overall, in the mid-1950s, US-affiliated firms in Britain accounted for around 12 per cent of total British manufacturing exports. Firms in certain products, such as sewing machines, tractors, and refrigerators, exported more than 75 per cent of their total output, while others in razor blades, washing machines and pharmaceuticals exported at least 60 per cent.[88] There were, however, certain exceptions to this high export propensity. Certain food and drink producers, such as Quaker Oats, Shredded Wheat, Pepsi Cola and Coca Cola, served the local British market, though some foreign firms in this sector – Nestlé for example – had large export businesses from Britain by 1962.

The third characteristic of foreign-owned companies examined in Table 11 is whether or not they engaged in research and development in Britain. Dunning's survey of US affiliates in the early 1950s found 56 per cent of the firms conducting 'some applied and development research'; 19 per cent 'some basic research'; and 25 per cent no research. Even higher levels of research activity were revealed in subsequent studies. A survey in 1970 established that 180 out of 270 leading US industrial subsidiaries undertook R & D. Moreover, their aggregate R & D spending was a higher percentage of total sales of US affiliates than for British industry as a whole. US-owned firms accounted for at least ten per cent of total privately financed R & D expenditure in Britain.[89]

Table 11 confirms the high level of research activity in the post-1945 period, but also suggests that it was quite widespread by 1935. The single case of R & D activity recorded in 1907 was that of Otto Mønsted, which manufactured oils and margarine at a plant in Southall, and engaged in considerable R & D before being sold to Maypole in 1910.[90] In the 1930s R & D activity was largely in the hands of US-owned firms: they provided 28 of the 33 cases noted in 1935. R & D activity was most extensive in chemicals and mechanical engineering (six cases each), followed by electrical and electronic engineering and metal goods (five cases each). STC established R & D laboratories at Hendon in 1927, while Kodak's research laboratories in Britain followed a year later. Other foreign firms which undertook R & D in Britain in the 1930s included ASEA, Rhône-Poulenc, Bakelite, Ford and Monsanto. Some of these R & D activities were considerable. By 1935, British engineers at Ford were contributing to the design of the Fordson tractor and also to car designs, while Kodak was engaged in fundamental research work

– and spending considerably more sums than its indigenous competitor.[91] This latter characteristic was not too unusual. Ford's R & D spending in Britain in the 1950s and 1960s was considerably higher than that of the British Motor Corporation.

After the Second World War the number of firms engaged in R & D grew. It seems likely that the great majority of the R & D undertaken in Britain by foreign companies was adaptive rather than basic: this remains a characteristic of multinational activity up to the present day.[92] However, there was certainly some basic research undertaken in sectors such as chemicals and pharmaceuticals, though not all research efforts were sustained. Johnson & Johnson, for example, established a central research laboratory at Slough at the end of the 1950s undertaking basic research, only to abandon it several years later in favour of a strategy of more product-related research dispersed around subsidiaries.[93] Du Pont, Ciba, Geigy, Chas. Pfizer, Dow Chemicals and Chesebrough-Ponds were among the foreign chemicals and pharmaceuticals firms which undertook R & D in Britain during the 1950s and early 1960s. Parke, Davis & Co., which had manufactured pharmaceuticals in Britain since 1900, established its first overseas research laboratories at Hounslow, outside London, in 1951. Pfizer, which established a British factory in 1953, opened a large microbiological research laboratory in 1959, and its research effort expanded further when it acquired the Exning Biological Institute two years later, which undertook research in dairy hygiene products and health products. This resulted in new products based on British research – like a 'slimming biscuit' known as Limmits.[94] The research activities in Britain of foreign pharmaceutical companies exercised a potent demonstration effect on their British competitors such as Glaxo and Beecham, stimulating them into adopting the research programmes which laid the foundations for the extraordinary development of the British-owned pharmaceuticals sector from the 1960s.

VI

The first foreign multinational manufacturers arrived in Britain in the 1850s, but it was from the 1890s that their numbers became substantial. Much greater numbers still arrived in the inter-war years, and even more in the 1950s. They clustered in particular sectors, notably chemicals, mechanical and electrical engineering, and – later – metal goods, motor vehicles and food products. For the most part, these were the high-growth sectors of British industry. US-owned companies predominated, though relatively less so before 1914 than afterwards. Foreign companies generally established greenfield factories in Britain, although acquisitions also became common after 1945. Over the whole period, foreign-owned firms favoured the south-east of England as their location, a preference only seriously challenged by Scotland in the late 1940s and 1950s.

Foreign-owned firms in Britain were always a heterogeneous population. Most of them were of modest size, while a few large firms controlled a substantial share of economic activity of the foreign-owned sector. The majority of foreign-owned firms were wholly-owned, but this left a considerable minority where other types of ownership were utilised. There were notable cases of longevity – such as Singer's operations in Britain – but a considerable number of investments were short-lived for one reason or another. Long-term business successes – such as Nestlé, Kellogg, Ford and Kodak – were matched by less fortunate cases. Yet some common characteristics of this diverse group can be observed, such as their propensity to engage in foreign trade. Foreign firms also grew increasingly willing to employ Britons at the highest levels of management, a policy which did not prevent them achieving – as a group – higher levels of productivity than their indigenous manufacturing competitors.

This article has not sought to explore the gains to the British economy from the foreign trade propensities, employment and new technologies of foreign companies, although individual contributions have been identified. Nor has it been possible to explore the various linkages of the foreign firms with the indigenous economy, or their stimulation (or otherwise) of competition and indigenous entrepreneurship. Both issues merit further investigation. It is evident, however, that by the 1960s foreign multinationals formed an important part of the British economy. In the mid-1960s Britain was firmly established as Europe's largest host economy, and accounted for 7.5 per cent of the total world stock of inward FDI. Inward investment represented 7.2 per cent of the British GDP in 1967, compared to the average for developed market economies as a whole of 3.2 per cent. This made inward FDI relatively much more important in Britain than in other large European economies such as Germany, where it was 1.9 per cent of GDP, or in the United States, where the figure was 1.2 per cent.[95]

Already by the time of the First World War foreign-owned manufacturing companies were responsible for much of the British production of certain electrical, chemical, machinery, and other products. In each generation, the overall market share of the foreign-owned sector appears to have grown, although the foreign role certainly waxed and waned in certain products. By the mid-1960s the foreign-controlled share of total British production was 80 per cent or more for a range of goods, including colour films, boot and shoe machinery, sewing machines, typewriters, tinned baby foods, and custard powder. It was over 50 per cent for a much longer list of products, including razor blades, calculators, agricultural implements, detergents, vehicles, tyres, vacuum cleaners, pens and pencils, frozen foods, potato chips, instant coffee, tinned milk and pet food.[96] Foreign firms in British manufacturing also employed considerable numbers of British workers; accounted for a significant percentage of total sales of British industry; and financed a substantial amount of R & D expenditure.

The foreign-owned sector of British manufacturing must be considered as one of Britain's major business success stories in the twentieth century. The dimensions of its evolution before 1962 have been further explored in this article, but much remains unclear about the precise reasons for the superior performance, in aggregate, over British-owned firms. To what degree was this derived from economies of scale and scope dependent on their multinationality? Were they simply 'better managed'? If so, how were foreign-owned firms able to isolate themselves from the debilitating effects of the British environment in which they chose to locate?

APPENDIX 1

UNITED KINGDOM STANDARD INDUSTRIAL CLASSIFICATION (1980): TWO DIGITS

11	Coal Extraction and Manufacture of Solid Fuels
14	Mineral Oil Processing
16	Production and Distribution of Electricity, Gas etc.
22	Metal Manufacturing
24	Manufacture of Non-Metallic Mineral Products
25	Chemical Industry
26	Production of Man-made Fibres
31	Manufacture of Other Metal Goods
32	Mechanical Engineering
33	Manufacture of Office Machinery
34	Electrical and Electronic Engineering
35	Motor Vehicles and Parts
36	Other Transport Equipment
37	Instrument Engineering
41/2	Food, Drink and Tobacco
43	Textiles
44	Leather and Leather Goods
45	Footwear and Clothing
46	Timber and Wooden Furniture
47	Paper and Paper Products
48	Rubber and Plastics
49	Other Manufacturing Industries

NOTES

The authors would like to thank the ESRC for funding this research under grant No. R000 23 2275 awarded to Geoffrey Jones. Many people provided useful information for this project and assisted with the analysis. We would like to thank, in particular, John Armstrong, Niklas Arvidsson, Mark Bostock, Fabienne Debrunner, Fritz Hodne, Hans Chr. Johansen, G. Kurgan-Van Hentenryk, Greg Marchildon, Ulf Olsson, Harm G. Schröter, Keetie Sluyterman, and Graham Taylor. John H. Dunning provided considerable help, including allowing access to his database on US companies in Britain. Mira Wilkins provided valuable comments on a first draft of the article. The staff of the Baker Library at Harvard Business School provided first-class service during the research on US corporate records. We would like to thank Richard S. Tedlow for facilitating access to the Baker Library, and Dennis Encarnation for permission to consult the records of the Multinational Enterprise Study project held at the Baker Library.

1. S. Young, N. Hood and J. Hamill, *Foreign Multinationals and the British Economy* (1988), pp.48–9, 80; W. Eltis and D. Fraser, 'The Contribution of Japanese Industrial Success to Britain and to Europe', *National Westminster Bank Quarterly Review* (Nov. 1992); J.H. Dunning, *Japanese Participation in British Industry* (1986).

2. J.H. Dunning, *American Investment in British Manufacturing Industry* (1958), p.290.

3. For Germany, see F. Blaich, *Amerikanische Firmen in Deutschland, 1890–1914* (Wiesbaden, 1984) and H. Pohl (ed.), *Der Einfluss ausländischer Unternehmen auf die deutsche Wirtschaft vom Spätmittelalter bis zur Gegenwart* (Stuttgart, 1992). For the United States, see M. Wilkins, *The History of Foreign Investment in the United States before 1914* (Cambridge, MA, 1989). For Japan, see T. Yuzawa and M. Udagawa (eds.), *Foreign Business in Japan before World War II* (Tokyo, 1990), and M. Mason, *American Multinationals and Japan* (Cambridge, MA, 1992).

4. G. Jones, 'Foreign Multinationals and British Industry before 1945', *Economic History Review*, 2nd series, Vol.XLI (1988).

5. J.H. Dunning (ed.), *Multinational Enterprises, Economic Structure and International Competitiveness* (Chichester, 1985), p.17.

6. J.H. Dunning, *US Industry in Britain* (1976), Part 2; S.W. Davies and B. Lyons, 'Characterising Relative Performance: The Productivity Advantage of Foreign-Owned Firms in the UK', *University of East Anglia, Economics Research Centre, Discussion Paper No.9106*.

7. J.H. Dunning, *Multinational Enterprises and the Global Economy* (Wokingham, 1993), pp.424–6, contains the best review of the evidence.

8. A full description of sources is contained in Professor Jones' End-of-Award Report to the ESRC. The database is deposited with the ESRC Data Archive, University of Essex.

9. Two examples of the problem are Brunner Mond, in which Solvay held around 20 per cent of the equity from its foundation until the formation of ICI in 1926, and British Siemens, in which Siemens of Germany took 15 per cent of the equity and a seat on the Board in 1929. In both cases the foreign firm had an important influence on the technology of the British company, but it did not really 'control' it. These investments have been regarded as portfolio rather than FDI. See W.J. Reader, *Imperial Chemical Industry: A History*, Vol.1 (1970), p.122; V. Schröter, *Die deutsche Industrie auf dem Weltmarkt 1929 bis 1933* (Frankfurt, 1984), pp.420–22.

10. D.F. Channon, *The Strategy and Structure of British Enterprise* (1973), p.64. We have also followed Channon in excluding the Thomson Organisation from the database, as the Thomson family shareholding was not directly linked to other holdings that family held in Canada.

11. G.D. Taylor provided valuable information on the Westons, and alerted us to a recent book on the family, C. Davies, *Bread Men: How the Westons Built an International Food Empire* (Toronto, 1987). Also valuable are W.S. Rukeyser, 'The $4-Billion Business Garfield Weston Built', *Fortune*, 1 June 1967, and S. Hunt, 'Willard Garfield

124   THE MAKING OF GLOBAL ENTERPRISE

Weston', in D.J. Jeremy (ed.), *Dictionary of Business Biography*, Vol.5 (1986).
12. Dunning, *American Investment*.
13. P. Dicken and P.E. Lloyd, 'Geographical Perspectives on United States Investment in the United Kingdom', *Environment and Planning A*, Vol.8 (1976), p.689.
14. Jones, 'Foreign Multinationals', p.430; Dunning, *American Investment*, p.17.
15. W. Feldenkirchen, *Werner von Siemens. Erfinder und internationaler Unternehmer* (Berlin, 1992), pp.72–86. There is a partial account of the origins of Siemens in Britain in J.D. Scott, *Siemens Brothers, 1858–1958* (1958), pp.17–58.
16. M. Wilkins, *The Emergence of Multinational Enterprise* (Cambridge, MA, 1970), pp.37–45. F.V. Carstensen, *American Enterprise in Foreign Markets* (Chapel Hill, NC, 1984), pp.13–26.
17. Wilkins, *Emergence*, p.185.
18. Further examples are given in Dunning, *American Investment*, pp.44–7.
19. Blaich, *Amerikanische Firmen*, pp.24–40.
20. Jones, 'Foreign Multinationals', pp.434–6.
21. E.J.T. Collins, 'Brands and Breakfast Cereals in Britain', in G. Jones and N.J. Morgan (eds.), *Adding Value: Brands and Marketing in Food and Drink* (1994).
22. V. Ward, 'Marketing Convenience Foods between the Wars', in Jones and Morgan (eds.), *Adding Value*.
23. US Dept. of Commerce, *Selected Data on US Direct Investment Abroad, 1950–76*.
24. Roussel Laboratories Ltd, *This is Roussel-London* (n.d.), p.3.
25. Dunning, *US Industry*, p.59. For similar evidence in the 1950s, see Dunning, *American Investment*, pp.90–92.
26. V. McNeill, 'Mustads: The Story of the Horseshoe Nail' (Bristol typescript, 1981); F. Hodne, 'The Multinational Companies of Norway', in G. Jones and H.G. Schröter (eds.), *The Rise of Multinationals in Continental Europe* (Aldershot, 1993), p.129.
27. Jones, 'Foreign Multinationals', p.442.
28. Scottish Record Office (SRO), Files SEP 4/159, 4/563.
29. Wilkins, *Emergence*, pp.212–13; Jones, 'Foreign Multinationals'; Dunning, *American Investment*, pp.19–34.
30. P. Hertner, 'German Multinational Enterprise before 1914: Some Case Studies', in P. Hertner and G. Jones (eds.) *Multinationals: Theory and History* (Aldershot, 1986), p.120.
31. H.G. Schröter, 'Die Auslandsinvestitionen der deutschen chemischen Industrie 1870 bis 1930', *Zeitschrift für Unternehmensgeschichte*, Vol.35 (1990), p.4.
32. Jones, 'Foreign Multinationals', p.431.
33. The number of German investments is, however, much less than that given in a Board of Trade study which claimed that 52 German firms (out of a total of 266) established factories in Britain between 1932 and 1938. It proved impossible to identify these firms. See C.M. Law, *British Regional Development since World War I* (Newton Abbot, 1970), p.176.
34. H. Nockolds, *Lucas: The First Hundred Years*, Vol.I (Newton Abbot, 1976), pp.255–9; Schröter, *Die deutsche Industrie*, p.388; G. Plumpe, *Die I.G. Farbenindustrie AG* (Berlin, 1990), p.191. For a general overview of German FDI in the inter-war years and later, see H.G. Schröter, 'Continuity and Change: German Multinationals since 1850', in Jones and Schröter (eds.), *Rise*, pp.30–35.
35. Information from Keetie Sluyterman.
36. P. Fridenson, 'The Growth of Multinational Activities in the French Motor Industry, 1890–1979', in Hertner and Jones (eds.) *Multinationals*, pp.159–61; A. Jemain, *Michelin. Un siècle de secrets* (Paris, 1982), p.114.
37. A.D. Chandler, *Scale and Scope* (Cambridge, MA, 1990), p.158.
38. M. Wilkins and F.E. Hill, *American Business Abroad: Ford on Six Continents* (Detroit, 1964), pp.192, 204.
39. Annual Reports; Dunning, *American Investment*, pp.59–78.
40. C.H.A. Dassbach, *Global Enterprises and the World Economy* (New York, 1989), pp.168, 181, 184, 305, 307, 309.

41. Dunning, *Multinational Enterprises*, p.424. The 1963 Census of Production showed that the net output per head of US-owned manufacturing enterprises (£2,157) was considerably higher than that of British-owned firms (£1,309). 'All other foreign' firms also had a higher net output per head of £1,610. Dicken and Lloyd, 'Geographical Perspectives', p.689.
42. Ciba's acquisition in 1947 of the small Aero Research Ltd, and its subsequent expansion, is discussed in E. Garnsey, 'An Early Academic Enterprise: A Study of Technology Transfer', *Business History*, Vol.34 (1992). See also Ciba-Geigy Plastics, *Fifty Years at Duxford* (1984).
43. P. Gammond and R. Horricks (eds.), *The Music Goes Round and Round* (1980), pp.45; G. Davies and I. Thomas, *Overseas Investment in Wales* (Swansea, 1976), pp.179–83.
44. Channon, *Strategy and Structure*, pp.109–10.
45. M.S. Moss and J.R. Hume, *The Making of Scotch Whisky: A History of the Scotch Whisky Distilling Industry* (Edinburgh, 1981), pp.156–7, 168; D. Daiches, *Scotch Whisky, its Past and Present* (Glasgow, 1976 ed.), pp.156–7.
46. G. Jones, 'The British Government and Foreign Multinationals before 1970', in M. Chick (ed.), *Governments, Industries and Markets* (Aldershot, 1990).
47. J. Slinn, *A History of May and Baker* (Cambridge, 1984), p.432.
48. J. Heer, *World Events, 1866–1966: The First Hundred Years of Nestlé* (Rivaz, 1966), p.57.
49. Chandler, *Scale and Scope*, pp.385, 388; C. Wilson, *The History of Unilever*, Vol 2 (1954), pp.344–50.
50. M. Wilkins, *The Maturing of Multinational Enterprise* (Cambridge, MA, 1974) pp.70–71; K. Geddes (with G. Bussey), *The Setmakers: A History of the Radio and Television Industry* (1991), p.173. P. Young, *Power of Speech* (1983), p.80; J. Rackham, 'Frederick George Creed', in D.J. Jeremy (ed.), *Dictionary of Business Biography*, Vol.1 (1984), pp.819–21.
51. Dunning, *US Industry*, p.14.
52. Annual Reports of Corn Products; D. Green, *CPC (United Kingdom): A History* (Stevenage, 1979); Dunning, *American Investment*, p.75.
53. T. Horst, *At Home Abroad* (Cambridge, MA, 1974), p.44.
54. Heer, *World Events*, p.219.
55. Annual Reports of Diamond National Corporation.
56. A. Teichova, 'The Mannesmann Concern in East Central Europe in the Inter-War Period', in A. Teichova and P.L. Cottrell (eds.), *International Business and Central Europe, 1918–1939* (Leicester, 1983), p.107.
57. Chandler, *Scale and Scope*, p.318; W.J. Reader, *Metal Box: A History* (1976), pp.52–4.
58. Annual Reports of A.G. Spalding and Brothers Inc. SEC Form S-1, Registration Statement.
59. Annual Reports of the Ruberoid Co; Anon, *A Study of the Ruberoid Company* (booklet, April 1955).
60. R. Jones and O. Marriott, *Anatomy of a Merger* (1970), Chs. 8 and 9.
61. D.J. Jeremy, 'The Hundred Largest Employers in the United Kingdom, in Manufacturing and Non-manufacturing Industries, in 1907, 1935 and 1955', *Business History*. Vol.33 (1991).
62. Dunning, *American Investment*, p. 96.
63. Dunning, *US Industry*, p.12.
64. Plumpe, *Die I.G. Farbenindustrie*, p.60.
65. Jones, 'Foreign Multinationals', p.440.
66. A. Attman, J. Kuuse and U. Olsson, *LM Ericsson 100 Years*, Vol.1 (Örebro, 1977), pp.197–203.
67. A. Montenegro, 'The Development of Pirelli as an Italian Multinational, 1872–1992', in Jones and Schröter (eds.), *Rise*, p.187.
68. E.J. Cocks and B. Walters, *A History of the Zinc Smelting Industry in Britain* (1968),

p.112.
69. Annual Reports of Scott Paper Corporation; W.J. Reader, *Bowater, A History* (Cambridge, 1981), p.239–44.
70. Annual Reports of the Haloid Company, Haloid Xerox Inc, and Xerox Corporation.
71. Law, *British Regional Development*, p.75; Jones, 'Foreign Multinationals', pp.443–4.
72. Dunning, *American Investment*, pp.45–6, 84–6.
73. Dicken and Lloyd, 'Geographical Perspectives', p.697.
74. Dunning, *American Investment*, pp.86–8; Law, *British Regional Development*, pp.177–8.
75. Files SEP 4/159, 4/563, SRO.
76. Davies and Thomas, *Overseas Investment in Wales*, pp.35–43.
77. Annual Report of Camco Inc., 1959.
78. Dicken and Lloyd, 'Geographical Perspectives', p.695.
79. Dunning, *US Industry*, p.22.
80. Dunning, *American Investment*, pp.110–12.
81. This happened after US Rubber's acquisition of North British Rubber in the late 1940s. See M. French, 'The Growth and Relative Decline of the North British Rubber Co., 1856–1956', *Business History*, Vol.30 (1988), p.408.
82. S. Bowden, 'Sir Charles Blampied Colston', in D.J. Jeremy (ed.), *Dictionary of Business Biography*, Vol.1 (1984), pp.755–8.
83. Dunning, *Multinational Enterprises*, Ch. 14. Information on importing activities was also recorded in the database, but it proved much harder to find than for exporting. In 1962 it was only possible to establish that 67 firms were importing, and 42 not.
84. Jones, 'Foreign Multinationals', pp.444–5.
85. H. Cox, 'Growth and Ownership in the International Tobacco Industry: BAT, 1902–1927', *Business History*, Vol.31 (1989).
86. Wilkins and Hill, *American Business Abroad*, pp.247, 304.
87. Annual Reports of Texas Instruments, Avon Products and Tampax Inc.
88. Dunning, *American Investment*, pp.291–8.
89. Dunning, *US Industry*, p.20; idem, *American Investment*, pp.168–73.
90. Letter from H.C. Johansen to Geoffrey Jones, 18 Dec. 1991.
91. Wilkins and Hill, *American Business Abroad*, pp.291–2, 303, 384; D. Edgerton, 'Industrial Research in the British Photographic Industry, 1879–1939', in J. Liebenau (ed.), *The Challenge of New Technology* (Aldershot, 1988).
92. Dunning, *Multinational Enterprise*, p.305.
93. J.N. Behrman and W.A. Fischer, *Overseas R & D Activities of Transnational Corporations* (Cambridge, MA, 1980), pp.298–300.
94. Annual Reports of Chas. Pfizer; *Focus on Pfizer* (pamphlet, Dec. 1961).
95. Dunning, *Multinational Enterprises*, p.20.
96. These estimates for 1966 are contained in the prepared paper of J.H. Dunning, printed in *A Foreign Economic Policy for the 1970s: Hearings before the subcommittee on Foreign Economic Policy of the Joint Economic Committee, Congress of the United States* (Washington, DC, 1970), pp.806–13.

Negotiating Technology Transfers within Multinational Enterprises; Perspectives from Canadian History

GRAHAM D. TAYLOR

Dalhousie University

The processes through which technology is transferred and diffused across national boundaries are complex, even when focused on direct transfers within multinational enterprises (MNEs); and conclusions about the quality (and even the quantity) of technology transferred through these processes by multinationals to host nations is a matter of considerable dispute, reflecting, to some extent at least, differences among observers over the broader impact of foreign direct investment (FDI) and the distribution of benefits between multinational investors and host countries.

In general, business enterprises prefer to transfer technology (particularly new technology and/or research capabilities) to companies in host countries that are controlled or at least affiliated with them through lines of ownership, financial dependence or long-term technical exchange contracts or a combination of these elements.[1] The quality of technology transferred through these processes, however, has been the subject of controversy. The product cycle theory suggests that firms possessing technological advantages are more likely to transfer to their foreign affiliates products and processes in areas which are already well established (and where returns on investment are declining) while reserving for themselves the most advanced and profitable lines. On the other hand, some studies have indicated that affiliates of multinationals are better equipped to adapt new products and processes more rapidly than their domestic competitors because of their access to the financial and managerial as well as technical advantages possessed by their parent firms.[2]

The product cycle theory and empirical studies also indicate that transfers of full-scale research and development capabilities by multinationals to foreign affiliates are exceptional and reflect special circumstances, such as the peculiar requirements of a particular national market or host-country government requirements. The emergence of world product mandating strategies may lead to the decentralisation of research operations in multinationals. Critics of FDI in Canada, however, have argued that the benefits of such arrangements to host countries in terms of strengthening long-term technological capabilities may be offset by reductions in the transfer of new products and processes in 'non-mandated' lines; and spillover effects may be limited as the industrial field in which research capability is enhanced is likely to be isolated from the host country's general economic and educational environment.

Counterpoised to this line of argument is the view that affiliates that are equipped with indigenous research capabilities are better positioned to diversify into new product lines in their mandated (domestic or export) markets than independent national firms that must rely on local financial and technical resources or the limited pool of advanced technology available on the open market. This view rests on the much-debated assumption that large-scale, integrated MNEs are the main source of modern product and process innovation.[3]

Historical approaches may provide some insights into these issues in several ways. First, much of the literature reviewed here rests on a body of information that is relatively 'time bounded', deriving from survey research and case studies of fairly recent vintage, primarily from the period since the 1960s. Broad-based historical reviews of processes of technological innovation and diffusion, and of the evolution of MNEs, have proliferated in recent years; and there have been significant studies of international technology transfer in particular industries, notably textiles, electrical power and equipment, and chemical products. Many of these studies encompass transfers within companies operating across national boundaries as well as through patent and other contractual arrangements among companies.[4] There is, however, still a need for historical analyses that cover a wide timespan and focus on the issues raised in the theoretical literature on the processes of technology transfer. In addition, historical studies of this nature can introduce a perspective that traces the dynamics of changing technological and organisational relationships within multinationals in response to changing external and internal conditions.

To a large extent the data upon which the theoretical literature draws is oriented toward measuring the results of technology transfers rather than the processes through which such transfers occur. Although some studies incorporate research surveys of managers, engineers and others that address questions of process, the methodology may be flawed, at least from the historian's point of view: beyond the issue of reliability of responses to surveys, there is the problem that such data cannot readily recreate the dynamics of decision-making. Given the sensitive nature of information about industrial technology, survey results constitute probably the best evidence accessible to researchers on contemporary technology transfers. For the historian who can procure access to business records in the more distant past, the reconstruction of discussion and decision-making within a firm (or among firms) is more feasible – although this advantage is offset to some extent by the accidental or arbitrary nature of business records preservation, which limits the potential range of companies that can be studied in depth.

Canada is a country whose industrialisation was largely the result of imported technology and has been particularly well-endowed with subsidiaries of foreign multinationals (broadly defined) throughout its history. Much of its resource and manufacturing development was carried out by foreign-owned firms, principally British and American; and many of these are still operating. The foreign presence was less significant in Canada's financial sector historically, and FDI in utilities diminished substantially after the Second World War. During the 1970s and 1980s the foreign (by this time mostly American) position in Canadian manufacturing and resource industries declined, hastened by the emergence of alternative investment opportunities for multinationals elsewhere and by nationalist government policies, particularly in the petroleum industry. Nevertheless, FDI remains a major source of capital and technology for Canada: in 1990, 29 per cent of the 100 largest non-financial firms, ranked by sales, were wholly or partially foreign-owned. Some of the largest established industries, such as automotives and newsprint, were overwhelmingly foreign-owned; and in 'high-tech' fields such as computers and electronics, pharmaceuticals and industrial equipment, domestic firms represented at best one-third of the total.[5]

Given the longevity of FDI and the close links of foreign-owned enterprises with the transfer of technology, Canada thus provides a potentially fruitful source for research on the subject. This paper examines the processes through which technology was transferred to three Canadian companies from foreign parent or affiliated firms from the 1880s to the 1950s, in each case focusing on the time period for which there is sufficient source material available to permit a reasonably full description of these processes in the context of the companies' general historical development. The paper then identifies some recurrent patterns in these cases that may provide guidelines for a more systematic analysis of the processes of technology transfer within MNEs.

II

Analysts of transnational technology transfers usually distinguish between different categories of technology, ranging from introduction of new products through transfers of processes of production and transfers of skilled technicians to establishment of research and development facilities, with this last category representing the most qualitatively substantial form of transfer, since the recipient is equipped to develop in-house technological capability, generating new products and processes for domestic or export markets. In general, however. the factors that promote or retard technological transfers are similar for all these categories. With respect to transfers within MNEs, these factors may be broadly divided into conditions external to the enterprise and those related to the internal strategy and organisation of the enterprise.

The major external factors relate to: market conditions in the host country; the distribution of resources in the host country; host-country government policies affecting FDI as well as technology imports and exports; and government policies in the parent company's country that affect investment abroad as well as technology transfers. The major internal factors relate to: the parent company's strategy, usually involving both domestic and foreign operations; the organisational structure of the parent company, relating in particular to linkages between the parent firm and its foreign affiliates; and the views and actions of key decision-makers in the parent firm and foreign affiliate, encompassing informal personal relationships as well as those based on the formal structure of the firms. The interconnection of these various external and internal factors vary from one situation to another, as will become evident in the three cases reviewed in this essay. The discussion at this point is intended to highlight certain features of the internal and external environment that appear to have a recurring impact on decisions involving technology transfers within multinational firms.[6]

Companies that embark on operations abroad that extend beyond importing or exporting of foreign goods or services generally do so in order to secure a position in a foreign market or enhance access to foreign resources vital to their production or marketing objectives, or both. In terms of the host-country market conditions, the existence of a developed infrastructure, integrated national market, a growing population experiencing rising living standards and the presence of domestic competitors are likely inducements for direct investment, particularly in industries featuring advanced technological processes and/or sophisticated consumer demands for new or specialised products.

On the resource side, the presence of accessible and substantial quantities of raw materials is an inducement; the presence of a large, relatively low-cost (compared to the parent's home base) labour supply may also be an incentive, although the quality of the labour market and the presence of a skilled, educated workforce may have more appeal to firms in capital-intensive industries using advanced technology. Canada is usually portrayed as a country historically richer in its raw material base than in its labour supply or domestic market potential. At the same time, the high standard of living and the presence of a relatively well-educated population have augmented its attractiveness to foreign investors, particularly since World War Two.

Host-country government policies figure prominently in the literature on FDI. General political stability and protection of private property rights are desirable features which have worked to Canada's advantage. Specific policies to encourage FDI and technology transfers come in a variety of positive and negative forms. As Bliss has noted, in Canada protective tariffs and other import restrictions were at least partly intended to attract foreign companies to set up branch manufacturing operations, as were the 'domestic production' requirements of the patent laws (as discussed in the next section).[7]

Governments at all levels in Canada (and elsewhere) have also introduced positive incentives – subsidies, tax concessions, loan guarantees, and so on – to entice foreign companies into their jurisdictions. None of these measures, negative or positive, necessarily encourage transfers of technology beyond the most rudimentary level. In recent years, some governments have also sought to impose technology transfer requirements on foreign firms operating within or entering their countries, a practice endorsed by the United Nations in the 1970s.[8] Determining the effect of such policies is problematical, since the flow of technology is usually dependent on other factors.

Government policies in the countries of domicile of parent firms also have had an impact on foreign investment and technology transfer decisions, perhaps to a greater extent than is generally recognised in the analytical literature. In two of the three cases examined here, critical changes in parent–affiliate relations were affected by US court decisions; and these are not isolated instances. In Canada, for example, some of the country's largest foreign-owned or affiliated firms, including Alcan and Imperial Oil, were influenced by American antitrust actions.[9] In addition, governments may affect parent firm decisions through tax policies, domestic-content laws on reimported products, and restrictions on capital and (less frequently) technology outflows. Wartime (and Cold War era) restrictions on trade in technology and strategic materials have also had an impact on multinationals.

While these various external conditions are important, decisions by firms to embark on foreign operations and transfer technology to these operations reflect as well the overall strategic objectives of these companies: local market and resource conditions and host-country government policies may encourage (or discourage) FDI but not all foreign enterprises will necessarily exploit these opportunities. Historically, strategies of expansion from domestic to overseas markets and vertical integration have propelled companies into FDI, With regard to transfers of technology, and particularly transfers of technological capability, strategies of diversification and decentralisation have been significant.

While the product cycle theory suggests that diversifying companies are more likely to introduce new products or services in their foreign operations only after their domestic markets are developed, a company may undertake foreign production of a specialised new product modified to suit particular host country conditions, or use a foreign market as a testing ground for an untried product or process. The development of continental or world product mandates by multinationals such as IBM or General Electric in recent decades, in which local branch companies are equipped with research and manufacturing capabilities to produce specialised product lines for export, represents an extension of corporate diversification strategies.[10]

These ventures also represent an extension of strategies of decentralisation pioneered by companies such as Jersey Standard and Du Pont in the 1920s, and applied to their foreign as well as domestic operations (see section V). Decentralisation has not necessarily translated into substantial transfers of technological capability by parent firms to subsidiaries, but can create an environment in which subsidiaries can negotiate for such transfers.

This negotiating dimension will receive some emphasis in the company histories examined below. The argument presented here is that once a company establishes a foreign affiliate – and sometimes even in the decision to move abroad – there are at least two sets of actors involved in the processes of transferring capital, technology and other resources from the parent to the foreign entity. While the situation for the subsidiary may be seen as essentially subordinate, the relationship is not necessarily one-sided, particularly for joint ventures or enterprises where the parent holds or exercises less than full, centralised control over decision-making. The parent firm's strategy may generally establish the parameters within which negotiations occur, but the subsidiary has some room for manoeuvre on the timing, quantity and quality of resources transferred; and in certain circumstances may be encouraged to take the initiative in negotiating. In this context, the personal qualities of the negotiators on both sides and the informal, personal and social links among them play a role, as will be seen more clearly in the following sections.

III

Although the relationship between Bell Telephone of Canada and the American Bell interests passed through several phases before it was finally sundered in the 1970s, its essential features were established in 1878–81 when the Canadian enterprise was set up, relying largely on American capital and technology. The complicated history of the creation of Bell Canada has been recounted elsewhere.[11] The focus here is on the technological dimensions of the relationship and the impact of the particular legal and market conditions in Canada on the strategy of the American company for establishing and maintaining a foothold across the border.

In *Anatomy of a Business Strategy*, G.D.Smith has reviewed the fairly rapid move of the American Bell company from a strategy based essentially on exploiting its patent monopoly to one based on vertical integration of manufacturing and service through the acquisition of Western Electric from Western Union Telegraph Co. in 1882. Five years earlier, when the initial Bell enterprise was set up by Gardiner Hubbard, Alexander Bell's father-in-law, neither the potential market nor the capital requirements of such an undertaking were apparent, and the venture was very much a local, almost a family affair. With relatively limited financial resources, Hubbard wisely decided to expand telephone service through licensing to independent franchisees across the country. Telephone equipment was leased to franchisees and manufactured in an electrical shop owned by Hubbard's fellow-Bostonian Charles Williams Jr. Between 1877 and 1880 the deficiencies of this approach became clear: Williams' factory could not keep up with growing demand, and the franchisees needed ancillary equipment not under the exclusive control of the Bell patent.

Meanwhile the fledgling company faced formidable competition from Western Union which held a rival telephone patent and possessed much larger manufacturing capabilities through its subsidiary, Western Electric. In 1879 Hubbard recruited a talented manager, T.N.Vail, but subsequently lost control of Bell to a shareholders' faction led by W.H. Forbes. After defeating Western Union in a patent suit, Forbes and Vail determined that the long-term survival of their firm required Bell to expand manufacturing capacity (by acquiring Western Electric) and strengthen its links with the service companies by standardising licence agreements and establishing an equity position in these companies. By 1889 when Vail left Bell (temporarily, as he returned as president from 1907 to 1919), the groundwork had been laid for a tightly knit system of telephone exchanges across the US, augmented by a long-distance communication network (American Telephone & Telegraph, which subsequently became the parent firm of all the local service exchanges) and a strong manufacturing base whose output of equipment would ensure the perpetuation of Bell's dominant position in the industry long after the initial patent expired in 1894.[12]

Bell's entry into Canada took place in the context of these major changes in the American company's strategy. in 1877 Alexander Bell had turned over the major part of his Canadian patent rights to his father, Melville Bell, a Brantford, Ontario, resident, who followed Hubbard's lead in licensing the patent out, and arranged for a neighbour, James Cowherd, to manufacture equipment under Williams' tutelage (in exchange, Williams received 25 per cent of the royalties under the Canadian patent). As with Hubbard in the US, Melville Bell's venture faced a more richly endowed competitor, Montreal Telegraph Co., which held Canadian rights to the Western Union patent, as well as difficulties in producing enough equipment to satisfy his licensees; and other manufacturers were busy making what were essentially pirated designs to meet the need.

In 1879 Melville Bell sold the Canadian rights to the Boston-based Bell company, now under Forbes and Vail, who in turn recruited Charles Sise, a native of Portsmouth, New Hampshire, and a former ship captain, Confederate agent and insurance dealer with business ties in Montreal, to reorganise affairs across the border. With characteristic energy and substantial sums of money that he coaxed from the somewhat reluctant Forbes, Sise negotiated an amalgamation of competing firms in 1880–81. Having made himself indispensable to the Americans in the process, Sise emerged as managing director of the Bell Telephone Co. of Canada, which directly or indirectly controlled most of the telephone exchanges in Ontario, Quebec and the Maritime Provinces. By 1890 Sise had become president, and exercised control over the company's affairs until his death in 1918, with his son assuming that position in 1925.[13]

For Forbes and Vail, the Canadian undertaking was perceived as a simple extension of their strategy for developing the US market. To that end they arranged for the American Bell Co. to acquire 33 per cent of the shares of the Canadian enterprise – sufficient to exercise control over major policy decisions while limiting their financial exposure. As Forbes put it to Sise: 'it is our policy [in Canada] as in the States, to bring in local capital, influence and management, since the whole field is too large for us to undertake to cover'.[14] Sise, however, was always quick to point out the special circumstances of doing business in Canada, and Bell Canada's consequent need for special treatment.

Although deciding early on to forego an effort to expand service into British Columbia, Sise continually pressed Forbes and his successors at American Bell to extend its financial commitments to enable the Canadian firm to maintain its position and fend off potential competitors across a large, underpopulated country. Between 1880 and 1900 Bell Canada increased its authorised capital from less than $1 million (Cdn) to $5 million (Cdn), with the Americans contributing one-third of the total to maintain their equity position.

The 'special circumstances' of Canada were particularly pertinent to manufacturing and technological development. The Canadian patent law of 1871 included a 'working clause' that required a patent holder to undertake manufacturing in Canada within one year of receiving the patent. In 1882 Bell Canada's federal charter extended its manufacturing rights; but after Cowherd's death a year earlier the company increasingly relied on imports, although Sise set up a small plant in Montreal that engaged primarily in repair work. In 1885 a rival company, Toronto Telephone Manufacturing, successfully challenged the Bell patent on the grounds that Bell's domestic equipment output was insufficient to supply the market. By this time Bell's position was too strong in the market for the decision to have a lasting impact; the Toronto company never actually commenced operations.[15] Nevertheless, Sise seized on this episode to argue that Western Electric should pass on to Bell Canada any 'improvements' in telephone technology.

When this issue was first raised, American Bell arranged for a process through which Western Electric would provide Bell Canada with copies of all new patent applications, with Bell Canada having the option to license the Canadian rights for a nominal fee. In 1895 Sise expanded the Montreal plant under a separate charter as Northern Electric Manufacturing Co., which was empowered to produce equipment in fields outside those directly tied to telephone apparatus; and four years later he set up another company, Imperial Wire & Cable.

These moves antagonised Enos Barton, president of Western Electric, since Bell Canada would be able to produce its own equipment (reducing imports from Western) while Western was banned from selling other electrical equipment in Canada through its existing agreements not to compete with Bell Canada in that market. This issue simmered along through 1899–1901, with American Bell acting as intermediary in a dispute between two of its affiliates. In the end Sise agreed to give Western Electric a 43 per cent share of Northern Electric, while procuring better terms for Western's imported products.

In some respects the outcome of this episode demonstrated the essentially subordinate role of Bell Canada in the relationship, particularly since Sise had initially offered Western only a 20 per cent share in Northern. At the same time, Bell Canada had neither the financial nor technical resources to match Western's capabilities; and the arrangement opened the way for a steady flow of Western's innovations to Canada, while discouraging Western from selling equipment not related to telephones to Northern's competitors in electrical markets in Canada. in 1914 Imperial Wire & Cable merged with Northern Electric, with Western Electric taking a 43 per cent position in the enlarged company.[16]

In the interim, major changes had taken place in the organisation of the American company. In 1899 AT&T was transformed into the parent firm in the Bell system. With a more liberal New York charter than the Boston-based American Bell, AT&T could mobilise more capital to acquire greater control over the operating companies, a policy pursued vigorously by its President, F.P. Fish, in 1901–7. In addition, Fish, a patent attorney by training, initiated measures to standardise equipment and facilities among the operating companies and centralise engineering activities. AT&T's expansion, however, precipitated financial problems that came to a head in the panic of 1907, and control passed into the hands of a group headed by J.P.Morgan, the New York investment banker, who reinstalled Vail as president.

Under Vail the process of integration of operating companies proceeded rapidly: engineering was consolidated in a department of Western Electric, and in 1911 a research branch was set up with the mandate to carry out 'investigations covering fundamental principles' in communications and related fields, including radio. In the 1920s the research branch became Bell Telephone Laboratories, and Western set up a subsidiary, Electrical Research Products, to market new products developed by Bell Labs.[17]

The transformation of Bell companies in the US, with an integrated and research-oriented system, resulted in a somewhat anomalous situation for Bell Canada, although the consequences were not immediately apparent. As AT&T extended its control over operating companies in the US, standardised service agreements were introduced which, among other elements, arranged for the provision of technical assistance and transfers of patent rights to improvements in telephone equipment from AT&T at no additional cost to the operating companies. Although Bell Canada and AT&T had negotiated agreements covering these (and other) areas on a yearly basis from 1898, there was no 'standard' service agreement: AT&T was not required to provide technical services to Bell Canada.

The Canadians were obliged to cover expenses for patents, as in the case of the loading coil, essential to long-distance communication, developed by Columbia University Professor Pupin in 1899: the American Bell company, which had been pre-empted by Pupin in this field, had paid the inventor 'handsomely' for the patent rights, providing its associated companies in the US with the benefits at no cost. The Canadian company was obliged to pay over $15,000 (the normal fee paid to American Bell for patent transfers was under $1,000) as expenses for taking out the Canadian rights, under which, as Sise noted at the time, 'we can have no monopoly on the invention'.[18]

More ominously for Bell Canada, given the widening research orientation of AT&T/Western Electric after 1911, the patent transfer agreement of 1880 between American Bell and the Canadian company referred specifically to 'telephones and telephone apparatus'; rights in other fields could be negotiated, but there was no standard contract or established guidelines to cover this situation; and even in the 1890s American Bell was inclined to apply a narrow interpretation to the agreement. Northern Electric had access to information on research carried out by Western's engineering department; but with Western as a large minority shareholder in Northern, relations between that company and Bell Canada took on more of an arms-length character than had been the case initially. (During the 1920s Bell Canada would complain to AT&T about the quality of material and service provided by Northern.) While Bell Canada was not necessarily interested in entering new telecommunications fields, even people at AT&T recognised that the 'patent situation . . . from the standpoint of the Canadian company is not satisfactory'.[19]

After Sise's death in 1918, L.B. MacFarlane, his successor as president of Bell Canada, had begun pressing for a revision of the Bell Canada – AT&T arrangements that would bring it more in line with those of AT&T's American operating companies, noting that Bell Canada had been a profitable investment for the US firm.[20] The opportunity for addressing at least some of these concerns occurred in the context of a general restructuring of AT&T's overseas business in the mid-1920s. From the 1880s Western Electric had been effectively the Bell companies' instrument for FDI, establishing manufacturing branches in Europe, South America, Australia and the Far East. Until the First World War these branches had been rather loosely linked to Western, with '[no] central policy and very little information [flowing] to central headquarters of problems and results'.[21]

At the end of the war, an effort was undertaken to integrate and systematise these foreign enterprises under a new company, International Western Electric Co. (IWEC), which included Northern

Electric in its penumbra as an 'allied company'. As part of the reorganisation, Bell Canada entered an agreement under which patent rights in Canada and Newfoundland held by Northern Electric were vested in IWEC, which then licensed them back to Northern and Bell Canada.[22]

AT&T's support for Western Electric's international business was moderate at best, and an investigation by the US Federal Trade Commission of its relations with General Electric and other companies in the international radio and telephone communications fields further diluted that enthusiasm. In 1925 Walter Gifford, the incoming president of AT&T, decided to jettison most of the company's foreign commitments, selling IWEC to the International Telephone & Telegraph Corporation. Northern Electric was not included in this transaction.[23] In the wake of that move Gifford, who had been considering the overall relationship of AT&T and Bell Canada for several years, initiated a general revision of agreements between the two companies.

Under the new arrangements, completed in 1925–26, Northern Electric was entitled to receive a wide range of technical advice and assistance from Western, including access to new research as well as Canadian patent rights to new technology developed by Western. A parallel agreement was made between AT&T and Bell Canada, providing the Canadian company with access to new developments from Bell Laboratories. A 'service contract' similar to those with US operating companies superseded the 1880 patent agreement; Bell Canada paid a fee for technical and other services, but since it would still have to cover ancillary expenses for acquiring Canadian patents, the fee was set at half the rate charged to other AT&T companies. The agreements also called for reciprocal sharing of technical information by Bell Canada and Northern Electric with their US partners; but given the vast differences in capabilities, these were at best pro forma elements.[24]

These agreements dramatically enhanced the competitive position of Bell Canada and Northern Electric. As one recent study comments: 'through its privileged access to the standards, methods and technology of the US Bell system, Bell Telephone [of Canada] . . . assumed the pre-eminent role in the Canadian telephone industry and guided the planning of Canada's national long-distance network'.[25] On the other hand, some critics have argued that under these agreements Canadian research and development capabilities in communications were allowed to atrophy. With a steady flow of new products and processes from the Americans, there were few incentives for Bell Canada or Northern to develop in-house research capabilities or engage in innovative work.[26] It seems unlikely that the Canadian companies could have developed a strong technical organisation before the Second World War, given the embryonic state of Canadian technical education in that era. In any case, after the sundering of their links with AT&T, Bell Canada and Northern Electric (now Northern Telecom) embarked on a fairly rapid expansion of their technical capabilities, entering the international tele-communications market aggressively in the 1970s.

Termination of formal ties between the American and Canadian companies was precipitated by a US antitrust suit that was initiated in 1949 with the aim of breaking up the AT&T/Western Electric re-lationship as representing a monopoly in the telephone equipment industry. Although AT&T was able to circumvent this draconian demand at the time, a consent decree negotiated in 1956 between the US government and the companies required Western Electric to grant non-exclusive licences to future patents not directly related to tele-phone apparatus. Western decided to phase out its existing arrange-ments with Northern, which had automatic access to Bell Labs' information. By 1957 Western had sold all but ten per cent of its share in Northern.

Since Northern had been a major conduit of technical information to Bell Canada, the termination of the Western–Northern linkage would seriously limit its access to the technology of AT&T. The US company in turn was prepared to disengage and began reducing its holdings in Bell Canada. In 1975 AT&T sold its last shares (by then down to a two per cent holding) to the Canadian company and cancelled the service contract.[27]

Throughout its history, the American Bell/AT&T relationship with Bell Canada was shaped principally by the US firm's strategic aims, modified at crucial points by external circumstances related to doing business in Canada. Initially, American Bell hoped to obtain a mono-poly position in Canada, as it was endeavouring to do in the US. Canadian patent laws required the establishment of manufacturing facilities in that country, which in turn led to a much greater commit-ment of financial and technical resources than the Americans may have intended. Similar circumstances also influenced the way AT&T/Western Electric moved into markets in Europe in the 1880s.

By this time the American company was moving away from its original patent monopoly strategy to one based on sustaining competi-tive advantage through advanced manufacturing and technical capabili-ties. After 1900 AT&T combined this approach with a policy of functional integration and standardisation of its service and technical relations with operating affiliates. By the 1920s the company had con-cluded that most of its foreign business could not easily be fitted into this emerging Bell 'system'. The Canadian connection, however, was retained so that Bell Canada became in effect a part of the system while remaining legally distinct as a foreign enterprise.

In the early years the terms of the relationship were influenced not only by the legal situation in Canada but also by the role of Charles Sise at Bell Canada who turned the Americans' interest in that market to the advantage of his company, justifying his requests for ever-expanding financial and technical assistance as necessary to fulfil the American company's objectives (even after Bell Canada abandoned pursuit of a service monopoly in 1907). After Sise's death, Bell Canada did not have a strong negotiator; but by that time AT&T executives Thayer and Gifford were prepared to expand and solidify the technical relationship initiated by Sise as part of their drive for systematisation. While Sise had had to haggle continually for new increments of American technology, his successors received a steady flow of assistance, in part because they displayed no inclination to develop their own technical capabilities. Under Sise, Bell Canada acquired resources through arms-length bargaining. His successors accepted a more clearly subordinate role in the Bell system but reaped the benefits of the system.

IV

In contrast to the enduring AT&T/Bell Canada relationship, Vickers' first foray into Canada was short-lived, virtually a footnote in industrial history. While Bell Canada was a lucrative vehicle for its Canadian and American shareholders, Canadian Vickers only produced profits for its British parent during the height of war production in 1917–19, and staggered through the 1920s under a massive debt burden before being sold off. But the company in these years was a recipient from its parent of a cornucopia of equipment and technical assistance, including the country's largest floating dry-dock (still in use more than a half-century later), an engineering division, aircraft design capabilities and an aircraft plant that eventually passed into the hands of Canadair Ltd (now owned by a Quebec-based multinational, Bombardier). During the 1950s the British firm re-acquired majority control of Canadian Vickers which operates as a diversified manufacturer in ship-building, structural steel and chemical engineering.[28] In addition, the aircraft manufacturing venture examined in this section contributed indirectly to the migration of various designers and engineers to Canada and induced other companies such as De Havilland and Boeing to set up more enduring operations in Canada.

The entry of the British company Vickers into Canada was less the result of any clear strategy than it was an *ad hoc* response to a particular situation. As Davenport-Hines observes, much of that company's foreign investment partook of this character, reflecting 'intuitive judgments made by its senior directors . . . [of] immediate market opportunities', particularly Albert Vickers, the major figure at the company between 1880 and 1914.[29] During the late nineteenth century, Vickers had been transformed from a general iron and steel producer to a diversified armaments manufacturer, making naval vessels, shells and weapons, particularly the Maxim machine-gun, and boasting a strong research capability in these fields. Although the arms race of the early 1900s provided the firm with a lucrative home market, Vickers was perennially interested in overseas sales, undertaking foreign manufacturing where necessary in a variety of countries including (by 1914) Spain, Italy, Japan, Turkey and Russia: preferably through joint ventures, keeping their financial commitments at about 25–30 per cent of total shares, much like American Bell in its early years. The Canadian venture was unusual in that it was almost wholly owned by Vickers alone.[30]

The particular situation in Canada was the passage of a Naval Service bill in 1910 and an accompanying Dry Dock Act under which the Canadian government offered subsidies to companies establishing shipyards for naval construction. Heretofore Canada had never had a navy of its own; and the Act was a matter of considerable political controversy, contributing to the defeat of the government that sponsored it a year later. Vickers had surveyed the Canadian shipbuilding market in 1907, concluding at the time that prospects were slight. The naval programme, however, presented Vickers with the opportunity to establish a dominant position in the field, with the added advantage (so it seemed) that Canada, as a loyal Dominion of the British Empire, would provide a more secure and stable host than many of the other places where Vickers had FDIs. In 1911 Vickers set up a subsidiary, capitalised at $5 million (Cdn) with the parent holding 94 per cent of the shares; leased a site near Montreal, Quebec – where the local government offered a 20-year exemption from property taxes – and arranged to transport a large floating dry dock from Vickers' major English shipyard at Barrow to Canada in the following year.[31]

Vickers' investment decision proved to be somewhat premature. As Vickers was to experience repeatedly, Canadian government policies toward military contractors were equivocal and parsimonious. The administration that came to power in Ottawa after the 1911 general election was unenthusiastic about the naval programme and delayed proceeding with orders until the outbreak of war in 1914. Although business picked up from that point, Vickers never achieved the pre-eminence in Canadian arms production anticipated in 1910–11. The

Canadian government parcelled out war supply orders to a wide range of companies; and Canadian Vickers was perceived by the British Munitions Ministry as an inefficient and uncompetitive supplier. This situation reflected a combination of circumstances, including incompetent local management – of which more later – as well as lack of political influence in Ottawa.

In addition, the Canadian company faced financial problems in expanding its facilities to meet wartime demand. A new issue of debentures that was intended for placement in London in 1914 had to be postponed for two years; and, when it was finally issued, the parent firm, which had already provided over £1 million pounds in capital and loans to Canadian Vickers, was obliged to guarantee a substantial portion of the total. Consequently the Canadian company reached full production only at the end of the war when orders were tailing off, and carried a debt burden of more than $4.8 million (Cdn) – which was never fully repaid – into the post-war era.[32]

Despite this less than exemplary record, Canadian Vickers was – and continued to be – recipient not only of fresh capital but also of technology from its parent. Under the 1911 charter of incorporation, Canadian Vickers was assigned Vickers' patent rights in Canada; initially this provision related only to the dry docks and 'appurtenances' but circumstances were to dictate an expanded commitment. In 1900 Vickers had entered a patent licence agreement with the US firm, Electric Boat, for construction of submarines in Britain. Shortly before the outbreak of war in 1914, Electric Boat and another American company, Bethlehem Steel, had contracted with the British Navy to produce submarines, but in December 1914 the US State Department proclaimed its opposition to the contract as a potential violation of American neutrality. Vickers then took over the contract, and arranged for Electric Boat and Bethlehem to provide Canadian Vickers with the technical and industrial resources needed to fulfil the contract. By the end of the war Canadian Vickers had produced 18 submarines and additional hulls (with Electric Boat providing the interior equipment) for Italy and Russia as well as Britain.[33]

At the end of the war both Vickers and its Canadian offspring faced the prospect of an abrupt termination of military supply contracts, although Canadian Vickers persisted for a time in an illusory expectation that there would be a post-war naval programme. In 1918 the parent company established a 'peace products' committee to develop a diversification plan ranging 'from locomotives to soft toys and from merchant ships to piano actions'.[34] In the process its less than perfect relationship with Canadian Vickers came under review. The Canadians narrowly averted the loss of the dry dock, which was to be towed back across the Atlantic to Barrow in 1920, only by arguing that this move would entail loss of the Canadian government subsidy of $100,000 (Cdn) a year.[35]

The dry dock remained in Canada, but Vickers was determined to overhaul the management of its troubled subsidiary. When Canadian Vickers was set up in 1911, the London directors had installed Frederick Orr Lewis, a Montreal merchant, as president, on the assumption that he 'had very good contacts', particularly with the Allan family who owned a steamship company and held minority shares in Canadian Vickers. Lewis, however, 'knew nothing at all about heavy industry', and provided at best part-time supervision of the company's affairs among his many activities.[36]

These failings had become apparent by 1914, but the parent firm delayed taking any remedial measures as war business picked up. By 1919, with an uncertain post-war era unfolding, the need for reorganisation was more pressing, hastened by changes at the top in the parent company. Albert Vickers, the dominant director for a generation, retired, to be succeeded by his nephew Douglas as chairman in that year. Although many of the older directors remained, the company recognised the need not only to move away from an exclusive preoccupation with armaments but also to re-examine its foreign business, much of which had been disrupted by the war. In the Canadian situation, they recruited an experienced shipyard manager, Arthur Gillham, to take over as president and reorganise the shipyard which faced serious labour troubles as well as diminishing contracts. They also dispatched a team from London to set Canadian Vickers on the path to diversification.

While the post-war slump and the cancellation of further naval contracts by the Canadian government dealt a lethal blow to the shipyard in 1920–21 – gross income fell by one-third in one year and net earnings by two-thirds – Gillham and his associates energetically pursued diversification. Accomplishing this task was no easy matter, particularly as they soon concluded that new financing would be needed, while the parent firm was adamantly opposed to further outlays. To circumvent this restriction, the subsidiary's managers appealed to the inherent bias of the parent firm's directors toward tradition: Vickers' peace products committee in 1918 could contemplate production of furry toy rabbits, but the directors clearly felt more at home with heavy industry. In 1922–23, Gillham persuaded London to provide short-term credit to Canadian Vickers to acquire a steel fabricating company, Phoenix Bridge & Ironworks of Montreal, so that his company could move into production of turbine engines.[37]

Canadian Vickers' managers tapped another rich vein of support in London with their proposals to establish aircraft manufacturing in Canada. The parent firm had entered this field during the First World War, producing a range of military planes at its Weybridge plant, most notably the twin-engine Vimy bomber. The company's most technically oriented director, Sir Trevor Dawson, was keen to promote post-war aircraft production, and in 1919 Vickers staged various barnstorming air races, including a transatlantic Vimy flight from Newfoundland to Ireland (eight years ahead of Lindbergh) to drum up interest.

Canada, with its vast wilderness and remote mining and logging camps, seemed a promising market. In 1920 Canadian Vickers negotiated with the nascent Canadian Air Board to outfit two Vimys with amphibian gear for use as seaplanes; and Dawson resurrected the old Vickers dream of securing a monopoly in government contracting supplying military and reconnaissance aircraft. The Air Board was cagey – and again Vickers would discover that dealing with Dominion officials was unpredictable at best – but Gillham and R.S. Griffith, who handled aircraft sales for Vickers in Canada, outbid rival US and British firms on a contract to supply the Canadian Air Force with an amphibious plane, the Viking.

Gillham persuaded Vickers to provide the Canadian firm with the resources to manufacture the woodwork and assemble the planes, despite objections from Weybridge, on the grounds that this would reap goodwill from a Canadian government that was moving away from its traditional imperial ties. By 1923 he had secured additional technical aid from Weybridge and an airplane designer, W.T. Reid. Over the next several years Reid organised a design team who created a range of new aircraft for the commercial market as well as the government. By 1925 Canadian Vickers was able to manufacture most airframe parts in-house, importing the engines from Britain.[38]

Aircraft manufacturing was not without its problems, particularly with Canadian officials who were inclined to alter specifications regularly and were dilatory about meeting contract payments. The aircraft venture did not in fact produce profits for Vickers, although by mid-decade it had a reputation as the most advanced company in the field in Canada. Meanwhile, however, financial problems plagued the company. Net earnings remained poor and Gillham was obliged on several occasions to draw on the company's cash reserves to meet its debenture and interest payments. Nevertheless the parent company might have allowed it to continue on its course, particularly as the Phoenix Bridge and turbine investments were beginning to bring in increased income by 1926–27. But at this point troubles on the home front precipitated a major reorganisation at Vickers in the wake of a merger with its equally troubled long-time rival, Armstrong-Whitworth Co., forced upon it by the Bank of England.

In 1926, in the midst of the Vickers–Armstrong merger negotiations, a Canadian group headed by Frank Ross, president of Montreal Dry Dock, approached Vickers with a proposal to purchase the Canadian enterprise, which was hastily embraced by the parent firm. A Canadian Vickers veteran later commented acidly that this was 'a very smart operation out of which Mr Ross and his associates did extremely well, but which left the company itself in a very bad position'.[39] For $4.5 million (Cdn), Ross acquired a firm whose assets were worth two to three times that amount, while Vickers in Britain absorbed over $2 million in accumulated debts. In 1928 Canadian Vickers merged with Montreal Dry Dock; the Ross group refinanced the enterprise, reaping a tidy profit at the crest of the late-1920s securities boom, and saddling the company with new debts that were not repaid until the Second World War revived the shipbuilding industry.

Ironically (in light of later assertions by Canadian nationalists on the impact of FDI on their country's technological capabilities), the Canadian investors decided early on to dismantle the aircraft manufacturing operation that represented probably the most significant transfer of technology by Vickers to its subsidiary. In 1929 the new owners closed the division down, and negotiated an agreement to be the exclusive suppliers of British-made Vickers planes in Canada. Most of the design and engineering staff returned to Britain; Reid went to the US and joined Curtiss Aviation. The rationale for this decision was understandable: the aircraft division had not been particularly profitable, and although the Canadian government proclaimed its enthusiasm for Vickers planes, Dawson's expectations of acquiring the lion's share of the Canadian aircraft market were never realised.[40]

More than the other companies examined here, Vickers appears to have been influenced in its foreign investment and technology transfer decisions by external factors, particularly by Canadian government procurement and tax policies. This is not surprising, as Vickers was quintessentially a military supply firm in this era even when it embarked on diversification after the First World War. Despite the fact that the Canadian subsidiary's most profitable venture in the 1920s was not directly tied to government contracting, an inordinate amount of attention was devoted by the directors in London to the aircraft enterprise, and substantial resources were transferred to Canadian Vickers for that venture. The decision by the parent firm to divest itself of Canadian Vickers was largely the result of measures imposed upon it (indirectly at least) by the British government in the Armstrong merger, combined with disappointment over the progress of aircraft contract arrangements with the Canadian government.

At the same time, the managers of Canadian Vickers displayed some skill in manipulating the situation to their advantage, at least temporarily, in the post-war years: retaining control of the dry dock – a major asset from the point of view of the Canadians who eventually acquired the company – and buying time in the 1920s by emphasising the potential government market for aircraft. Ultimately, their efforts could not offset real financial losses, and the Canadian government proved to be an unreliable client; but in the process they had procured for Canadian Vickers a remarkable transfer of resources and technical capabilities that testified to their negotiating abilities if not to their business acumen.

V

Canadian Industries Ltd (CIL) was established as a joint venture between the British company, Nobel (later Imperial Chemical) Industries Ltd and the American firm, E.I. du Pont de Nemours.

This was a somewhat unusual arrangement at the time of its founding, although it has become far more common in recent years. It was in part a by-product of wide-ranging international patent-sharing agreements between the two firms, and in the 1940s the US antitrust authorities charged that CIL was essentially a vehicle for a cartel arrangement intended to suppress competition in the chemical industry in Canada. This view was apparently shared by the American courts, which ordered the dissolution of the joint venture along with the patent agreements in 1952; subsequently ICI took over majority control of CIL while Du Pont set up a separate subsidiary in Canada.[41]

CIL was, however, an operating company that manufactured a wide range of chemical products in Canada; a recipient of Canadian patent rights from both parent firms; and it maintained modest research and export operations by the time American antitrust officials began their investigations in the 1940s. During the Second World War, CIL's subsidiary, Defence Industries Ltd, was a major supplier of explosives and other chemical products to the Canadian government, cited as 'one of the largest industrial enterprises ever undertaken in Canada'.[42] To a great extent, of course, the transfer of capital, patent rights, technical assistance and manufacturing capabilities to CIL was the result of the Du Pont/ICI relationship; but these developments also reflected the growth of the Canadian market for industrial products and the efforts by CIL's managers to procure the maximum benefits available to them from their well-endowed parents, as well as strategies of diversification and decentralisation pursued by both Du Pont and ICI, particularly between the 1920s and the 1940s. These two firms also established joint ventures in Latin America and Australia, but the Canadian enterprise was by far the largest and most technologically advanced of these undertakings.

Between 1880 and 1910 both the Du Pont Powder Co. and Nobel Explosives (UK) had entered the Canadian market where large-scale mining and rail construction projects stimulated demand for their products. Canadian duties on imported black powder were relatively low, as were transport costs from the US; but Nobel could offset Du Pont's advantage to some extent by its technical capabilities in dynamite production. More significantly, key figures in both firms were inclined early on to prefer co-operation over competition, particularly in a small market such as Canada.

Du Pont had erected a 'powder trust' among competing US firms in the 1880s, while the Nobel group developed a similarly dominant position in Europe with its Glasgow-based member as the leading company. In 1888 the American and European 'trusts' negotiated an agreement to keep out of each other's markets; Canada was left open for competition at this point. By the early 1900s both Du Pont and the British Nobel company were reorganising their respective federations into integrated, consolidated enterprises; and Du Pont in particular was looking toward diversifying into more broad-based product lines albeit still (at this time) in the explosives industry. Coleman du Pont, president of the American company, was interested in reviewing international arrangements; and the emerging figure at British Nobel, Harry McGowan, was receptive.

In this context the Canadian situation was re-examined in 1909 – during which time Du Pont also faced antitrust prosecution relating to its control of the US powder market, a development that reinforced the impetus for renegotiating its international position. In 1910 the two companies agreed to set Canadian Explosives Ltd (CXL) as a joint undertaking, established on the base of an Ontario enterprise, Hamilton Powder Co., in which both held shares. Nobel held 55 per cent of the shares of CXL, which was capitalised at $15 million (Cdn), with Du Pont holding 45 per cent. Despite Nobel's dominant position, CXL was to be regarded by both partners as a joint vehicle, entitled to receive sufficient assistance to achieve economies of scale in production and access to new developments in the explosives field, to ensure that it would maintain a strong position in the Canadian market.[43]

Between 1910 and 1920 CXL functioned largely as a single-industry branch operation. Wartime demand for military explosives led to a rapid expansion of capacity and takeover of several smaller companies. By 1920 capitalisation was raised to $22.5 million (Cdn). There was, however, little in the way of transfer of new technology from either parent. Although CXL's president was a Canadian, William McMaster, former head of Hamilton Powder, the company's activities were closely monitored by McGowan of Nobel. Circumstances began to change within both of the parent firms at the end of the First World War, which in turn would lead to a change in their relationship and the role of the Canadian company.

Du Pont and Nobel were each branching into new fields of chemical research and development. During the war Du Pont moved into product lines such as plastics and lacquers that provided an alternative end-use for materials used in military smokeless powder, and into dyestuffs. Nobel followed suit, although in a more hesitant fashion: by the mid-1920s, however, McGowan was seeking a merger with the British chemical firm, Brunner Mond, that would give it a position roughly equal to Du Pont.

In 1919 the Americans proposed broadening CXL's activities to encompass the new fields Du Pont had entered. At this point they had secured a technical advantage over Nobel which was reflected in the reorganisation of the Canadian firm's shares in 1920, with Du Pont and Nobel now each holding 47 per cent and each agreeing not to increase its position via the Canadian minority shareholders. Du Pont, however, still preferred co-operation with potential rivals in international markets; and Nobel's prospective alliance with Brunner Mond would give it a firm foothold in the field of synthetic nitrogen where Du Pont's early efforts were lagging. When Du Pont and Nobel renegotiated their general patent agreements in 1925, they arranged for CXL to become the mutual recipient of Canadian rights to selected chemical products and processes developed by either parent, with the additional provision that it would have preferential consideration in the introduction into Canada of any new products 'not covered by the [general patent and process] agreement'. Following the Nobel–Brunner Mond merger later that year, CXL was reconstituted as CIL to reflect its broader mandate.[44]

As this account suggests, the Du Pont–Nobel/ICI relationship was not quite the cosy cartel arrangement later perceived by US antitrust investigators. Both sides were continually manoeuvering for best advantage. Du Pont was wary not only of its British partners but also of the US government, particularly in the late 1930s when a new era of trust-busting commenced.[45] Chief executives on both sides were receptive to the concept of co-operation, particularly McGowan and his American counterpart, Irenee du Pont, in the 1920s; but managers in their research departments were inclined to secretiveness and delay in sharing new processes.[46] In these circumstances, CIL's access to the full benefits of its parents' technology was by no means ensured through the Du Pont/ICI agreements alone.

This task was taken up by CIL's president, Arthur Purvis, during the decade following reorganisation of the company. A British native, Purvis had risen rapidly through the ranks at Nobel, and, as a protege of McGowan, could be seen – as many Du Pont people did – as essentially an 'ICI man'. At the same time, he was recognised as a 'forceful character' who linked CIL's development to his own ambitions, which some observers believed to embrace a political career in Canada. During the 1930s he chaired a Canadian Royal Commission on Unemployment and headed the British purchasing board in North America in the early days of the First World War; his career was cut short, however, when he was killed in a plane crash in 1941. At the outset of his tenure as CIL's president, Purvis proclaimed that 'the logical future of CIL lay in going into all the lines practicable in which its parent companies could give it technical assistance'.[47]

Purvis's room for manoeuvre was limited of course by CIL's financial as well as technological dependence on ICI and Du Pont. But in the 1920s both companies had moved toward more decentralised structures with substantial autonomy accorded to division heads in operating decisions. A manager who ran his division or department profitably could exercise a fair amount of independence. Despite some misjudgements – in particular an over-expansion into synthetic fertiliser production in the early 1930s – Purvis proved to be an able leader. The return on investment averaged over 12 per cent a year for CIL during the 1930s (considerably better than ICI's overall performance); and even in the worst years, 1932–33, earnings per share and dividends were kept above 1927 levels. In 1933 CIL, which held substantial shares in the Canadian subsidiary of Dunlop Tire & Rubber, temporarily took over management of that enterprise under an agreement with its British parent and reduced its operating losses, although even Purvis could not completely salvage this unhappy situation. Even Wendell Swint, one of Purvis's harshest critics at Du Pont, acknowledged that CIL was 'a well run company'.[48]

Purvis's tactics for coaxing new product lines and technology out of Du Pont and ICI generally featured a combination of warnings and appeals for justice accompanied by references to past good performance. Warnings fell into two categories. Sometimes Purvis would argue that unless CIL were allowed to enter a new product line the Canadian market would be lost to a competitor outside the Du Pont/ICI network of agreements. This line was pursued to enable CIL to expand into dyestuffs in 1928–29 when German and Swiss companies posed serious threats. Du Pont was sceptical, regarding this initiative as a thinly disguised effort to salvage the floundering fortunes of ICI's predecessor company in that field, British Dyestuffs. Eventually Du Pont agreed to transfer its Canadian dyestuffs business to CIL and even to allow CIL to sell these products under its own brand name.

Alternatively, CIL would propose to enter an export market in an established product line, maintaining that it was under pressure from the Canadian government to do so, an argument that had some substance in the Depression years. Both Du Pont and ICI were predictably hostile to these proposals, viewing CIL as restricted to its home market (although US antitrust considerations blocked them from imposing this restriction formally). Purvis could use the threat to procure concessions elsewhere. In 1934–35 CIL began selling ammunition in South America in competition with another Du Pont affiliate, Remington Arms. This adventure helped precipitate a general overview by Du Pont and ICI of the relationship with CIL. Under the 1936 agreement CIL was obliged to foreswear future export ventures (without express permission); but was designated as 'the vehicle for all Canadian undertakings, whether manufacture or sale', by Du Pont or ICI, a substantial expansion of its position under the 1927 arrangement.

These tactics were not always successful, particularly if CIL was seen to be seeking access to new technology not securely under the control of Du Pont or ICI. In 1937 CIL proposed undertaking a joint venture with a Quebec company, Shawinigan Chemicals, in the production of methanol, using a German process. ICI and Du Pont concurred that the methanol project would probably open the way for production of a much wider range of products in such quantity that CIL would again be pushing for export operations; and although they approved the methanol venture, sufficient obstacles to expansion and diversification were erected as to discourage CIL from pursuing the matter.[49]

Despite occasional setbacks, CIL significantly diversified its product lines through the 1930s, receiving substantial technical assistance in setting up manufacturing of synthetic ammonia (for fertiliser), chlorine and cellophane, as well as expanding its production of paints and plastics. In 1939 Du Pont passed on Canadian patent rights to nylon and helped CIL establish a plant in the following year. During World War Two, CIL's subsidiary, Defence Industries Ltd, provided engineering and managerial assistance to the Canadian atomic energy project at

Chalk River, Ontario, paralleling Du Pont's work in the United States.[50]

Purvis's successors were less independent-minded, but as the Second World War ended, the prospect of antitrust action against Du Pont and ICI largely affected their relationship with CIL. Faced with pressures from Canadian Combines Act officials as well, the parent companies in 1945 renounced any intent to restrict CIL's exports; and in the following year the nylon licensing agreement was revised. In 1948 the general patent and process agreement between Du Pont and ICI was terminated and replaced with one that provided for non-exclusive licensing and an end to technical co-operation between the companies. Although ICI in particular hoped to maintain CIL and other joint ventures with Du Pont, the Americans were looking at setting up a separate Canadian enterprise by this time, anticipating the 1952 US court decision that ordered the break-up.

These post-war changes were something of a mixed blessing for CIL. On the one hand it could now move more readily abroad which would help absorb some of the increased output fostered by the expansion of wartime manufacturing capacity. But its access to technology from its parents was at risk at a time when both ICI and (particularly) Du Pont were introducing a wide range of new products and processes in synthetic textiles and other fields. While the flow of technology slowed, however, CIL's own research capabilities were expanding, partly as a result of its war-related activities but also as a by-product of the deepening research orientation of the parent firms.

During the First World War, CXL had set up a small laboratory at its powder works at Beloeil, near Montreal, which concentrated primarily on developing specialised shotgun cartridges. In 1934 Purvis expanded it into a central research operation tied in with his ambitious synthetic fertiliser project. Before 1939, however, the lab employed fewer than 20 people in modest facilities. By 1947 this staff had increased fivefold, and ICI and Du Pont agreed to allow the lab to move into 'pure research' to a limited extent. More significantly, Du Pont helped reorganise its operations to link research projects directly to the activities of the manufacturing divisions, which in turn contributed to its larger budget. CIL's research expenditures almost doubled in five years, and by 1951 the company was exploring the possibility of entering the petrochemical field. Although uncertainties over the future of the company delayed new initiatives at this point, after the division of 1952 both successor firms continued to develop their research capabilities.[51]

Even before the US court announced its decision in US vs. ICI et al., both companies had decided to proceed with a division of CIL and other

joint ventures; ICI retained control of CIL while Du Pont set up its own
company. Following protracted and sometimes acrimonious negotia-
tion, a 'segregation' of patents, licences, production facilities and other
assets was agreed on in 1954. Essentially, CIL retained product lines
most closely associated with ICI, including explosives, ammunition and
heavy chemicals as well as areas developed in the 1920s, including
fertilisers, paints and plastics. Du Pont Canada kept product lines most
closely tied to Du Pont, including cellophane, nylon and other synthetic
fibres. On balance, Du Pont Canada probably emerged with a more
advantageous situation, as it was well positioned in markets that were
only beginning to be exploited and where technological advances were
substantial.[52]

As in the case of Bell Canada, CIL's acquisition of resources and
technology was determined more by internal than external factors,
principally the strategic aims of the parent firms; but in CIL's case, these
strategies were oriented more toward the broader relationship between
the two parents than toward the particular circumstances in the
Canadian market. While CIL was not simply a mechanism for technological exchanges between Du Pont and ICI, it is fair to say that the
capabilities bequeathed upon CIL were inextricably tied to the general
patent and process agreements; and as those agreements became less
viable the flow of technology to CIL diminished.

Within the framework of those agreements, however, CIL had some
scope for manoeuvre; and, as in the case of Bell Canada under Sise and
Canadian Vickers in the 1920s, CIL, particularly under Purvis, pursued
opportunities for expanding operations and acquiring new technologies.
Purvis's ambitions sometimes exceeded the limits permitted by the
parent firms, particularly on the issue of exports, but on the whole ICI
and Du Pont were prepared to give their subsidiary considerable leeway
as long as it was profitable for all parties involved and did not threaten
the structure of relations established by the patent and process
agreements.

VI

In two of the three cases reviewed here, internal rather than external
factors seem to have been more important in determining investment
and technology transfer decisions; and in the third case (Vickers), the
principal external factor – government procurement policies – was
important largely because the company's basic strategy focused on
military contracts. This is not to say that external considerations played
no role in these decisions; and, again, in two of the cases US court

decisions were crucial in shaping the parent–subsidiary relationship. But the major factors in each case appear to be more directly related to parent firm strategies and the initiatives taken by managers in the affiliated companies.

Bell Canada was set up initially largely as an extension of American Bell's domestic market strategy, and changes in the relationship between the Canadian and US firms reflected (albeit somewhat belatedly) changes in American Bell's links with its domestic operating companies. Du Pont and Nobel established CXL in the context of their broader 'co-operative' relationship, and the Canadian firm's expansion and diversification occurred within that evolving system. Vickers entered Canada to exploit a particular opportunity – the naval construction programme – but after the First World War, Canadian Vickers' diversification followed the path laid out by the parent company.

While the particular circumstances of the Canadian market were of less saliency than the overall strategies of the foreign companies, local management in each case played at least some role in decisions relating to transfers of capital and technology, frequently invoking the argument that the special requirements of operating in Canada dictated these transfers. Their successes were probably due more to their ability in presenting the argument than to the actual circumstances. Sise based his case for transfer of telephone manufacturing capability to Bell Canada on the 1871 patent law and the 1885 court decision, even though the likelihood that successful domestic competition would emerge was remote. Gillham tied his pleas for the dry dock and aircraft manufacturing capability to the (at best) problematical commitment of the Canadian government to post-war military contracts. Purvis cited pressure from the Canadian government in his quest for export opportunities and new product lines, although there is little evidence that the Canadian government contemplated reprisals against CIL for failing to export its products. Canadian managers were always careful to link their particular needs to the interests and strategies of their parent companies, but it is important to note that they took the initiative in each situation and, within the limits accepted by the parent firms, established the terms under which resources were transferred.

The parent firms' willingness to transfer resources, particularly advanced technology, however, was closely linked to the degree of control they exercised over the affiliated companies. Sise, for example, got his manufacturing plant but had to share control of that operation with Western Electric; and it was only after Sise's departure from the scene that Bell Canada was substantially integrated into the Bell system with its attendant technological benefits. In that later situation, Bell Canada basically traded part of the autonomy Sise had won for it in order to procure technology at a lower price. Vickers was prepared to pour large amounts of assistance into its Canadian subsidiary because it exercised virtually complete control over that enterprise. CIL's relations with Du Pont, particularly in the Purvis era, were punctuated by distrust and recriminations in part because Du Pont managers suspected CIL of maintaining closer ties with ICI; and the American company moved with alarming alacrity (from ICI's point of view) to sunder relations in the 1940s, with all parties concerned looking to protect their own long-term interests.

While it may be hazardous to generalise on the basis of a relatively limited number of examples, in the three cases examined here it seems fair to conclude that transfers of technology were shaped primarily by three elements: the strategies of the parent firms, particularly those emphasising diversification and decentralisation; the initiatives and negotiating skills of the managers of the affiliated firms; and, balanced against this last point, the extent to which the affiliates were ultimately dependent upon the parent firms.

NOTES

Financial assistance for the research for this essay was provided through a research grant from the Social Sciences and Humanities Research Council of Canada in 1987–89.

1. E. Mansfield and A. Romeo, 'Technology Transfer to Overseas Subsidiaries by US-Based Firms', *Quarterly Journal of Economics*, Vol.95 (Dec. 1980), pp.737–50; E. Mansfield, 'Technological Change and the International Diffusion of Technology', in D. McFetridge (ed.), *Technological Change and Canadian Industry* (Toronto 1985), pp.80–87; D. de Melto *et al.*, *Innovation and Technological Change in Five Canadian Industries* (Ottawa, 1980); H. Crookell', The Transmission of Technological Access Across National Boundaries', *Business Quarterly*, Vol.30 (Autumn 1973), pp.52–60.

2. K.E. McMullen', Lags in Product and Process Innovation Adoption by Canadian Firms', in A.M. Rugman (ed.), *Multinationals and Technology Transfer:The Canadian Experience* (New York, 1983), pp.50–72. See also L.T. Wells, 'International Trade: The Product Life Cycle Approach', in L.T. Wells (ed.), *The Product Cycle and International Trade* (Cambridge, MA, 1972), pp.3–39. For a different perspective, see J.N. Behrman and H. Wallender, *Transfer of Manufacturing Technology Within Multinational Enterprises* (Cambridge, MA 1976); W.H. Davidson, *Experience Effects in International Investment and Technology Transfer* (Ann Arbor, MIch, 1980).

3. R. Caves, 'Multinational Enterprises and Technology Transfer', in A.M. Rugman (ed.), *New Theories of the Multinational Enterprise* (New York, 1982), pp.254–76; R.C. Ronstadt, 'Research and Development Abroad by US Multinationals', in R. Stobaugh and L.T. Wells (eds.), *Technology Crossing Borders* (Boston, 1984), pp.241–64; Science Council of Canada, *Multinationals and Industrial Strategy: The Role of World Product Mandates* (Ottawa, 1980). Critical views are offered by A.J. Cordell, *The Multinational Firm, FDI and Canadian Science Policy* (Ottawa, 1971); L. Eden, 'Multinational Response to Trade and Technology Change: Implications for Canada', in D. McFetridge, *Foreign Investment, Technology and Economic Growth* (Calgary, 1991), pp.153–62.

4. Some examples of studies of the international diffusion of specific technologies include: J. Tilton, *The International Diffusion of Technology: The Case of Semiconductors* (Washington, DC, 1971); T.P. Hughes, *Networks of Power: Electrification in Western Society, 1880–1930* (Baltimore, MD, 1983); D. Headrick, *The Invisible Weapon: Telecommunications and International Politics, 1851–1945* (New York, 1991).
5. See G.P. Marchildon, 'Canadian Multinationals and International Finance: Past and Present', *Business History*, Vol.34 (July 1992), pp.1–16.
6. See M. Wilkins', The Role of Private Business in the International Diffusion of Technology', *Journal of Economic History*, Vol.34 (1974), pp.166–88, for an analysis of the conditions promoting or deterring international technology transfers among business enterprises (not restricted to transfers within MNEs).
7. M. Bliss, 'Canadianizing American Business: The Roots of the Branch Plant', in I. Lumsden (ed.), *Close the 49th Parallel Etc.* (Toronto, 1970), pp.27–43. See also S. Scheinberg, 'Invitation to Empire: Tariffs and American Economic Expansion in Canada', *Business History Review*, Vol.47 (1973), pp.218–38.
8. United Nations Conference on Trade and Development, *Guidelines for the Study of the Transfer of Technology to Developing Countries* (New York, 1972). See also M. Blomstrom, 'Host Country Benefits of Foreign Direct Investment', in McFetridge (ed.), *Foreign Investment, Technology and Economic Growth*, pp.93–5.
9. See M. Wilkins, *Maturing of Multinational Enterprise* (Cambridge, MA, 1974), pp.293–7; G.D. Taylor, 'From Branch Operation to Integrated Subsidiary: The Reorganisation of Imperial Oil under Walter Teagle, 1911–17', *Business History*, Vol.34 (July 1992), pp.49–68; D.C. Campbell, *Global Mission: The Story of Alcan* (Toronto, 1985), pp.227–44.
10. Although the term 'world product mandate' is of fairly recent vintage, the concept is not entirely novel. In the 1930s, for example, International Paper introduced geographically separate divisions, concentrating its newsprint operations in Canada and its kraft paper production in the United States. See A.D. Chandler, Jr., *Strategy and Structure* (New York, 1962), pp.422–3; J. Niosi, *Canadian Multinationals* (Toronto, 1983), pp.133–5.
11. See G.D. Taylor, 'Charles F. Sise, Bell Canada and the Americans: A Study of Managerial Autonomy, 1880–1905', in D. McCalla (ed.), *The Development of Canadian Capitalism* (Toronto, 1990), pp.150–54. See also C. Armstrong and H.V. Nelles, *Monopoly's Moment: The Organization and Regulation of Canadian Utilities, 1880–1930* (Philadelphia, 1986), pp.66–73; R. Collins, *A Voice From Afar* (Toronto, 1977), pp.65–84; R.C. Fetherstonhaugh, *Charles Fleetford Sise* (Montreal, 1944), pp.111–42.
12. G.D. Smith, *Anatomy of a Business Strategy: Bell, Western Electric and the Origins of the American Telephone Industry* (Baltimore, MD, 1985), Chs. 2–4; see also R.W. Garnet, *The Telephone Enterprise: The Evolution of the Bell System's Horizontal Structure, 1876–1909* (Baltimore, MD, 1985), Chs. 3–6.
13. On Sise's extraordinary early career before his association with the Bell Telephone Co., see Fetherstonhaugh, *Sise*, pp.1–110. Both of Sise's sons, Charles, Jr and Paul, were born in Montreal after Charles Sise Sr emigrated there, and both held major managerial positions in Bell Canada and its affiliate, Northern Electric Co.
14. Quoted in ibid., p.131.
15. Armstrong and Nelles, *Monopoly's Moment*, p.343, indicate that Sise suspected that the decision by the Patent Commissioner, Joseph Tache, was based on political factors (that it was a prelude to an attempt to set up a crown enterprise to control the country's telephone and telegraph systems). Nothing seems to have come of this effort at this time, although nationalisation proposals were floated later and several of the prairie provinces 'provincialised' their telephone systems in 1905–7.
16. American Telephone & Telegraph Records, New York City, Box 1272. C.F. Sise, president, Bell Tel. Co. of Canada, to J.N.Hudson, pres., Amer.Bell Telephone Co., 2 Aug. 1898; E.M. Barton, president, Western Electric, to F.P. Fish, president,

AT&T, 26 Sept. 1901; Sise to H.B. Thayer, Western Electric, 20 Dec. 1901. AT&T Records, Box 1046, Sise to Hudson, 10 Jan. 1896. Western Electric Co. Records, New York City. 'Northern Electric Co. and Its Predecessors – Historical Data', 1948. See also Taylor, 'Sise' pp.158–60.

17. Garnet, *Telephone Enterprise*, Chs. 8–9; L.S.Reich, *The Making of American Industrial Research: Science and Business at GE and Bell, 1876–1926* (Cambridge, MA, 1985), pp.142–60. Vail also advanced the concept of 'regulated monopoly' under which AT&T would provide long distance service to independents as well as its own operating companies, and accept public regulation of rates, a system that endured up to the 1980s.

18. Bell Canada Records, Montreal. American Bell Tel Co. Letterbook No.5. Sise to A.Cochrane, president, American Bell Telephone Co., 22 May 1901. AT&T Records, Box 75. 'Bell Telephone Co. of Canada – Service Contract', 1948. See also Reich, *American Industrial Research*, pp.147–8.

19. AT&T Records, Box 7, Service Contracts File. A.J.Guernsey, vice-president and general counsel, AT&T, to H.B. Thayer, president, AT&T, 16 Nov. 1922. Guernsey noted that under the existing arrangements, even in the field of telephone equipment improvements, Bell Canada would not be assigned rights unless AT&T decided to take out patents in Canada.

20. Western Electric Records. L.B. MacFarlane, president, Bell Canada, to H.B. Thayer, president, Western Electric, 16 Nov. 1918.

21. G. Swope Oral History, Oral History Collections, Columbia University, New York City, 14 Oct. 1947. Swope worked for Western Electric from 1895 and was involved with its international business from 1913–19 when he left the company to take over running International General Electric Co. See Wilkins, *Maturing of Multinational Enterprise*, p.147.

22. AT&T Records, Box 7. A. Bracelen, general solicitor, AT&T to W.S. Gifford, vice-president, AT&T, 14 June 1922.

23. Wilkins, *Maturing of Multinational Enterprise*, pp.70–71; R. Sobel, *ITT: The Management of Opportunity* (New York, 1982), pp.41–4.

24. Western Electric Records, HC-135, 'Outside Companies' Western Electric/Northern Electric contracts, 22 Sept. 1925; AT&T Records, Box 75. Bell Telephone Co. of Canada – Service Contract, 17 April 1926.

25. L. Surtees, *Pa Bell: A. Jean de Grandpre and the Meteoric Rise of Bell Canada Enterprises* (Toronto, 1992), p.93.

26. See A.J. Cordell, *The Multinational Firm, FDI and Canadian Science Policy* (Ottawa, 1971), pp.49–50.

27. Surtees, *Pa Bell*, pp.97–101, 197–8.

28. Vickers Records, Cambridge University, Hist.Doc.609. V. Pritchett, 'Notes on the History of Vickers Ltd., Montreal, Canada', 30 Nov. 1956. See also J.D. Scott, *Vickers: A History* (1962), pp.318–19, 326–7. This section of the paper focuses on the history of Canadian Vickers in 1911–27, as the records of the company after its reacquisition in 1956 were more limited. In 1981 Canadian Vickers was sold to Versatile Corporation, a large shipbuilding company in British Columbia. *Financial Post*, 21 Feb. 1981, p.4.

29. R.P.T. Davenport-Hines, 'Vickers as a Multinational before 1945', in G. Jones (ed.), *British Multinationals: Origins, Management and Performance* (Brookfield, VT, 1986), p.45.

30. On the early development of Vickers, see Scott, *Vickers*, especially Pt. II; C. Trebilcock, *The Vickers Brothers: Armaments and Enterprise, 1854–1914* (1971).

31. Vickers Records, Hist.Doc.608. 'Canadian Vickers Ltd: A Short History of Formation and Sale'. See also Davenport-Hines, *Vickers*, p.54; G.D. Taylor, 'A Merchant of Death in the Peaceable Kingdom: Canadian Vickers 1911–27', in P. Baskerville (ed.), *Canadian Papers in Business History*, Vol.I (Victoria, BC, 1989), pp.217–19. The selecion of a shipyard site in Quebec probably reflected political considerations (never a minor factor in Vickers' decisions): the Minister of Marine in

the Canadian government at the time was a MP from Montreal; and the government hoped to offset French Canadian hostility to the Naval Service Act by locating the major yard in Quebec. See N. Brodeur, 'L.P. Brodeur and the Origins of the Canadian Navy', in J. Boutilier (ed.), *The Royal Canadian Navy in Retrospect* (Vancouver, 1982), p.18.

32. Vickers Records, Hist. Doc. 608, 'Canadian Vickers: A Short History'; Davenport-Hines, *Vickers*, pp.54–5.

33. Taylor, 'Canadian Vickers', pp.220–21. The most thorough account of this episode is G. Smith, *Britain's Clandestine Submarines, 1914–15* (New Haven, CT, 1964). See also C.C. Tansill, *America Goes to War* (Boston, 1938), pp.43–6; G.N.Tucker, *The Naval Service of Canada*, Vol.I (Ottawa, 1952), pp.235–6, 287; M.L. Hadley and R. Sarty, *Tin Pots and Pirate Ships: Canadian Naval Forces and German Sea Raiders, 1880–1918* (Montreal, 1991), pp.99–100,120–1. Vickers' relationship with Electric Boat also included a minority interest in the US company (which apparently was sold sometime after the First World War) and a complicated set of agreements relating to market divisions, which continued to 1937. See Scott, *Vickers*, pp.63–6; R. Franklin, *The Defender: The Story of General Dynamics* (Boston, MA, 1986), pp.53–4, 75.

34. Scott, *Vickers*, p.137.

35. Vickers Records, Microfilm Reel 303. Minutes, executive committee, Canadian Vickers, 13 Nov. 1918.

36. The quote is from J.D. Scott, interviews with Mr Hatcher and Mr Dixon (both Canadian Vickers employees), 30 May 1960. Vickers Records, Hist.Doc.609. Scott, 'Notes on a visit to Canadian Vickers'.

37. Vickers Records, Microfilm Reel 303. Minutes, Canadian Vickers board meetings, London, 14 Feb. 1923; 11 Sept. 1923; 23 Oct. 1923. Vickers Records, Hist.Doc.609. Scott, interview with G.Mossop, 24 May 1960. Mossop was the financial officer sent by Vickers to Canada in 1919.

38. For a more detailed account of Canadian Vickers' aircraft manufacturing, see Taylor, 'Canadian Vickers', pp.226–32.

39. The quotation is from J.D. Scott's interview with Hatcher. See also Davenport-Hines, *Vickers*, p.55; Pritchett, 'Notes on History of Canadian Vickers'. Armstrong's financial problems, incidentally, were partly the result of a disastrous investment in a pulp and paper mill at Corner Brook, Newfoundland, which eventually passed into the hands of another British firm, Bowater. See Scott, *Vickers*, pp.153–5; W.J. Reader, *Bowater: A History* (Cambridge, 1981), pp.32–4, 139–40.

40. Vickers Records, Hist.Doc.609. Horace H. German, 'Memoirs re Canadian Vickers Ltd. in the Canadian Aircraft Industry', Feb.1959. German was the vice president of the Marine and Aviation division of Canadian Vickers in the 1920s, leaving the company in 1930.

41. *US v. Imperial Chemical Industries et al.* 105 Federal Supplement 215 (1952). See also Wilkins, *Multinational Enterprise*, pp.293–4; G.D. Taylor and P.Sudnik, *Du Pont and the International Chemical Industry* (Boston, MA, 1984), pp.166–8.

42. Records of E.I.du Pont de Nemours Co., Eleutherian Mills Historical Library, Greenville, DE, series II, Pt. 2, Accession 1460, Box 32. 'A Short History of Canadian Industries Ltd'. See also G.D. Taylor, 'Management Relations in a Multinational Enterprise: The Case of Canadian Industries Ltd., 1928–48', *Business History Review*, Vol.LV, No.3 (1981),pp.337–58.

43. On the establishment of Canadian Explosives Ltd, see Taylor and Sudnik, *Du Pont*, pp.39–41; W.J. Reader, *Imperial Chemical Industries: A History*, Vol.I (1970), pp.173, 194–6,210–11.

44. On the general context of Nobel–Du Pont relations in this era, see Taylor and Sudnik, *Du Pont* pp.124–30; Reader, *Imperial Chemical Industries*, Vol.II (1975), pp.32–56; D.A.Hounshell and J.K.Smith, *Science and Corporate Strategy: Du Pont Research and Development, 1902–80* (Cambridge, MA, 1988), pp.190–205. CIL was initially a holding company with subsidiaries in explosives, paints, cellulose products and ammunition. Later these and other companies acquired by it were reorganised into

divisions.

45. Du Pont negotiators went to some lengths to try to circumvent potential antitrust charges. In the general patent and process agreement with ICI in 1929, for example, provision was made for mutual compensation for patent exchanges with a regular review process, to avoid the appearance that Du Pont and ICI had set up a 'patent pool'. Unfortunately, by the 1940s US court rulings not only extended the antritrust penumbra to reach such agreements but also to cover joint ventures such as CIL. See Wilkins, *Maturing of Multinational Enterprise*, pp.292–4; G.W. Stocking and M.W.Watkins, *Cartels in Action* (New York, 1946), pp.448–57.

46. See Hounshell and Smith, *Science and Corporate Strategy*, pp.199–201. ICI researchers, in particular, felt that Du Pont adopted dilatory tactics in exchanging information while belittling ICI's own achievements; and in 1948 Du Pont moved quickly to cancel the patent and process agreements, even before antitrust charges reached the stage of court proceedings. See Reader, *Imperial Chemical Industries*, Vol.II, pp.433–8.

47. On Purvis, see Taylor, 'CIL', pp.744–6; Reader, *Imperial Chemical Industries*, Vol.II, pp.213–14.

48. Imperial Chemical Industries Records, London, 'Canada and Canadian Industries Ltd., 1926–39', manuscript, Appendix F. The Swint quote is from *US v. ICI et al*, Trial Transcript, 6 June 1950. Swint, as a member of Du Pont's Foreign Relations Committee in the 1930s and 1940s, was one of his company's main liaisons with CIL.

49. 'Canada and Canadian Industries Ltd., 1926–39'; Reader, *Imperial Chemical Industries*, Vol.II, pp.214–18.

50. 'Short History of Canadian Industries Ltd.'; H.H.Lank and E.L.Williams, *The Du Pont Canada History* (Montreal, 1982), pp.61–106. On Defence Industries Ltd and Canada's atomic energy project, see R. Bothwell, *Nucleus: A History of Atomic Energy of Canada Ltd.* (Toronto, 1988), pp.57–60, 112–16.

51. ICI Records. 'CIL 1945–52'. The reorganisation of research in 1948 was not without controversy: many of those who worked in the Central Lab felt that they were tied too closely to applied research and dependent on the manufacturing divisions. After the separation in 1952, Du Pont Canada estalished an independent R & D division with its own budget and control system. See Lank and Williams, *Du Pont Canada History*, pp.192–3.

52. See Taylor and Sudnik, *Du Pont*, pp.167–8; 'CIL 1945–52'; Lank and Williams, *Du Pont Canada History*, pp.161–72.

I.G. Farben in Japan: The Transfer of Technology and Managerial Skills

AKIRA KUDO
University of Tokyo

I

This article deals with the technology and management transfer from the German to the Japanese chemical industries during the 1920s and 1930s.[1] Before 1945, I.G. Farbenindustrie Aktiengesellschaft (hereafter referred to as I.G. Farben), the giant German chemical firm, exported goods such as dyestuffs and nitrogenous fertiliser to Japan, and licensed its synthetic ammonia process to Japanese companies. It also made direct investments in Japan, both in manufacturing and in sales outlets. Through these three forms of international business activities – export of products, licensing, and direct investment – I.G. Farben transferred to the Japanese chemical industry, intentionally or not, its production technology and managerial skills. Its technology and management transfer also produced far-reaching effects on other facets of the Japanese chemical industry, including its distribution system. In fact, I.G. Farben was one of the two German companies which affected business management in Japan most profoundly, the other being Siemens in the electrical machinery industry.[2]

This article divides the period under study into the 1920s and the 1930s, the two decades when the Japanese market took on significantly different characteristics. This will be followed by a brief overview of the activities of I.G. Farben during the two decades, with a review of the technology and management transfer which was effected by its business activities. Throughout, the focus is on production technology, marketing policy, the distribution system, and personnel management. Financing issues are omitted due to the shortage of available information.

II

It is necessary to begin with a brief outline of the Japanese market for chemical products from 1910 through the 1920s. In pre-First World War years, the major German chemical companies were already exporting their products to Japan on a considerable scale. Dyestuffs were an important export item, particularly synthetic indigo, which was especially favoured in the Orient. Each company had its Japanese agent; BASF established its agent in 1881 and Bayer changed its agent in 1891.[3] By 1913, immediately before the First World War, the Japanese market had become very important for German dyestuff producers. In that year Japan ranked as the eighth largest export market for German dyestuffs, importing 15.83 million marks' worth of the products, or 4.9 per cent of total German dyestuff exports of 321.20 million marks. Among the eight German dyestuff manufacturers, the largest three, BASF, Bayer and Hoechst, overwhelmed the others in export sales in Japan, with two of the three, BASF and Hoechst, dividing between them as much as two-thirds of the exports to Japan. In addition, the two companies had stronger interests in the Japanese market than the six other German dyestuff producers. They saw Japan not only as an important export market in itself but also as a sales base for East Asian markets, including China. In fact, Japan with its political stability and communications infrastructure had become an important foothold for business activities in the large Chinese market.[4]

With the outbreak of the First World War, the German chemical manufacturers were denied access to the Japanese market. In an attempt to fill the suddenly created vacuum, many small dyestuff manufacturing firms cropped up, and, also, large firms like the Mitsui Mining Co. began to undertake dyestuff manufacturing operations. The trend was further accelerated by the Japanese government, which, in an effort to foster a modern chemical industry, promulgated the Law for Promoting Dyestuff and Medicine Production and other laws, and established a government-owned Nihon Senryo Seizo Kabushiki Kaisha (Japan Dyestuff Manufacturing Co. Ltd, hereafter referred to as Nihon Senryo). Thus the First World War marked the birth of a modern chemical industry in Japan.

After the war, the Japanese market became even more important for the German chemical industry. The rapidly developing Japanese textile industry was in need of ever-increasing quantities of dyestuffs. Also, the spread of fertiliser-intensive farming methods in the agricultural sector was creating a lucrative export market for the German nitrogen industry with its newly developed synthetic ammonia process. In addition, the Chinese market, following the revolution of 1911 that overthrew the Ch'ing dynasty, seemed ready to grow by leaps and bounds. Thus, it was only natural that the German chemical firms were greatly attracted by the Japanese market, and competed fiercely with each other in order to put their pre-war sales networks back into shape, regain their export shares, and capture the newly expanding segments of the market.

In the immediate aftermath of the war, the Japanese demand for dyestuffs and nitrogenous fertiliser was met to a large extent by supplies from the United States and other European countries, but, before long, German products began to dominate the market. This was because the newborn Japanese chemical industry was not yet competitive enough to dominate the domestic market, while the German chemical industry had a significant competitive edge over its international competitors in chemical production as a whole, even though the degree of its supremacy varied from one product to the next.

Moreover, the Japanese government had not yet adopted a protectionist policy effective enough to stem the inflow of foreign chemical products. To be sure, the government felt the need to protect the country's infant chemical industry, on the one hand, but, on the other hand, it also found it imperative to serve the interests of the textile industry and agriculture by allowing them access to cheaper chemical products imported from abroad. As a result, the government adopted what could basically be characterised as a 'weak protectionist policy', or a policy of selective protection of the infant chemical industry, one which kept the import tariffs at relatively low levels, while fostering sentiments of economic nationalism by encouraging the population to 'buy Japanese'. Direct investments by foreign chemical firms were also welcomed, in principle, for the same reason, even though the government was reluctant to allow the investing foreign companies to gain control of management of the joint ventures, and the Japanese partners of the joint ventures, too, were insistent on keeping them under their own control.[5]

Despite its 'weak protectionist' stance, the government sometimes took bold steps to sustain sections of the domestic chemical industry under threat from foreign competition. For instance, it enforced, in June 1924, an import licence system to protect the dyestuff industry which was badly in need of protection. This system was, in effect, meant to discriminate against German goods. One of the counter-measures devised by the German dyestuff industry was reorganisation of its distribution outlets within Japan.

At the time, major German dyestuff companies belonging to an industry-wide *Interessengemeinschaft* (community of interests) were being pressed hard to rationalise their business organisations in response to the subsiding post-war hyperinflation. And the consolidation of their sales outlets outside Germany was one of the most important and difficult tasks, because each member company considered its own traditional sales outlets, trade rights and trade marks as too precious to be subjected to reorganisation and reshuffling. Nevertheless, the effort to consolidate the German sales outlets in Japan was completed relatively smoothly, most likely because each German company took a serious view of the growth potential of the Japanese industry's production capabilities and the adverse effects of the discriminatory import licensing system.

Interestingly enough, in the course of deliberation on the consolidation of sales organisations in Japan, BASF presented a plan which called for an immediate and complete integration of the sales branches of all the German companies concerned, while Hoechst proposed an export quota system and Bayer suggested a partial integration as a compromise between the two. This conflict of plans preceded and anticipated a dispute at the top management level concerning the reorganisation of the community of interests, namely, a conflict between a merger plan proposed by Carl Bosch of BASF and a shareholding plan by Carl Duisberg of Bayer. Eventually, the immediate integration measure won its day. In December 1924, the Doitsu Senryo Gomei Kaisha (German Dyestuff Co.) was established at 37 Akashi-cho, Kobe, as the sole representative for the community of interests with the exception of Cassella. Established with a capital outlay of 300,000 yen, the office was staffed by two employees from BASF, and one each from Hoechst, Bayer, Agfa, and Griesheim-Elektron, with Richard Veit of Bayer appointed as chief manager. It was just one year after this that Bosch's plan was accepted and, as a result, I.G. Farben was established back in Germany.

Much the same pattern of reorganisation took place in other fields. For fertiliser products like nitrogenous fertiliser, H. Ahrnes & Co. Nachf., located in the Yaesu Building at Yaesu-cho, Kojimachi-ku, Tokyo, was established as the sole representative for the community of interests from the outset. As shown in Table 1, sales organisations for medicine, photographic products and titan were reorganised or newly established one after another.

As a consequence of this reorganisation, a strategy of the community of interests in Japan was to be carried out through a set-up composed of three strata. Situated at the top was a council of the community of interests composed of the chief executives of the eight participating companies. This council would directly involve itself in making decisions on matters of crucial importance. Placed directly subordinate to this council was the Japan Commission (later renamed East Asian Commission), charged with the task of devising the community's strategy toward Japan and carrying it out with the council's consent.

TABLE 1

I.G. FARBEN'S DIRECT INVESTMENT IN JAPAN AS OF 1945

Company	Place	Purpose of establishment	Capital (million yen)	Shareholding ratio (%)
Asahi Bemberg Kenshi Kabushiki Kaisha	Osaka	Rayon manufacturing	46.00	1.81
Nihon Tokushu Seizo Kabushiki Kaisha	Tokyo	Pesticide manufacturing	1.00	10.00
Bayer Yakuhin Gomei Kaisha	Kobe	Sales of medicine	0.15	100.00
Doitsu Senryo Gomei Kaisha	Kobe, Tokyo	Sales of dyestuffs	0.30	26.23
H. Ahrens & Co. Nachf.	Tokyo	Sales of nitrogenous fertiliser	0.20	100.00
Agfa Gomei Kaisha	Tokyo	Sales of photographic products	0.10	100.00
Titan Kogyo Kabushiki Kaisha	Tokyo	Sales of titan	3.50	4.17

Source: Finance and Accounting Section, I.G. Farben Control Office of the Office of Military Government for Germany (US), Survey, 1947, Hoechst-Archiv.

Hermann Waibel of BASF was appointed as the first chief of this commission. At the bottom of the hierarchy were sales organisations, such as Doitsu Senryo, each responsible for directly handling the sales of a specific variety of goods in Japan. This hierarchical set-up was basically kept intact even after the establishment of I.G. Farben.[6]

It is hardly necessary to emphasise the significant place I.G. Farben occupied, not simply in the German industry, but in the world chemical industry as a whole. Naturally, for the newborn Japanese industry, I.G. Farben was a formidable giant. It was capitalised at 650 million marks (some 300 million yen) at its establishment, whereas the Mitsui Mining Co., the largest Japanese mining company which was diversifying into chemical production, was capitalised at only 52.50 million yen, and the government-owned Nihon Senryo at a mere eight million yen.

The Japanese dye industry and the government repeatedly requested technical co-operation and/or licensing from I.G. Farben. Although I.G. Farben did not openly reject these requests, it was tacitly following a policy of not granting such requests. One well-known example of I.G. Farben's tacit refusal to grant such requests involved the transfer of technical know-how about the Haber–Bosch process. The patent for this process was confiscated by the Japanese government during the First

World War, and the exclusive right to use the patent was sold to Toyo Chisso Kumiai (Oriental Nitrogen Association) established by major *zaibatsu* groups. However, Japanese chemical firms, including those of the *zaibatsu* groups, had no knowledge of how to put this process to commercial use. As soon as the war was over, therefore, some companies contacted BASF in the hopes of acquiring the necessary know-how. BASF, however, demanded an outrageous fee of 68 million yen, and the Japanese firms had to give up the idea of acquiring the technology from BASF. Indeed, by quoting the prohibitively high fee BASF made it known that it had no intention of offering licensing or technical co-operation. It should be kept in mind that the term 'licensing' here is used in a broad sense, because BASF's patent was still under confiscation by the Japanese government when this episode took place.[7]

Another illustration of I.G. Farben's lack of interest in offering technical co-operation is found in the reaction of the top executives of the community of interests to a proposal for technological co-operation which Fritz Haber made to them in 1924 upon his return from a trip to Japan. Haber possessed great prestige at BASF and the community of interests because of the remarkable success of the Haber–Bosch process, and he proposed that the community should offer technological co-operation to Japan in the field of inorganic chemistry as an indispensable means of compromise to entice the Japanese government into abolishing the import licence system for German chemical products. However, the community council flatly rejected his proposal. Especially obstinate in opposing Haber's proposal was Carl Bosch, the very person who had worked closely with Haber in the development of the Haber–Bosch process, and who was then chairman of the board of directors of BASF and one of the leading figures of the community. Bosch maintained that, if the community started co-operating with the Japanese in the field of inorganic chemistry, the Japanese would then press hard for co-operation in the field of dye production as well. Calling attention to '*der fast krankhafte Ehrgeiz der Japaner*' (the almost morbid ambition of the Japanese), Bosch asserted that 'our objective, under any circumstances, ought not to be to offer any help whatsoever to the Japanese in their efforts to build up a profitable chemical industry, and in particular, a dye industry of their own, but rather to slow their progress in these efforts as long as possible, and moreover to reduce these efforts into a failure as best as we can'.[8]

Moreover, when Jiro Inabata, managing director of Nihon Senryo, made a tour of Europe, visiting Kuhlmann (Compagnie Nationale de Matières Colorantes et Manufactures de Produits Chimiques du Nord réunies Etablissements Kuhlmann) and St Denis (Société Anonyme des

Matières Colorantes et Produits Chimiques de St Denis) of France, and Durand & Huguenin AG of Switzerland to look into the possibility of securing technological co-operation, his efforts were frustrated by I.G. Farben, which informed Inabata through Ciba (Gesellschaft für chemische Industrie in Basel) that no company that was a member of the German–Swiss–French three-party dyestuff cartel could give technological assistance to Japan without the consent of the other members.[9]

It is true, however, that there were some occasions when I.G. Farben gave positive consideration to offering technological co-operation. For instance, it considered offering technological co-operation to Nihon Senryo in the field of rayon and aluminium production as a means of discouraging the latter from developing synthetic indigo. It should be pointed out, however, that I.G. Farben brushed the idea away as soon as it discovered that Nihon Senryo was not competent enough to develop synthetic indigo.[10]

I.G. Farben's strategy can be understood in the light of the fact that it is usually difficult for a leading firm in the chemical industry, unlike its counterpart in the electrical machinery industry, to maintain its technological supremacy over its competitors by using its patents as a leverage. It should also be recalled that the Japanese government had requisitioned German patents during the First World War, and that in April 1921 the government promulgated a Revised Patent Law which made chemical material ineligible for patent protection.

In some fields of chemical production, such as nitrogenous fertiliser, Japanese firms introduced the necessary technologies from France and Italy after these had been diffused from Germany during the First World War, while in other fields they used technologies devised by themselves. In the field of dyestuffs, Japanese firms were trying hard to develop the products for themselves by copying German products. Mitsui Mining's effort to develop synthetic indigo and Nihon Senryo's to develop naphthol dyestuffs were two outstanding examples. Needless to say, the lifting of patent protection in itself did not immediately guarantee that high-technology products could be easily developed. There are a wide variety of intricate details that had to be learned or discovered before the previously patented information could be put to practical application. Nevertheless, there is no denying that these developmental efforts posed a serious threat to I.G. Farben.

Thus, in order for I.G. Farben to protect its technology, which became ineligible for patent protection, it had no choice but to deny licensing to Japan. Not only that, I.G. Farben even went so far as to dump its synthetic indigo products in the Japanese market in the hope of discouraging Mitsui Mining's effort to develop these.[11] It also had recourse to a number of other measures, including reorganisation of its sales base in Japan, as mentioned already, and readjustment of its sales policies, to be explained shortly. In addition to these, I.G. Farben concluded a series of bilateral agreements with individual Japanese firms and with the Japanese industry as a whole as a means of securing its outlets.

One such agreement signed in the field of dyestuffs was a gentlemen's agreement of August 1926 on German dyestuff export to Japan between I.G. Farben and the Japanese dyestuff industry – known as the Saito–Waibel Agreement after with the representatives who signed it. The agreement stipulated, in essence, that in exchange for the Japanese government's abolishing its current import licence on German products, I.G. Farben would voluntarily restrict exports to Japan of those products which the Japanese were capable of producing domestically. Put differently, the agreement implied that I.G. Farben was free from any import restriction on products currently not being produced in Japan, like indigo. The arrangement envisioned by the agreement was a kind of international division of labour between the chemical industries of the two countries. Incidentally, it was not until the agreement was concluded that the two governments signed a new Japanese–German Commerce and Navigation Treaty, which they had been negotiating. This reveals the important place dye products occupied in trading between the two countries. The Saito–Waibel Agreement, which came into effect in April 1928, was finalised far quicker than other bilateral agreements between the two countries. This was because the import licence system, introduced by the Japanese government as one of the measures to pursue selective protection, was restraining I.G. Farben's activities. Thus, the conclusion of this agreement, which obliged the Japanese government to lift its current import licence system, and allowed German indigo and other expensive dye products free access to the Japanese market, was basically a welcome accomplishment for I.G. Farben.[12]

In the field of nitrogenous fertiliser, on the other hand, the Japanese market still had some room to absorb imports, despite the rapid growth of domestic production. As shown in Figure 1, nitrogenous fertiliser became, by 1929, Germany's single most important chemical exported to Japan, far surpassing other chemicals, including dyestuffs. Partly because Japan was designated by the international fertiliser cartel as a market for open competition, foreign companies in the late 1920s competed fiercely against each other for larger shares of the Japanese market, giving rise to a phenomenon called, 'gaian dumping' (gaian

FIGURE 1
GERMAN CHEMICAL EXPORTS TO JAPAN, 1929–36

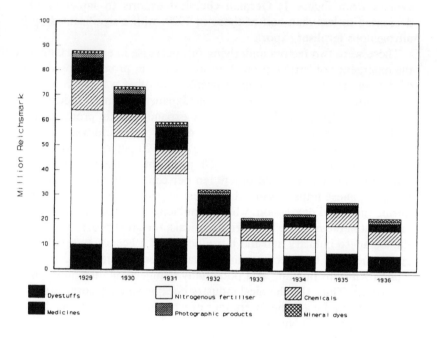

meaning foreign ammonium sulphate). It was against this backdrop that in December 1930 I.G. Farben, acting on behalf of the CIA (Convention Internationale de l'Azote), consulted with the Japanese fertiliser industry, and worked out a draft agreement called the Fujiwara–Bosch Draft Agreement which was meant to put an end to the heated price competition. It called upon the Japanese industry to refrain completely from exporting its nitrogenous fertiliser, and upon the foreign industries to curtail their exports to Japan in exchange for this, but it miscarried because of strong domestic opposition. Several months later, in April 1931, a Tentative Agreement on Domestic and Foreign Ammonium Sulphate was signed, but this, too, failed to come into effect.[13] It was only in the 1930s that agreements between the international cartel and the Japanese chemical industry began to materialise.

III

The rapid growth of the Japanese market continued well into the 1930s. However, German exports to the Japanese market were seriously thwarted by the collapse of the international gold standard and by the fragmentation of the world economy into several economic blocs. As is evident from Figure 1, German chemical exports to Japan in 1932 decreased to less than half of those of 1929, with a significant drop in nitrogenous fertiliser export.

There were two factors underlying this decrease in exports. One was the emergence of 'strong protectionism' in Japan, prompted by the fall of the yen and the rise in import tariffs. The other was the continued gain in the productivity attained by the Japanese chemical industry. In the field of dyestuffs, Japanese firms expanded their production so rapidly as to account for 3.2 per cent of the total world-wide sales by 1938. In the same year, Mitsui Mining had a 20 per cent share of the domestic market, Nihon Senryo 60 per cent, Mitsubishi Chemical Industries ten per cent and others ten per cent.[14] In the field of fertilisers, Japanese firms continued to invest in plants and equipment even during the world depression, when manufacturers abroad were foreseeing a glut in the market. In pharmaceuticals, the great progress made by the Japanese industry and the introduction of a licence system by the government led to a decrease in German exports. In fact, I.G. Farben named Kitazato Institute as a potentially strong competitor in the field of serum.[15] Thus, the chemical industry became an early cornerstone of industrialising Japan, the forerunner of what are now known as 'Newly Industrialising Economies' (NIEs).

The Manchurian Incident of September 1931 marked a turning point for the Japanese government's policy toward foreign capital, with the previous policy of welcoming foreign capital investment replaced by that of rejection. Foreign capital was to be either phased out or Japanised, and foreign firms were prevented from exercising control over the management of their joint ventures.[16] As shown in Table 1, I.G. Farben's direct investments in manufacturing firms, if not those in distribution firms, were seriously restricted, with the result that its participating ratio in Asahi Bemberg, a rayon manufacturer, remained no more than 1.81 per cent in 1945, and that in Nihon Tokushu Seizo, an insecticide manufacturer, as low as ten per cent.

I.G. Farben's response to this policy change was, for the time being, to pursue the strategy devised in the 1920s, trying to conclude bilateral agreements with the Japanese chemical industry. With the advance of Japanese products, which were capturing ever greater shares of the market, it was becoming increasingly difficult to keep the market open for free competition among members of the international cartel. On the other hand, however, the international cartel had grown stronger, making it possible for I.G. Farben to carry out negotiations with the

Japanese to its own advantage through collaboration with the participating companies of the international cartel. In the field of dyestuffs, where the Saito–Waibel Agreement had been reached early, I.G. Farben concluded in the early 1930s, either on its own or on behalf of the international cartel, agreements with Mitsui Mining, which had developed synthetic indigo, and with Nihon Senryo, which had developed naphthol dyestuffs.

The international cartel in the field of dyestuffs had its origin in the German–French agreement of 1927. In 1928 it grew into a three-party cartel with the participation of Switzerland. February 1932 saw the establishment of a four-party cartel, consisting of the dyestuff industries of Germany, France, Switzerland and Great Britain. This cartel was further expanded with the conclusion of separate agreements with the industries of the United States, Italy, Czechoslovakia and Poland.

In May 1935, six parties of the international cartel – consisting of I.G. Farben, Swiss companies, French companies, ICI (Imperial Chemical Industries) of Britain, Du Pont and Nacco (National Aniline & Chemical Co.) of the US – signed the Mitsui Indigo Agreement with Mitsui Mining. This agreement stipulated that Mitsui export its products only to China (including Manchuria, Hong Kong and Dalian) and within the bounds of a quota to be assigned to it. In return, the six parties concerned were to accept quotas for their exports to Japan. The distribution of the Japanese market including Korea and Formosa was 85 per cent for Mitsui and 15 per cent for the six parties. The prices in the Japanese and Chinese markets were also set at the same time.

I.G. Farben also signed for itself an agreement with Nihon Senryo in March 1931, called the Variamine Blue Agreement. There were several patent disputes between I.G. Farben and Nihon Senryo concerning Variamine Blue B, Naphthol AS, and their equivalents. The agreement was to solve these disputes and to restrain competition. Nihon Senryo agreed to honour the patents of I.G. Farben and not to export its products outside China. In exchange for this, both sides agreed to divide up the Japanese market between themselves, with I.G. Farben enjoying a 68 per cent share and Nihon Senryo 32 per cent for Variamine Blue B. Concurrently, it was also agreed that both sides would sell their products at the same prices in the Chinese market.[17]

In addition, I.G. Farben, acting on behalf of the six parties of the international cartel, concluded a sales and price agreement on sulphur black dyes exports to China with Mitsui Bussan (Mitsui & Co.) in 1931. And, in October 1931, I.G. Farben alone signed the Alizarine Blue Agreement with Mitsui Bussan, which represented Mitsui Mining. This latter agreement stipulated that I.G. Farben would have a 60 per cent share of the Japanese market, and Mitsui the balance.[18] In February 1934, I.G. Farben concluded the Astraphloxine Agreement, again with Nihon Senryo, restricting the latter's export of the product and specifying the two parties' shares of the Japanese market.[19]

In the field of nitrogenous fertiliser, the Fujiwara–Bosch Draft Agreement had failed to materialise, as noted earlier, owing to a large extent to the collapse of the CIA. The CIA was re-established in July 1932. In March 1934, the CIA succeeded in concluding an Overall Ammonium Sulphate Agreement with the Japanese nitrogenous fertiliser industry through I.G. Farben. This was followed by the signing of the second agreement in February 1935, and the third agreement in November 1935. I.G. Farben was satisfied by these three agreements because they imposed a quota on Japanese exports to China, and so was the Japanese industry because they reduced or eliminated German exports to Japan and China.[20]

By the mid-1930s, I.G. Farben had to acknowledge that the Japanese market had been saturated with Japanese products. Of the two alternatives to product export which were theoretically available, namely, direct investment and licensing, the former was virtually out of the question since the Japanese government was bent on rejecting the inflow of foreign capital. I.G. Farben thus opted to change its strategy, beginning to offer Japanese firms the licences to use its know-how for the production of dyestuffs and nitrogenous fertiliser, and to export plants to the licensees. The new strategy seems to have much in common with those which advanced countries of today adopt in their relations with NIEs. However, in the case of synthetic oil, the situation was different. I.G. Farben could not export the product to Japan, and it was ready from the outset to respond positively to enquiries about licensing arrangements for synthetic oil production.

Concurrently with the adoption of the licensing strategy, I.G. Farben began to emphasise intelligence activities in Japan and East Asia. To be sure, German marketing subsidiaries in Japan, such as Doitsu Senryo, had been fairly active in collecting information,[21] but they became far more active as the licensing issue developed. For instance, Max Ilgner, executive chief of the Public Relations Office of I.G. Farben, made a tour of inspection in East Asia from 1934 to 1935, and wrote a detailed three-volume report entitled 'Report of the Far Eastern Tour, 1934–35'.[22] Several other reports, including 'The Japanese Chemical Industry', were also compiled, most likely by the Research Division.[23]

In the field of dyestuffs, there is a record suggesting that in 1934 or thereabouts, I.G. Farben concluded a licensing agreement with Nihon Tar Industries (later renamed Mitsubishi Chemical Industries). But the agreement did not seem to bear much fruit: when an engineer from Mitsubishi visited I.G. Farben's plants, I.G. Farben deeply suspected him of being an industrial spy.[24]

In sharp contrast to this, the licensing strategy proved quite successful in the field of fertilisers, where the Japanese market's vigour continued well into the 1930s, assuring high profit rates and enticing new entrants into the industry. Although the fertiliser producers had already been using the Casale process and the Claude process, they were eager to introduce I.G. Farben's Haber–Bosch process. This zeal to introduce the process must have derived, at least partly, from its having been rated by Japanese specialists to be the best. It should be pointed out, moreover, that Japanese curiosity and inquisitiveness, which astonished an I.G. Farben engineer, must have also contributed to the introduction of the process. This engineer observed that 'Japanese mentality is always in quest of something new, and it matters little whether the "new" thing is really superior to the older one or not'.[25]

The patent for the Haber–Bosch process had expired by then, so the arrangements made between I.G. Farben and Japanese fertiliser manu-facturers were for technological guidance, to be specific, but in a broad sense they might be regarded as licensing arrangements. I.G. Farben offered licences to a total of five companies, beginning with a licensing arrangement made with Taki Seihisho (Taki Fertiliser Works) in Hyogo Prefecture in May 1935. The four other licensees were Yahagi Industries (later renamed Toa Chemical Industry), Nihon Tar Industries, Dainippon Tokkyo Hiryo (later renamed Nitto Chemical Industry) and Dainippon Sugar Manufacturing.[26]

In the field of synthetic oil, I.G. Farben started to negotiate with Japanese companies earlier than it did in the field of nitrogenous fertiliser. In the early 1930s, it approached South Manchurian Railways, and later contacted more than a dozen companies including the Mitsubishi Mining Co. and Ogura Petroleum. However, no licensing agreement resulted from these contacts. The most important reason for the failure of these efforts seems to have been the stiff opposition mounted by the Japanese Navy, which developed its own process and was interested in seeing private companies put this into commercial use. I.G. Farben continued trying to sell its synthetic oil technology to Japan even after the outbreak of the Pacific War. However, it was not until January 1945, when the Second World War was drawing to an end, that I.G. Farben was able to conclude with the Japanese Army what became its first and last licensing contract on synthetic oil production.[27]

IV

Since I.G. Farben made little direct investment in manufacturing in Japan, its technological transfer to Japan was limited in scope. Nonetheless, its technological influence was not insignificant in the fertiliser industry where it licensed the Haber–Bosch process to five companies.

The case of Taki Fertiliser Works, the manufacturer of superphosphate fertiliser in Hyogo and the first of five companies to receive technological assistance from I.G. Farben, is instructive. The technological agreement stipulated as follows. First, I.G. Farben would provide all the drawings and specifications necessary for building the plant and equipment and all the other pertinent information necessary for putting these into operation; second, I.G. Farben would provide engineers and foremen to train the operators of Taki Fertiliser; and, third, I.G. Farben would assume the responsibility for placing orders for and supplying machinery, equipment and apparatus. In short, I.G. Farben committed itself to offering not only the licence for the Haber–Bosch process for use in the production of synthetic ammonia but also peripheral technology as well as the know-how for ammonia sulphate production, all in one package. Taki Fertiliser Works at the time was trying to diversify from the production of calcium superphosphate, which did not require much technological expertise, into the technologically more sophisticated area of synthetic ammonia production, and, as such, the company must have been in need of securing technological co-operation in as comprehensive a manner as possible.

It should be kept in mind, however, that the contents of the contract signed by Nihon Tar Industries, a member of the Mitsubishi *zaibatsu*, were similar to that of Taki Fertiliser, except that Nihon Tar Industries adopted the state-of-the-art Winkler reactor as a means of generating hydrogen gas. It is plausible that Nihon Tar Industries, with its avowed intention to become 'an I.G. Farben of the Orient', concluded the agreement on terms as comprehensive as possible with the intention of learning the most from I.G. Farben. It can be presumed, however, that the comprehensive nature of the technological transfer agreement should be interpreted as reflecting the wide technological gap between Germany and Japan rather than the intent of Nihon Tar Industries.[28]

I.G. Farben did send a team of its engineers, chemists and foremen to Japan to supervise the building and operation of the plants. Though only five of them (two engineers and three foremen) stayed for an extended period of time, the team consisted of 12 members at its peak (two engineers, two chemists and eight foremen). From a historical point of view, they were like a large number of foreign advisors who assisted in Japan's modernisation in the early Meiji period. Unlike the famous foreign advisors of the earlier time, who were mainly government employees, these I.G. Farben technicians were a group of unknown foreign advisors dispatched at a private level to supervise the construction of chemical plants.

Of all the machinery procured for the sake of implementing the technological licensing agreement with Taki Fertiliser Works, I.G. Farben's own products consisted only of high-pressure apparatuses, pipelines and fittings, and measuring instruments. I.G. Farben procured the rest from other companies: specifically, these consisted of high-pressure compressors and gas circulating pumps from Borsig, water gas plants and conversion plants from Bamag, high-pressure centrifugal pumps and rotary vacuum pumps from Klein, Schanzlin & Becker, Cu-lye pressure pumps from Hydraulik, ammonia hydraulic pumps from Balke, free jet turbines from Escher Wyss, transformers for electric heaters from Siemens-Schuckert, centrifuges from Gebr. Heine, saturators from Schütze, and synchron motors from AEG. This list is a virtual exhibition of German machinery, with the exception of the products of Escher Wyss, a Swiss firm.[29]

Under the supervision of the German engineers, the German-made machines were assembled and installed. This process by which the German engineers trained Japanese junior engineers into supervisors constituted an important aspect of technology transfer, understood in a sense broader than the transfer of technological know-how itself. The training was provided at the site of construction, and along the line of command and supervision which stretched down from the German chief engineer at the top, to the German engineers and foremen below him, to a group of young Japanese junior engineers. The Japanese junior engineers, through their daily contacts with the Germans, learned not only about engineering skills but also about how to supervise their own subordinates, the Japanese foremen and rank-and-file workers.[30]

The Taki Fertiliser plant and equipment, which embodied the Haber–Bosch process, were later taken over by a joint venture with Sumitomo Chemical Industries and produced ammonium sulphate in the early post-war period. The imported facilities at other companies followed a similar fate after the war.

There were several other instances of technology transfer. In the field of dyestuffs, the activities of research laboratories and their travelling engineers were instrumental in the transfer of German dyestuff technology. More specifically, the 1930s saw dyestuff manufacturers' associations in several localities establish syndicated plants and laboratories and invest in technology improvement. These moves were a concerted response to I.G. Farben's activities.

German exports also played an important role in transferring German technologies to Japan. Mitsui Mining's synthetic indigo and Nihon Senryo's naphthol dyestuffs, both modelled after I.G. Farben's products, were the products of unintended technology transfer. In the case of synthetic oil, the contacts that companies had with I.G. Farben in the process of negotiating on licensing contracts provided them with channels for technology transfer, such as experiments with crude coal, written estimates, and factory tours. Moreover, the factory tours and the access to drawings granted to visiting Japanese scholars, government officials and military officers also served as an important channel for technology transfer.

I.G. Farben affected the marketing practices and the distribution system of the Japanese chemical industry primarily through export of its manufactured goods, but the establishment of its sales bases also amplified these effects. In the summer of 1927, the head of the East Asian Commission and *Japan-Herren* (personnel responsible for business in Japan, actually employees of Doitsu Senryo) met at I.G. Farben's headquarters to discuss I.G. Farben's overall strategy in Japan. The main purpose was to re-evaluate the company's marketing policy and distribution system in Japan, and the discussions allow an insight into the influence I.G. Farben exerted on the distribution system.[31]

Let us first look at the re-examination of the distribution system. The history of the German dyestuff distribution system in Japan in the period from the late nineteenth century to the outbreak of the Second World War may be divided into three phases. The first period was from the early Meiji era to immediately before the outbreak of the First World War, the period when imports from Germany were handled by agents. Products manufactured by German companies were imported by foreign-owned or Japanese-owned sales agents, and were then sold to Japanese dyestuff wholesalers which were franchises of the German companies. The second period was from the eve of the First World War to its conclusion, or the period of 'direct import' when the sales agents came under direct management of the German firms. With this change, the route along which imported dyestuffs were distributed also changed, so that products manufactured by the German firms were imported by their respective agents or branches under their direct management, and were then sold to the franchised wholesalers. The first of such direct sales agencies was Friedrich Bayer & Co. Gomei Kaisha, established by Bayer in Kobe in 1911. Other German companies followed suit, reorganising their sales agencies and franchised wholesalers on a large scale.

The third period started in 1924, when the sales agencies under direct German control were consolidated into Doitsu Senryo Gomei Kaisha.[32]

As mentioned above, the German dye companies which were consolidated into I.G. Farben expanded their distribution networks in Japan by nurturing large wholesalers into their special agents or franchises. In other words, they built a franchise system, drawing upon the existing wholesale system. In this sense, German dyestuff companies had the effect of accelerating the stratification of the dyestuff wholesalers, and, in effect, reinforced the traditional wholesale system.

Even before the establishment of I.G. Farben, the German dyestuff companies had been talking about the need to reorganise the franchise system drastically. The most serious drawback of this system, it was argued, was that it was unavoidably accompanied by increased distribution costs. The minutes of the aforementioned meeting contain several interesting figures showing the high distribution costs in Japan. At the level of Doitsu Senryo, the distribution costs, inclusive of handling fees and warehouse charges of five per cent, amounted to as much as 9.08 per cent of gross revenues. When clerical and other handling charges of 1.77 per cent due in Germany were added to this, the total cost percentage rose to 10.85 per cent, an exceptionally high ratio by international standards. At this meeting, the possibility of abolishing the special agent system and replacing it by a direct sales system was discussed. However, the meeting concluded that a drastic change of this sort would be extremely difficult to implement. Ironically enough, the existing system had grown so firmly rooted that it could not easily be discarded.

Textbooks on Japanese business history usually point out that the pre-war market, in which a wholesale distribution system was dominant, was quite different from the American or European system.[33] One observation of the dyestuff market points out that in the period from the turn of the century to the 1920s, when non-traditional manufactured goods started to flow in, the market was sometimes affected more profoundly by European companies than by American companies. This was particularly true in already high segmented markets, such as dyestuffs, in which the situation was closer to that of European countries, and in their efforts to adapt themselves to the Japanese market, European companies made the characteristics of that market all the more conspicuous. The viability of this hypothesis cannot be demonstrated here. However, unlike the distribution system for automobiles and electric appliances, which were formed under the influence of American companies, the dyestuffs distribution system seems to have been strongly affected by European companies.

The summer 1927 meeting also discussed marketing policy. It was decided, for instance, that in order to meet the various demands of Japanese users, company engineers, be they Japanese or German, were to participate in *Reisetätigkeit* (tours of production centres) across the country. This measure was linked to the reorganisation of laboratories which was implemented simultaneously. One objective of sending specialists on these tours was to investigate firsthand the competitive situation, but another, more important, objective was to help customers solve their problems by providing advice on dyeing and printing technologies. Through these activities, the specialists were expected to help promote the sales of new and expensive dyestuffs like naphthol, indigo paste, and indanthren.

In order to accommodate its marketing practice to swift changes in customer tastes, a peculiar trait of the Japanese market, the meeting decided that special *Musterkarten* (brochures of samples) specifically targeted to the market should be prepared. Unlike the existing, voluminous and comprehensive brochures, these compact brochures were designed to cater for the needs of selected strata of customers, could be produced at lower costs, and could prove more effective. It would also make sense to leave out some of the dyestuffs which were not being imported to begin with. The meeting also decided that samples be explained in Japanese, and that the brochures be produced in Japan.

This line of thinking on the marketing policy was based on the understanding, gained through experience, of the nature of the Japanese market. The minutes of the meeting stated that 'only through a ceaseless and thoroughgoing study of the Japanese market, the one which is exposed to violent changes in fashions and tastes, can we hope to fully open up the prospects for expensive dyestuffs with new uses to be accepted there'. It was also pointed out that

> considering the particular situation of Japan, it is urgently necessary to see to it that information on our new products, sample brochures and handling methods be disseminated among customers promptly, and that the introduction of new products, as long as they can attract interest in the Japanese market, be executed and monitored carefully.

Another improvement in marketing practice was to cut down inventories. Previously, inventories had tended to pile up, partly because of the frequent changes in the dyeing and printing methods brought about by sudden changes in trends, and partly because of the need to prepare for the possibility of a sudden imposition of import bans. The meeting concluded on the one hand that while it was definitely impossible to abide by the company's policy of maintaining inventories of six-month supplies the inventories should not be allowed to exceed an eight-month supply. At the same time, the meeting deliberated on the means of reducing inventories and found it essential that products of low-to-medium price range, which were being supplied in increasing volumes by Japanese manufacturers, should be sold in the Chinese or other markets nearby, or shipped back to Germany, or even disposed of. The meeting agreed, furthermore, that new additions to inventories should be prevented by all appropriate means, for instance by keeping closer watch on the market and accurately forecasting the demand in the coming season. Here again, how to cope with the rapidity of fashion changes was the most crucial issue.

The meeting also re-examined the marketability of each product in detail. For instance, there was deliberation on sulphuric dye, a black dye much in demand for its use in school uniforms. The attempt to introduce powdery indanthren black BB as a substitute for sulphur black dye had turned out to be unviable because of the proposed product's lack of price competitiveness. Indian carbon was a better choice. But the existing CL variety of Indian carbon left something to be desired in terms of its colour shades, and the SN variety was not pure enough. A mixture of Indian carbon composed primarily of the CL variety but with improved colour shades was desirable. This combination, argued the meeting, would yield a reasonably priced dyestuff. The headquarters of I.G. Farben should send a telegram to Doitsu Senryo informing it of this decision, and instructing it to develop this new Indian carbon. With this substitute for sulphur black, I.G. Farben would be able to expand its sales and regain much of the share it had lost in the sulphur black market.

On the whole, this re-examination was geared not so much to applying I.G. Farben's marketing policy directly to the Japanese market as to re-adapting it to the Japanese realities. Nevertheless, the revised policy was quite different from those being followed by its Japanese competitors. As such, the new policy must have exerted some influence on the Japanese industry, and have been copied by it gradually, although this remains to be confirmed by evidence. At any rate, there is no denying that I.G. Farben's approach was radically different from those of Japanese firms. To take Nihon Senryo, for instance, it was not until after Katsutaro Inabata became president in 1926, when the company began to divest itself of its earlier characteristic as a semi-government corporation and become a more genuinely private entity, that the company launched a campaign to advertise its products to plants and laboratories, resuming distribution of its samples and brochures.[34]

It was the German dyestuff industry that had introduced innovative marketing policies to the Japanese market in the pre-WWI days. Take, for instance, an observation of the policy for marketing indigo products adopted by H. Ahrnes & Co. Nachf., BASF's sales agent in Japan, as excerpted from a document compiled by an association of dealers in painting and dyeing materials in Osaka. This observation is revealing of how active and aggressive German dyestuff manufacturers were in their approach to the Japanese market. BASF's agent made

> very strenuous efforts to promote BASF products. Not only did it prepare a very detailed brochure and distribute it widely, it also sent specialists all over the country to visit indigo dye works, literally door to door, instruct the owners of the works on the use of the products, and explain details of their advantages and disadvantages in comparison with natural indigo.

It was also the German industry that introduced the practice of cash transactions, as attested to by the same document.

> Under the traditional practice of indigo transaction in Japan, which was based on consignment, customers used to settle their bills only after three to six months following delivery, by which time they would have mostly used up the dyestuffs. We found this practice undesirable, and so, when we began to deal in synthetic indigo, we decided to follow the advice of German trading houses and to stick fast to cash transactions from the beginning despite all the difficulties.[35]

The meeting of 1927 did not simply re-examine the company's marketing policy and distribution system in Japan, but also considered reducing its staff of local employees. According to the minutes of the meeting, the main objective was to discharge older Japanese employees who were 'not competent enough' but were 'becoming an increasingly heavier financial burden for Doitsu Senryo', and thereby to 'rejuvenate' the local staff as a whole. On the surface, this personnel rejuvenation scheme appears to have been dictated by the management's concern for cost curtailment.

Much the same concern seems to have underlain the discussion on the method for paying severance allowances to the employees to be discharged. At the time the payment of lump sum retirement allowances for white-collar workers was beginning to take root in Japan, and in fact Doitsu Senryo was advised by outsiders to pay the retirement allowances as a lump sum. The management of the company, however, was reluctant to follow this advice, and tried to negotiate payment by a long-term instalment or retirement pension plan.

When looked at from a different angle, the two episodes above may be interpreted as manifesting I.G. Farben's willingness to introduce the German practice, that is, the corporate pension system, to Japan. Unfortunately, little is known about how the personnel rejuvenation scheme was actually carried out and how the retirement allowances were actually paid. Even if these were known, their effects on the Japanese personnel management practice must have been negligible. Nevertheless, the fact that these possibilities were actually discussed at a time when the retirement allowances for white-collar workers were not firmly established in Japan deserves special attention.[36]

V

The First World War gave rise to a modern chemical industry in Japan. In the post-war period, the government adopted a policy of selective, or limited, protectionism to nurture this infant industry. Given the growing importance of the Japanese market, I.G. Farben first re-established its sales outlets in Japan and then undertook their reorganisation, which resulted in the establishment in 1924 of Doitsu Senryo as the sole agent of the German dyestuff industry in Japan. During the 1920s, I.G. Farben refused to agree to Japanese companies' requests for licensing arrangements, and its strategy toward Japan was basically formed around product export. In pursuing this strategy, I.G. Farben tried to conclude several bilateral agreements. The only agreement concluded during the decade was the Saito–Waibel Agreement on dyes, which enabled I.G. Farben to gain a foothold in the Japanese market in exchange for voluntary restrictions on exports.

In the 1930s, 'strong protectionism' emerged in Japan, making the market less accessible to I.G. Farben's exports. Meanwhile, the strengthening of the international cartel enabled the company to conclude several agreements with Japanese companies on market share and prices, either on its own or as a member of the international cartel. The agreement with Mitsui Mining on indigo and the Agreement on Domestic and Foreign Ammonium Sulphate were two examples. In the late 1930s, when the prospects for further expansion of its product export to Japan were foreclosed, I.G. Farben eventually changed its Japanese strategy to one oriented towards licensing. It made at least one licensing agreement in dyestuffs and five licensing agreements in synthetic ammonia and nitrogenous fertilisers.

Through its technology and management transfer during the 1920s and 1930s, I.G. Farben exerted significant influence on the production technology, marketing policy, and distribution system of the Japanese chemical industry. Much technology was transferred to Japan in the course of implementing agreements in the field of nitrogenous fertiliser, through the dispatch of I.G. Farben's engineers and foremen to Japan, and through I.G. Farben's procurement of plants and equipment from Germany. It is also worth noting that these employees of I.G. Farben played an important role in training Japanese junior engineers not only in engineering but also in supervisory skills. In marketing practices, too, I.G. Farben introduced several innovations, such as sales activities by travelling engineers and improvements in sample brochures, which sought to cope effectively with the rapidly changing fashion trends in Japan and with specific requirements of users. As for the distribution system, I.G. Farben nurtured large Japanese wholesale dealers as its special agents, and consequently reinforced the traditional wholesale distribution system.

NOTES

The author acknowledges with gratitude the assistance of Fumiaki Moriya for translation and Lynn Cornell for retyping.

1. This is a revised, English version of an earlier paper prepared in German and presented at a symposium on the History of Japanese–German Technological Transfer held in Tokyo in July 1990 by the German Institute of Japan Studies. The proceedings of the symposium was published as E. Pauer (ed.), *Technologietransfer Deutschland: Japan von 1850 bis zur Gegenwart* (München, 1992). A Japanese version of the paper, with some revisions, was included in the author's book, *I.G. Farben no Tainichi Senryaku: Senkanki Nichidoku Kigyokankeishi (I.G. Farben's Japan Strategy: A History of Japan–German Business Relations during the Interwar Period)* (Tokyo, 1992). The English version was first published in *Annales of the Institute of Social Science*, University of Tokyo, No.34, 1992.

2. For an overview of German technology and management transfer to Japan, see E. Pauer, 'German Companies in Japan in the Interwar Period: Attitudes and Performance', in T. Yuzawa and M. Udagawa (eds.), *Foreign Business in Japan before World War II: The International Conference on Business History*, 16 (Tokyo, 1990). As for Japanese technology and management transfer to Germany, see A. Kudo, 'Japanese Enterprises in Germany: Attempts at Technical-Industrial Cooperation prior to the Second World War', in H. Pohl (ed.), *Der Einfluss ausländischer Unternehmen auf die deutsche Wirtschaft vom Spätmittelalter bis zur Gegenwart* (Stuttgart, 1992).

3. Beziehungen der BASF zu Japan, BASF-Archiv; Bayer Japan Kabushiki Kaisha, *Nihon to tomoni 75-nen (75 Years Together with Japan)* (Tokyo, 1986), p.12. See also E. Verg *et al.*, *Meilensteine: 125 Jahre Bayer 1863–1988* (Köln, 1988), p.586.

4. Documents housed in Hoechst-Archiv.

5. R. Miwa, '1926-nen Kanzei Kaisei no Rekishiteki Ichi' (Historical Implications of the Revised Tariff of 1926), in T. Sakai *et al.* (eds.), *Nihon Shihonshugi: Tenkai to Ronri (Japanese Capitalism: Its Development and Logic)* (Tokyo, 1978), pp.176–8 and 181–2; M. Udagawa, Business Management and Foreign-Affiliated Companies in Japan before World War II', in Yuzawa and Udagawa (eds.), *Foreign Business in*

Japan, pp.2–3. See also T. Hara and A. Kudo, 'International Cartels in Business History', in A. Kudo and T. Hara (eds.), *International Cartels in Business History: The International Conference on Business History*, 18 (Tokyo, 1992).

6. Protokoll über die Besprechung der Firmen Ludwigshafen, Leverkusen und Hoechst üder das Japan-Geschäft am 11. Dezember 1923; Protokoll über die Sitzung der Japan-Kommission am 13. Mai 1924; etc., Hoechst-Archiv.
7. H. Morikawa, *Zaibatsu no Keieishiteki Kenkyu* (*Studies in the Business History of Zaibatsu*) (Tokyo, 1980), pp.168–75.
8. Bosch (BASF) an die Herren des Gemeinschaftsrates, 19 Juni 1925, etc., Hoechst-Archiv.
9. I.G. Farben an CMC, Geigy und Durand & Huguenin, 2 Mai 1929; Ciba an Geigy, 27 Mai 1929, Firmenarchiv Geigy VE/IGK 15, Ciba-Geigy-Archiv.
10. Auszug aus der Niederschrift über die Sitzung des Arbeitsausschusses, 23 Nov. 1926, Hoechst-Archiv, etc.
11. Doitsu Senryo an die Abteilung Export 1, 21 Juni 1926, etc., Hoechst-Archiv.
12. Dokkoku Dai-13 Go (Document No.13 on Germany), Gaimusho Gaiko Shiryokan Shozo Joyakusho 6 (File of Treaties, No.6, housed in the Archive of the Japanese Ministry of Foreign Affairs).
13. J. Hashimoto, 'Ryuan Dokusentai no Seiritsu' (The Emergence of a Monopoly in Ammonium Sulphate), *Keizaigaku Ronshu* (Journal of Economics, University of Tokyo), Vol.45 No.4 (1980), pp.59–63.
14. I.G. Farben Control Office of the Decartelization Branch, Economics Division, of the Office of Military Government for Germany (US), *Activities of I.G. Farbenindustrie AG in the Dyestuffs Industry*, 1946, p.15, Hoechst-Archiv.
15. I.G. Farben Control Office of the Decartelization Branch, Economics Division, of the Office of Military Government for Germany (US), *Activities of the Former 'Bayer' I.G. Farbenindustrie AG in the Pharmaceutical Industry*, 1946, pp.90 and 134, Hoechst-Archiv.
16. Udagawa, 'Business Management', pp.2–3.
17. I.G. Farben Control Office of the Decartelization Branch, *Activities of I.G. Farbenindustrie AG in the Dyestuffs Industry*, pp.86–7 and 90–91, Hoechst-Archiv.
18. K. Suzuki, 'Senji Keizai Toseika no Mitsui Bussan, III' (Mitsui Bussan under Wartime Economic Control, III), *Mitsui Bunko Ronso* (*Journal of the Mitsui Research Institute for Social Economic History*), No.20 (1986), pp.211–12 and 221.
19. I.G. Farben Control Office of the Decartelization Branch, *Activities of I.G. Farbenindustrie AG in the Dyestuffs Industry*, pp.88–9.
20. H. Ahrens & Co. Nachf., 29. März 1934 mit 2 Anlagen: Agreement, M. Kobayashi and H. Bosch, 23 March 1934, T74/11 CIA Internationale Konventionsverträge 1923–34; Exposé über die internationale Stickstoff-Verständigung, 25 März 1935, T74/10, BASF-Archiv.
21. Doitsu Senryo seems to have engaged in the following intelligence activities beginning in 1928: submission of summary reports of travels to Ludwigshafen every two months; submission to the headquarters of one copy each of complete reports, that were judged to be of possible interest to the headquarters; and compilation of biannual reports giving overviews of Doitsu Senryo's performance in dyestuff business and important developments in the dyestuff market (such as the trends in competition, changes in fashion, effects of business cycles, and the performance of local dyestuff manufacturers). In order to ensure that these activities be performed satisfactorily, a proposal was made to make the pre-existing system of information gathering, under which German employees had been responsible for collecting and handling information on specific items of expensive dyestuffs, also applicable to the low-priced items which had become subject to the Saito–Waibel Agreement. It was also decided that Doitsu Senryo should file with the headquarters a report each year on its judgement as to whether each product introduced during the year would be marketable or not. Moreover, for any dyestuff that it found unfit for the market, Doitsu Senryo was to specify why not, and to propose viable measures for making it acceptable in Japan.

182   THE MAKING OF GLOBAL ENTERPRISE

Waibel, Voigt, Bericht über die Besprechung über das Japan-Geschäft, 31 Aug., 1–3 Sept. 1927, Japan China 1920–36 Allgemein. Habers Reise nach Japan 1924 84, Hoechst-Archiv.

22. The report briefly surveyed the political, economic, social and cultural situations of each area or country of the region. Volume one was devoted to the discussion of the situation in Japan and Manchuria. M. Ilgner, 'Bericht über eine Reise nach Ostasien 1934/35', n.p., n.d. Even though the date of compilation of the report is unknown, it is certain that it was compiled by the middle of 1936, at the latest. '1934–1935 Dr Max Ilgner Ostasien 81' in 'IG AG Marktforschung T52/11', BASF-Archiv.

23. Die Chemiewirtschaft Japans, BASF-Archiv.

24. Rundschreiben Leverkusen, 2 Juli 1934, Hoechst-Archiv.

25. Besprechung über Auslandsprojekte, 9 Juni 1939, BASF-Archiv.

26. I.G. Farben Control Office of the Decartelization Branch, Economics Division, of the Office of Military Government for Germany (US), *Activities of I.G. Farbenindustrie AG in the Nitrogen Industry*, 1946, pp.116–17, Hoechst-Archiv. However, the name of Taki Seihisho is missing from this document. Moreover, what this document regards as a contract signed with Mitsubishi Shoji was actually technological licensing granted to Dainippon Tokkyo Hiryo.

27. A. Kudo, 'I.G. Farben's Japan Strategy: The Case of Synthetic Oil', in *Japanese Yearbook on Business History*, No.5 (1989).

28. Contract; Stickstoff-Besprechung, 15 Juni 1935; Vertrag, 17 Feb. 1936, BASF-Archiv.

29. H. Ahrens to Taki Seihisho (Taki Fertiliser Works), 11 Sept. 1937, housed in the Archive of Taki Kagaku (successor to Taki Seihisho); Akira Kudo, 'Japanese Technology Absorption of the Haber-Bosch Method: The Case of the Taki Fertiliser Works' in D.J. Jeremy (ed.), *The Transfer of International Technology* (Aldershot; 1992).

30. A recollection by Mr Genzo Ema, a young engineer at that time.

31. Waibel, Voigt, Bericht über die Besprechung über das Japan-Geschäft, 31 Aug. 1–3 Sept. 1927, Japan China 1920–36 Allgemein. Habers Reise nach Japan 1924 84, Hoechst-Archiv.

32. Bayer Japan Kabushiki Kaisha, *Nihon to tomoni 75-nen*, op. cit., pp.7–8 and 13; Harada, *Senryo (Dyestuffs)* (Tokyo, 1938), p.211.

33. J. Hirschmeier and T. Yui, *The Development of Japanese Business, 1600–1973* (1975), pp.179–80; Y. Suzuki, E. Abe and S. Yonekura, *Keieishi (Business History)* (Tokyo 1987), pp.196–7. Also note the following point made in K. Toba, 'Nihon no Marketing: Sono Dentosei to Kindaisei nitsuiteno Ichi Kosatsu' (Japanese Marketing: An Analysis of its Traditional Nature and Modern Nature), *Keieishigaku (Japan Business History Review)*, Vol.17 No.1 (1982), p.5: 'One significant difference with the American marketing system was that Japanese manufacturing firms were undertaking marketing activities only on a very limited scale by themselves, and their inaction in this regard was made up for by wholesalers, inclusive of trading firms, who were performing extremely active roles in the country's distribution system'.

34. Nihon Senryo Seizo Kabushiki Kaisha ('Nissen' for short; Nihon Dyestuff Manufacturing Co. Ltd), *Nissen 20-nenshi (20 Years History of Nissen)* (Osaka, 1936), p.65.

35. Osaka Enogu Senryo Dogyo Kumiai (Osaka Paints and Dyestuff Manufacturers' and Dealers' Association) (ed.), *Enogu Senryo Shoko Shi (History of Manufacturing and Transactions of Paints and Dyestuffs)* (Osaka, 1938), pp.1201–2.

36. The only legal provision existing at the time that addressed itself to the procedure of discharging workers was Clause 2, Article 27 of the Ordinance concerning the Enforcement of the Revised Factory Law of 1926, which stipulated that a worker to be discharged should be either given at least 14 days' notice, or be paid at least 14 days worth of wages. This provision is regarded as having paved the way for the establishment of a retirement allowance system in Japan. See M. Numagoshi, *Taishoku Tsumitatekin oyobi Taishoku Teate Ho Shakugi (Annotation of Laws concerning*

Retirement Compensation Reserve Funds and Retirement Allowances) (Tokyo, 1937), p.38. It was, however, not until the late 1930s that the payment of a retirement allowance for a discharged worker was explicitly written into law.

After Henry: Continuity and Change in Ford Motor Company

ALAN McKINLAY and KEN STARKEY
Glasgow University
Nottingham University

Since 1979 the Ford Motor Co. has fundamentally reoriented its global strategy, restructured its management processes and attempted radically to revise its labour relations. From 1945 to the late 1970s Ford's management structure and culture stressed continuity, caution and control. Since 1979, however, Ford has concluded that the organisational sources of its post-1945 profitability had become serious impediments to building durable competitive advantage. The process of change has differed significantly in Ford's European operations from that of the American parent company. In part, this reflects the corporation's contrasting competitive position in these markets: American vulnerability between 1979 and 1982 coincided with a surge in European competitive advantage and profitability. Equally, however, the contrasting experience of the post-1979 change process reflects the limits of Detroit's direct control over Ford of Europe. Within Ford of Europe we focus primarily on the experience of the British company, Ford UK. This essay considers the radical changes of the 1980s against the background of Ford's developing strategy, structure and management processes since 1945. The second section reviews Ford's employee involvement programmes in America and the European company's first serious appraisal of Japanese production methods. This is followed by an examination of changes in Ford's product development process; the functional area in which the European company has achieved the most significant break with Fordism.

I

The essential elements of Fordism as the definitive form of mass production – direct control of the labour process and elaborate managerial hierarchies policed by financial specialists – were established at different moments in the development of the Ford Motor Co. If the de-skilling logic of scientific management was embedded in the pre-1914 assembly lines of the Model T, then Fordism's characteristic managerial organisation was a post-1945 phenomenon.[1] General Motors' dominance of the

American auto market in the 1930s was paralleled by Ford's failure to develop a multidivisional structure, the classic institutional structure of modern big business.[2] In 1945 Henry Ford's grandson Henry II became Chairman of a company on the verge of collapse, both financially and in terms of domestic market share. Henry Ford II immediately remodelled the company on Sloan's General Motors.[3] The philosophical touchstone of Ford's reorganisation was Peter Drucker's classic 1946 account of General Motors, *Concept of the Corporation*.[4] For Drucker, Alfred Sloan had perfected the multidivisional structure to such an extent that it constituted 'a basic and universally valid concept of social order'.[5] The Sloan structure addressed 'the fundamental problem' of the mass production enterprise – 'the managing of managers'.[6] Indeed, so central was the General Motors model that it assumed an iconic significance for Henry Ford II who kept a General Motors organisational chart on his office wall for over 40 years.[7]

But if General Motors' organisational chart was the regulative ideal of Ford's post-war management then finance specialists rapidly emerged as the midwives of Fordism. Under Robert McNamara, finance became the cornerstone of corporate power in Ford, overwhelming manufacturing and product development.[8] Every decision had to be justified in financial terms, an unbending principle which generated constant tension between finance and operational functions. The tight financial monitoring of all management decisions was singled out with pride by the company's own publication celebrating the first decade of Ford of Europe.[9]

> One of the many stringent tests which all Ford cars have to pass is to sustain a crash at 30mph into a concrete barrier with less than five inches of steering column penetration. This means that the steering column must not move more than five inches towards a driver. In management terms in Ford, the nearest thing to that concrete barrier is probably the finance staff – and many projects are fated to crumple entirely on impact.

As this revealing metaphor suggests, finance became both an ubiquitous and unyielding obstacle for every initiative in Ford. Reflecting on his personal experience over the last two decades a senior product planner explained:

> Finance is all about total attention to detail and total overkill. They're empowered to ask dumb questions and to inhibit things. I don't think it's a lack of confidence in the quality of management, just an obsession with control.

The central management skills in this regime were enforcing procedures and quantifying social relationships wherever possible. As the logic of this quantitative discourse was elaborated over three decades it enveloped ever more routine management tasks. Ford pushed rational processes to their irrational conclusion: an 'iron cage' of bureaucracy which systematically squeezed out discomforting information and radical initiatives. The accumulating dysfunctionalities of a planning process designed to police managerial decision-making and individual performance inhibited innovation. In 1988 one European product planner explained that during the 1970s, even senior Ford managers had very little discretion but were reduced to being 'administrators of pseudo-information flows', manipulating internal reporting systems rather than confronting external competitive realities.

Ford's reputation for analytical rigour was matched only by the intensely political nature of the organisation. The boardroom infighting of the Ford family was symptomatic of the organisation as a whole.[10] As we have argued elsewhere, the formal planning process became the arena for personal and functional struggles of Byzantine complexity, spanning entire careers and waged with unrelenting ferocity.[11] Political acumen was an essential prerequisite for the aspiring Ford manager. A finance specialist who worked in both Ford of Europe and the American parent company during the 1970s explained:

> One group of Directors or Vice Presidents wouldn't attend a meeting where certain individuals were present. Those kind of feudal politics were a fact of life in Ford. Self-preservation meant that you had to develop as wide a knowledge of the personal and functional animosities as any technical skill. To succeed – to survive – you had to develop antennae very quickly indeed.

Ford's functional 'chimney' structure and the politicised nature of corporate culture combined to limit lateral information flows and inter-disciplinary decision-making. The result of Ford's intense specialisation of managerial knowledge was a collective trained incompetence: an inherently reactive organisation which systematically eliminated its capacity for radical innovation in product or process.[12]

II

Before 1945, Ford's extensive overseas operations were treated as a portfolio of independent businesses by Detroit.[13] After 1945 the loose control Ford US exercised over its foreign subsidiaries stood in stark contrast to the tightly controlled regime being constructed by

McNamara in Detroit. Henry Ford II examined the corporation's overseas holdings within two years of assuming the chairmanship. Over the
following decade a series of divestments saw Ford withdraw from
France and Spain while it extended its British and German manufacturing operations.[14] Between 1949 and 1961 Ford US reacquired ownership
of all its European interests, including the purchase of the share capital
of Ford of Britain. The legal foundations of an integrated European
company had been laid.

Ford and IBM pioneered the development of the multinational as a
planned global organisation in which national subsidiaries were allocated specific roles within the corporation's regional and world-wide
strategies. The formation of Ford of Europe in 1967 was the first step in
the creation of an integrated network of complementary plants stretch-
ing across the continent.[15] In contrast, General Motors relied on co-
operation between its German and British subsidiary companies, Opel
and Vauxhall, which pursued independent strategic agendas.[16] But in
1967 Ford of Europe was itself a loose confederation of national manufacturing companies in Britain and Germany and sales companies
throughout the continent. Over the next decade Ford of Europe became
an increasingly integrated regional division of the global corporation:
the continent rather than the nation state became the geographic unit of
strategic management and production. In theory, Ford of Europe remains simply an organisation co-ordinating the activities of independent
national companies, In practice, however, Ford of Europe rather than
the national companies had become the locus of all strategic decision-
making and financial planning by the early 1970s. Increasingly, through
the 1970s, despite their full range of executives and directors, national
companies such as Ford UK and Ford Werke have existed primarily to
satisfy particular legal requirements and act as the public face of Ford of
Europe. All functional managements report directly to the appropriate
Ford of Europe vice-president regardless of their national location. The
essence of Ford of Europe's control system has remained constant: the
separation of activities into cost and revenue centres. Ford's management information system consolidates cost, revenue and profit only at
the European level. 'Ford UK', one European executive explained, 'is a
legal fiction'.

The confused, fragmented structure of Ford's European businesses
before 1967 was most clearly expressed by the lack of integration
between the design and production facilities in the British and German
national companies. Not only was product planning and development
carried out independently in Ford's two main European companies it
was a highly informal process compared to the rigorous planning being

perfected in Detroit.[17] The economic pressure for integration steadily increased after the foundation of the European Community in 1957. The Treaty of Rome signalled the end of tariff barriers which had sealed the continent's core automotive markets, isolating the British market which remained sheltered behind a 28 per cent tariff wall. Britain's exclusion from the Common Market until 1973 undoubtedly disadvantaged Ford UK compared to Ford Werke in investment terms. British tariffs penalised intra-company trading while the German company became the focus of investment designed to satisfy growing demand in the Common Market as a whole.[18] Between 1960 and 1968, Ford Werke's net fixed assets increased by 405 per cent, compared to Ford UK's 147 per cent.[19] By 1973 Ford Werke had emerged as the lead national company in Ford of Europe in design and production while Ford UK's influence rested on its profitable position in the British market.[20]

From its foundation, the executive management of Ford of Europe has been based on long-serving European operational managers and short-stay Detroit postings. Unlike GM whose overseas operations were a corporate backwater with little contact with Detroit headquarters until the early 1980s, in Ford international service was a vital rite of passage in a successful corporate career from the mid-1950s. All the principal players in Ford America's turnaround in the 1980s – Philip Caldwell, Don Petersen and Harold 'Red' Poling – had served in, or had corporate responsibility for, Ford of Europe. An international posting was the one way to gain executive experience while remaining insulated from the vicious politicking which racked Ford US during the reign of Henry Ford II. The one functional area in Ford of Europe in which Americans have rarely served is manufacturing, which was dominated by a powerful British manager – Bill Hayden – from 1973 to 1990. Hayden was a constant feature in the extremely fluid executive team of Ford of Europe. Hayden was a member of the first generation of Ford of Europe managers which was acutely aware that their trans-national responsibilities took priority over their loyalty to any national company. Hayden exemplified all the strengths and weaknesses of traditional Fordism: analytical, ruthless and a committed company man, Hayden was the archetypal 'Dagenham Yank'. Despite the nominal power of American expatriates in Ford of Europe, the regional company's profitability and long superiority over GM in Europe effectively dissuaded these 'executive tourists' from straying from their passive stewardship role during their two or three year international sojourns. From 1967, manufacturing management were critical players in the pursuit of an integrated European production system to maximise scale economies.[21]

Hayden's permanence and personal commitment to manufacturing on a European rather than a national scale gave him enormous influence in Detroit.[22] Ironically, Hayden's reputation as a bluff traditional Ford manager was to make him a critical, if always ambivalent, figure in the diffusion of the radical changes which have swept through the American and European companies since 1979.

From its inception Ford of Europe has been by far the largest of the corporation's four regional companies: Europe, Asia Pacific, Latin America, and the Middle-East and Africa. The relationship between Detroit and the regional companies has been principally financial rather than on a strict command and control basis.[23] Detroit prefers to set financial and market targets for the European company rather than detailed operational parameters. Through the 1980s Ford of Europe has been expected to generate 25 per cent of corporate earnings, achieve a 12 per cent market share in Europe as a whole and compete in every major market segment. By 1973 Ford had established a series of European management committees to monitor every important activity: these remain in place today. The cornerstone of this committee structure is the Executive Committee which is convened by the Chairman of Ford of Europe and considers strategic, financial, technical and political issues. Beneath this lead committee a series of operating policy committees, chaired by European functional vice-presidents, monitor budget performance, product planning, and sales and pricing strategy. The essential parameters of business policy are established, therefore, by Ford of Europe, not its constituent national companies. Within this committee structure, finance staff exercise a decisive influence, a hegemony which can be challenged only in exceptional circumstances and overruled only by a Chairman backed by the full weight of Detroit.

Contemporary business planning in Ford of Europe is a highly formalised budgeting, financial and analytical process. The cornerstone of the Ford planning process is a series of interlocking financial plans for each national company for periods of between one and five years. The development of each strategic plan is an almost continuous process with final approval of one budget in November of each year followed in January by the first stage of the next cycle. Overall responsibility for co-ordinating the planning process lies with the finance function which also controls sales and manufacturing projections. It is finance, not manufacturing, which reacts to changing market circumstances and also adjusts production schedules to currency fluctuations. Beneath this strategic role, finance exercises a pervasive influence over all managerial decisions which must quantify their expected return and probable impact on budget plans. Although the highly interdependent nature of car

production makes it impractical for managers to assume profit responsibility, individual managerial performance is rigorously scrutinised. All
profit variables are categorised into factors which can and cannot be
controlled by management and allocated to particular managers: 'Every
Ford manager's ego has been bruised by a run-in with Finance'.[24]

Ford played a vital role in pushing forward the pace of integration and
rationalisation in the European car industry. In the decade after 1965
the rate of intra-company trade in cars expanded four times faster than
car production.[25] Similarly, intra-firm trading across Europe accelerated
during the 1970s as Ford created an international production system.
Between 1974 and 1984 intrafirm imports to Ford UK rose from 1.4 per
cent to 24.1 per cent by value, before stabilising at over 40 per cent in
the mid-1980s.[26] The gradual, if always problematic, development of a
common product range across Europe – Capri, Fiesta and Escort –
consolidated the predominance of Ford of Europe over national companies. Within a decade of its formation, Ford of Europe's integrated
command structure had become a formidable competitive asset. By
1976 internal Ford estimates were that its pursuit of scale economies
through plant specialisation was reaping a 10–15 per cent efficiency
advantage above the unintegrated General Motors in Europe. Before
1980 Ford was content to use its German company as the efficiency
benchmark for the European car industry. During the last decade Ford
strategists have used Japanese car makers as *global* paragons in productive efficiency and product quality.

III

For over 50 years 'Fordism' has been the regulative ideal of Western
management. 'Fordism' refers to an organisational form in which elaborate management hierarchies systematically strip away worker autonomy and knowledge in highly integrated divisions of labour. Both
labour and machinery in the Fordist factory perform finely defined
tasks. Fordism's relentless search for maximum productivity through de-
skilling is premised on the existence of stable and predictable mass
markets for standardised commodities. The conservative symbiosis between market and production at the heart of Fordism has been destabi-
lised by the fragmentation of demand and the arrival of competitors
setting radically new performance standards in product and process.
Faced with this new industrial competition Ford has been attempting to
manage the transition from mass production to 'mass customisation'. In
mass customisation strategies the capacity to produce a range of different products at the lowest possible aggregate cost is more important

than reducing the cost of any single product to the technically attainable minimum. For Ford's corporate management, the shift to a work regime characterised by increasingly flexible technologies and adaptable work-forces demands a qualitatively new role for management: from planning and controlling to enabling and mobilising. For Ford this shift in pro-duction organisation defined the strategic importance of human re-source management (HRM): to overcome the endemic low trust labour relations of Fordism and cultivate the consensual culture required by mass customisation.[27]

In their seminal study of the global auto industry, Womack, Jones and Roos (1990) single out Ford US as a leading Western practitioner of the 'lean production' system pioneered by Japanese companies.[28] The dif-fusion of 'lean production' from Ford US to the European company has, they suggest, remained incomplete. This section explores the contrast-ing experience of the American and European companies. Lean pro-duction is a highly integrated manufacturing process spanning not just all levels of the corporation but also its supplier network in pursuit of rapid response to changing consumer demand. The efficiency advantage of lean production over mass production is paralleled by equally dra-matic improvements in product innovation and quality. It is this novel combination of *simultaneous* gains in efficiency, innovation and quality which has exposed the weakness of Western manufacturers' reliance on strategies which define scale economies and product variability, cost and differentiation, as irreconcilable alternatives.

The key to Ford US' corporate renewal was the cathartic experience of a crisis which threatened the company's very existence. Between 1980 and 1982, Ford US experienced a confluence of overlapping crises – financial, imploding market share, and an archaic product range – which combined to undermine the validity of Ford's previously unquestioned planning systems. Even the worst-case scenarios built into Ford's finan-cial forecasts understated the collapse of the company's cash position.[29] This was a creative crisis in a double sense. First, these crises could not be resolved sequentially, slowly nor solely by added financial stringency and an intensification of Ford's traditional control systems.[30] Second, 1980–82 saw a crisis of Ford's corporate imagination, an executive team stripped of the historical certainties of Fordist management, of in-cremental strategic changes accompanied by marginal adjustments to organisational structure. Indeed, one participant in these fraught board-room discussions described the 'desperate panic' which threatened to immobilise the Detroit board during the initial phase of the crisis. For Ford's Detroit management, survival in the emerging global market-place in which the rules of competition were being radically rewritten entailed challenging the assumption that the prime management imperative was to maximise control over the workforce. Importantly, however, during the financial crisis and the first stages of strategic change there was no concerted effort by Detroit management to formulate a vision of a reconstituted, revitalised Ford Motor Co. Rather, as Richard Pascale (1990) demonstrates, the starting point for change at all levels in Ford US was essentially negative: a rejection of the strategy, structure and management processes which had been refined since 1945. In effect, the Detroit board attempted to replicate its experience of creative crisis in every Ford plant in America. During this phase of corporate renewal, the central task of Detroit executives was to mobilise change, maintain momentum and direction, rather than to articulate what the defining features of the emerging corporation should be. Donald Petersen, then President of Ford US, was a pivotal figure in this process, championing the new emphasis on employee involvement and product design in Ford's American plants.[31]

Ford US was largely untouched by the quality of working life (QWL) programmes developed by General Motors in the early 1970s.[32] The deep recession which hit the American auto industry in 1979 coincided with the emergence of union and corporate executives within Ford committed to the rapid expansion of co-operative management–union programmes. During the 1970s, QWL initiatives were restricted to non-contractual issues, including work organisation and workloads. From 1979, however, the distance between co-operative programmes and collective bargaining has slowly been reduced as efficiency and quality have become issues for informal negotiations. A watershed in this process was the launch of employee involvement (EI) in 1979 as a joint initiative between Ford US and the United Auto Workers (UAW) with agreed goals of improving work experience, increasing efficiency and quality and reducing absenteeism.[33] UAW endorsement of EI legitimised the programme which rapidly blossomed into thousands of small-scale projects. As EI expanded it highlighted the excesses of Ford's control system and, in turn, stimulated demands from line management for similar involvement in joint programmes. The outcome – participative management (PM) – consolidated what Pascale (1990) describes as 'a set of tributary actions . . . flow(ing) into a river of change'. Pascale's imagery captures the uncontrolled, organic nature of the EI process which contrasts sharply with the mechanical, structural orientation of classical Fordist management.[34]

Ford's first attempt to reflect on the experience of change was embodied in the 1984 'Statement of Mission, Values, and Guiding Principles' (MVGP). People, products and profits are described as its basic values –

a linguistic ordering conveying a significant change in strategic priorities. MVGP forms a code of conduct that encapsulates policy towards employees, customers, dealers and suppliers. These guiding principles include commitment to the following: quality in all aspects of the business, customers, continuous improvement, EI and teamwork at all levels, specified levels of competitiveness and return on assets. MVGP combines Ford's traditional emphasis on low cost with the new stress on product differentiation through quality and design.

Between 1979 and 1982, the pressure on Ford of Europe to emulate the experience of its American parent was minimised by the vital contribution of European profit and revenue flows to sustaining corporate liquidity. Beyond fiscal pragmatism, however, lay deeper organisational differences between the American and European organisations. No European executive played a transformational role comparable to Donald Petersen in Ford US. Above all, Ford of Europe experienced no creative crisis similar to Ford US. Embedded assumptions about the nature of competition, the prioritisation of efficiency over innovation remained largely unquestioned. In Europe the main symbol of changed corporate thinking was the 'After Japan' (AJ) campaign which began in late 1979. AJ began as an innocuous study trip by Bill Hayden, then Vice-President of Manufacturing in Europe. Before Hayden's visit Japanese success in the West was largely attributed to a pricing advantage sustained by government support rather than manufacturing superiority. Ford of Europe's efficiency comparators were other European manufacturers and Ford's own national companies. Ford Werke was consistently the most efficient manufacturer in Europe, while Ford UK was the most efficient in its domestic market. Hayden, mesmerised by Japanese efficiency, concluded that to focus on narrowing the productivity gap between Ford's UK and German operations was now far too restrictive, but if AJ represented a major reorientation in terms of Ford of Europe's competitive benchmarking then it also contained contradictory elements. Unlike their American counterparts, Ford of Europe executives returned from study trips impressed not so much by the social relations of lean production but by the discipline and sheer intensity of labour in Japanese factories.[35]

The major HRM element of AJ was the attempt to introduce quality circles in 1980–81, a period in which Ford UK also attempted unsuccessfully to impose a draconian new disciplinary code on the shopfloor.[36] The mixed messages from Ford UK betrayed a deep uncertainty about the nature of changing labour relations. Unlike the legitimising concordat struck between the corporation and the UAW in America, Ford UK's management made no effort to win the support of union executives in forming quality circles – nor did they see the need to. As one bemused executive put it: 'Quality is like Motherhood, how could *anyone* be against it?'[37] Not surprisingly, given decades of adversarial industrial relations, what Ford UK management regarded as a seminal trust-building exercise was received with deep suspicion by the unions who regarded quality circles as a covert manoeuvre to undermine established bargaining procedures. Initially regarded as the first step in the rapid 'Japanisation' of production organisation, Ford UK was forced to reconsider its strategy and timetable for implementing change. Inside Ford of Europe's manufacturing function, human resource management (HRM) advisers drew on the American experience and successfully argued that radical change could not be introduced at the shop-floor level without first securing an enabling agreement from national union leaders.

Ford UK's 'Japanisation' initiatives were rejected by the British manufacturing unions and only temporarily ratified by the salaried unions. Despite Ford UK's limited success in introducing HRM initiatives on to the shop-floor, significant reforms were achieved though conventional collective bargaining. In particular, critical aspects of Ford's HRM agenda were endorsed by the manual unions, such as the elimination of archaic demarcation lines, the creation of broader job roles and the acquisition of new skills in search of a more versatile and flexible workforce. Manufacturing executives conceptualise this process as a challenge to the corporation's embedded assumptions about work organisation. In particular, Ford managers regard the negotiated reduction of 500 production job titles to 50 as a frontal assault on the de-skilling logic of Fordism. Production operators' roles were expanded so that tasks vary according to operational requirements while line workers accepted responsibility for indirect work such as minor maintenance. Such initiatives were intended to enhance manpower flexibility, increase the intensity of capital usage, and ensure greater continuity of production. Ford UK's 1985 contract negotiations included the novel departure of increasing wage rates for the acquisition of supplementary skills rather than greater output.[38] Workforce resistance to the imposition of new work practices was central to the national Ford strike of 1988, the first for a decade. The resulting settlement tempered the 1985 enabling agreement ratified by national union officials by adding that reforms of work practices also had to be endorsed through local negotiations.[39] Both the 1985 and 1988 Agreements contain significant elements of change and continuity in Ford's approach to industrial relations. If the 1980s marked a pause in the long-term de-skilling of work, then Ford management continued to insist on the centrality of managerial prerogative in reshaping work organisation.

Two processes formed the backdrop to the 1985 Agreement. The first was the closure of the Dagenham foundry, which ended fully integrated production in Ford UK's heartland. The second was heavy investment in flexible robotisation and the beginnings of the gradual transition from separate lines for each model to a one-line system for mixed model production between 1979 and 1981.[40] The first stage of this massive investment programme coincided with the collapse of the American company's finances, a period in which British profits provided a vital fiscal breathing space for the embattled corporation. In this context, Ford's corporate strategists concluded that it was imperative that the British company avoid any damaging dispute which could jeopardise revenue flows during a period of world-wide financial vulnerability. At this vital moment, Ford's ambiguous interpretation of Japanese lean production became vitally important: Ford UK manufacturing executives unilaterally introduced a draconian new disciplinary code in November 1980 which threatened to destabilise industrial relations.[41] The resulting running battles with the Halewood workforce were vital in convincing hard-line Ford UK manufacturing executives of the futility of trying to bludgeon through change.[42] The tension between Ford's global agenda and British manufacturing management's explosive attempt to strengthen direct control on the shop-floor is indicative of the relatively weak operational chain of command between Detroit and the European company.

The initial phase of robotisation at Dagenham revealed much about Ford UK's schizophrenic policies toward labour relations. In 1981–82 Ford introduced specimen robots to prepare for the transition from Cortina to Sierra production. But although Ford was careful to familiarise the Dagenham workforce with the new technology there were no substantive negotiations with shop stewards about restructuring work organisation. By imposing job design unilaterally, management failed to capitalise on the considerable goodwill the workforce displayed towards the new technology. The construction of the new robotised production facility was completed during the summer shutdown. On their return, the workers discovered that their rest areas – personalised by calendars, kettles and posters – had been demolished and their possessions discarded.[43] Such insensitivity undermined the residual benefits from the one-year familiarisation process. This incident highlights the yawning gulf separating the strategic aspirations of the Detroit and European boardrooms from the highly autocratic practices of plant-level ment. As one Dagenham production manager put it: 'when you've got them by the balls, the head and heart soon follow'.

If AJ had a limited impact on work organisation then it constituted a watershed in Ford's approach to management and, equally important, was perceived by senior managers as a critical symbolic moment in the corporation's development. Since 1945 Ford managed its managers in the same way as it managed the shop-floor: specialised, hierarchical and tightly controlled. The autocracy of the assembly line was simply the cutting edge of a pervasive corporate culture. Ford's famous 'Blue Book' defined the tasks and authority of every employee in the factory, manual *and* managerial. The precise allocation of managerial roles and responsibilities was designed to maximise the visibility of individual managers, to expose their decisions and actions to intense surveillance from above.

In Ford US, PM was an attempt by middle managers to win some leverage in the change process. Moreover, this bottom-up initiative was championed by the executive management of Ford US. PM broadened managerial spans of control. Again, Ford of Europe's experience of change differed significantly from that of the American company. In Europe, AJ was the trigger for major changes in the company's management structure and culture. Ford of Europe's initial appraisal of Japanese manufacturing was quickly followed by studies of the managerial infrastructure of the Japanese corporation, but if the common denominator was the concern with cost and efficiency then the second wave of Ford studies revealed profound differences in the Japanese and Western approaches to managing managers. Ford's finance staff concluded that in Japanese corporations financial control was not the prerogative of a specialist function but was shared throughout the organisation. The target set by these 1980 comparisons was a 30 per cent reduction in finance staff within three years.[44] This target was achieved in 1986 by stripping out innumerable layers of procedural controls. Indeed, our respondents identified the diminished power of finance as the vital enabling factor in reshaping corporate culture. Implicitly, a senior finance functionary acknowledged their changed role within Ford's decision-making process:

> We used to analyse everything to death. We'd bludgeon every investment decision until it stopped moving. It's more judgemental now – we don't check obviously correct proposals a thousand times for minor defects. The old system used to focus on the defects at the expense of the project as a whole; that's reversed now.

Importantly, cultural change was as much a consequence of the rationalisation of administrative structure as of corporate initiatives such as PM. The AJ rationalisation process was driven by operational management specifying which controls were superfluous to *their* needs. This bottom-up approach was a radical departure from Ford's traditional pattern of top-down cost-cutting. For line management, reduced administrative controls were a potent symbol of their increased personal responsibility *and* of finance's diminished power-base within the company. In contrast to the American experience, in Ford of Europe PM was a top-down initiative designed to facilitate bottom-up corporate restructuring. Essentially, cultural change and the beginnings of project rather than functional management were unintended consequences of administrative rationalisation rather than its prime objective.

The highly visible role of senior executives was vital to the success of the change process in Ford US. Throughout the 1980s the Ford US executive team balanced traditional and transformational leadership styles.[45] Donald Petersen's evangelical role in promoting EI/PM was complemented by Phil Caldwell and Harold Poling who exemplified Ford's traditional reliance on strict financial control. In Ford of Europe, however, there was no similar creative tension in the executive team. There was no equivalent of Donald Petersen in the European company. Rather, operational efficiency was championed by the powerful figure of Bill Hayden until his departure for Jaguar in 1991. An adviser intimately involved in the relationship between Ford US and Europe observed that throughout the 1980s Detroit made no sustained effort to force EI/PM to the top of the European agenda. 'The pressure was to keep producing profit and keep doing the job you're doing. Well, what kind of pressure was that? That was a cost-profit pressure.'

The 'executive tourists' seconded from Ford US lacked the political muscle in Europe to displace the traditional cost-based strategy. From 1984, deteriorating business performance strengthened the hand of European advocates of further rationalisation at the expense of the American HRM agenda. Poor financial performance, following hard on the heels of indifferent new product launches, led to highly public disagreements between board members. Management conferences intended to strengthen PM became public forums for confrontations between members of the European executive team. 'They were', as one stunned audience member put it, 'kicking the shit out of each other'. Hayden's role as manufacturing's advocate of traditional managerial prerogative was a conservative counterweight to the EI/PM change initiatives. A Dagenham production manager recalled that he was reassured by Hayden's interpretation of PM:

So Hayden said, 'Now, you've all heard this EI stuff. But at the end of the day I'm paid to run this bloody place and I'll listen to all you've got to say if there's time, if there isn't I won't listen. I make the decisions that I think are right and you'll just have to learn to live with that: that's your contribution to EI'.

Nevertheless, during the second half of the 1980s Ford UK made significant changes to its management structure, processes and culture. The leading area in this respect was product development, and it is to this that we now turn our attention.

IV

Compressing product development lead times and continually improving product performance and styling have emerged as vital competitive factors in volatile demature markets. Perhaps the most profound changes in Ford have been in product development. Before the 1980s Ford's product design and engineering process epitomised

> old-fashioned Ford thinking: if you specialise you will get people who are so expert that you will design the best of everything individually. Therefore, when you put it all together you will have the best product.

This approach assumed that product development was amenable to rigidly defined systems – 'doing things by the book'. The message of AJ was that the system actually squeezed out essential features of leading edge product design: 'The manual was an incredible piece of work, but a manual doesn't build cars'. Over-specialisation within product development was exacerbated by the need to co-operate with the manufacturing function. Historically, the relationship between these two functions was 'very aggressive and confrontational'. The nature of inter-functional relationships was most apparent at 'hand-over' points in the sequential process from product development to manufacturing. Manufacturing and product development managers ruefully recounted that immense process problems were routinely caused by inadequate communication with product designers.

> The Mark III Cortina had at the top of the seat pillar . . . the biggest patch of solder there had ever been on a Ford car since the V8 pilot. It meant that we had part-solders and lead-diskers in their dozens and the lead-diskers had to wear air-fed masks, hoods, total body protection from the lead. The manufacturing problems that resulted from that – apart from the technical prob-

lems – . . . were such that manufacturing went back to product engineering and said, 'When you replace this car you either replace it with a car that has a zero solder or only a very small one'. And that's the first time we were ever obliged to engineer a vehicle to take account of manufacturing problems.

This fractious relationship was policed by Ford's powerful financial specialists. Overall control of the sequential design process lay with cost analysis which specified detailed trade-offs between cost and quality for every component. The decisive role of the 'high priests' of cost control in product development was most graphically demonstrated in the design process for the Fiesta, Ford's first small car. Rival products were stripped and each component priced to the last quarter of a cent to set targets for Ford designers. The 'high priests', according to Seidler's (1976) detailed account of the Fiesta design process,

> knew all the rules by heart and all the . . . quality standards, the rigorous criteria for durability for weight and cost. . . . These . . . were the great enemies, the two culprits on which they had to pass judgement: excessive weight and abnormal cost. And these were the men who finally told the experimental engineers: 'This is what we think about the parts that make up the cars of the competition, their weight and their cost of production. You be the referees, you find better ways'.[46]

Ford's reputation for developing 'robust' designs to extend the product life cycle was both a reflection of stable market-places and the inherent conservatism of a product development system which systematically suppressed product innovation.[47] The financial logic of the Fiesta design process contrasts sharply with that developed during the 1980s. From the American Taurus project in 1982 Ford designers have focused on benchmarking against the best designed and engineered rival products rather than concentrating solely on cost.[48]

Ford's post-AJ European product strategy has been based on more precise definitions of market segments, a greater range of speciality model derivatives and an acceleration of the model replacement cycle. Between 1970 and 1977 Ford of Europe offered two new models targeted at three market segments compared to eight new models for four market segments in the period 1978–86.[49] Despite the Fiesta's success in increasing Ford's southern Europe market penetration, the tight margins of the small car segment and the design leadership of the German car firms in high value-added products was jeopardising Ford of Europe's target of contributing 25 per cent of total corporate earnings.

The launch of the Sierra in 1983 marked Ford's drive for design leadership. The Sierra project was championed by Bob Lutz, then President of Ford of Europe. Unlike his predecessors Lutz was a 'product freak . . . almost indifferent to costs and profits in his search for innovation'. For Lutz, the Sierra marked Ford's transition from mass production of utility vehicles to mass customisation:

> the Japanese have taken over the no-nonsense, no-frills, high-value for money, reliable transportation part of the market. My goal is to be a mass producer of the type of cars BMW and Mercedes have a reputation for making. We are moving up in technology and credibility so we get the same price elasticity as they have.[50]

Reaction to the Sierra was double-edged: it revolutionised the agenda in mainstream car design, but proved vulnerable in the market-place.[51] The Sierra marked a sharp break from Ford's traditional strategy of providing high utility but low functionality products. The Sierra development process also broke with the strictly controlled Fordist models of design and engineering. Matrix management was used to span the specialised functions and modular engineering allocated responsibility for clusters of components to teams of eight to ten engineers rather than individual specialists. In effect, the Sierra development process represented Ford's traditional product development process stretched to its limits, an experience important as much for the systemic failings it revealed as the product it delivered.

Western companies have turned to Japan to learn about best practice in product development. Clark and Fujimoto's 1991 analysis of product development in the global auto industry highlights two major sources of Japanese competitive advantage: speed and flexibility.[52] In the wake of the Sierra's troubled launch and AJ, Ford's European product development function initiated its own examination of its management practices – the Insight project. Essentially, the 'Insight' team compared product development in Ford to Mazda, in which Ford holds a 25 per cent ownership stake.

The Insight team delivered a powerful indictment of Ford's product development process:

> increased efficiency can only be achieved by better utilisation of available talent through improved teamwork. In our strongly functional organization these improvements require the elimination of artificial barriers to communication and in their place must come a stronger focus on, and identification with, the product and the 'customer'. To facilitate these changes some organization restruc-

turing is needed in order to build cross-functional, multi-discipline teams dedicated to product programs. The organizational change is a means to an end, not an end in itself. Improved efficiencies will result from more delegation, development of broader skills and the substitution of a 'not invented here' attitude by supportive team-goal oriented behaviour.

Compared to Mazda, the Insight team concluded that Ford of Europe was bedevilled by poor communications and inefficiency. Above all, Ford's failings were ascribed to an unquestioning adherence to vertical reporting procedures. Ford's strict formal control system prohibited lateral information flows both within product development and with manufacturing engineers. 'Procedure', Insight concluded, 'sometimes takes precedence over problem solving.' Mazda's fluid project-based organisation fostered swift, flexible responses. In contrast to Mazda's 'environment of harmony' Ford was characterised by an 'environment of competition'.

> There is insufficient communication and cooperation between engineering areas and between Manufacturing and Product Development. Sometimes we get the feeling that different areas work for different companies.

Inter-functional rivalry dissipated time and effort as information filtered up – and decisions down – the Ford hierarchy. Mazda was three times as efficient as Ford in terms of the hours required to engineer a Sierra equivalent vehicle. The majority of Mazda managers were in flexible project-based teams. Indeed, this was the most disconcerting aspect of Mazda's organisation for the Ford investigators. Managers accustomed to 'thinking structurally' were surprised to find their Japanese counterparts working in transient teams rather than fixed positions: 'there was no embarassment about being a minister without portfolio'.

At first sight the most striking feature of the changing nature of Ford's product development process is the modesty of its ambition. The Insight project highlighted Japanese best practice and the inadequacies of Ford's product development process, but it offered no blueprint for bridging the chasm. Since 1985 Ford has inserted cross-functional teams within the product development process as a transitional step towards simultaneous engineering. The traditional linear approach to product development first designs the car and *then* the manufacturing process. Simultaneous engineering collapses these distinct activities into a single process in which project teams synchronise product *and* process design.

The Japanese-inspired experiments of the 1980s were Ford's attempt to negotiate the transition from sequential to simultaneous engineering.

The Insight project was important in preparing the ground for structural change in product development. The objective was to shift the focus of product development from individual components and subsystems to complete car programmes. For Ford managers, the move from functional to programme management was critical in allowing the company simultaneously to develop three important products – Fiesta, Escort and Mondeo – in the late 1980s. In 1989, however, internal reviews of the relationship between product development and manufacturing concluded that they remained locked into essentially functional, sequential roles. Since 1989 Ford has attempted to use matrix management to cut across functional boundaries in order to ease the transition to simultaneous engineering – the integration of product and process development. This process remains incomplete and Ford executives anticipate that continuous reorganisation of product and process engineering will gradually dissipate functional loyalties and create an integrated form of programme management. In product development, therefore, the company remains in a transitional phase between Fordism and flexibility.

V

Between 1980 and 1986, Ford US achieved one of the greatest turnarounds in corporate history, overtaking General Motors for the first time in over 50 years. Ford US made no effort to measure the contribution of programmes such as EI/PM to turnaround. In Ford US the process of change was essentially unmanaged and bottom-up. Detroit executives' rejection of past strategies and practices was their point of departure rather than a blueprint of a rejuvenated corporation. The process of change in Ford of Europe differed significantly from that of the American parent company. Above all, Ford of Europe experienced no comparable financial or creative crisis during the early 1980s. Indeed, to the contrary, there were enormous pressures on the European company to maintain the revenue flows and repatriated profits which shored up Ford's world-wide finances during this period. The loose operational control exercised by Detroit over its regional companies and the composition of Ford of Europe's executive management also diluted the impact of American initiatives. Ford of Europe pursued a deeply ambiguous change strategy during the 1980s. This ambiguity was implicit in the seminal AJ initiative which was essentially an efficiency drive triggered by comparisons with Japanese competitors. But if AJ bore the hallmarks of traditional Fordist management then it also opened up new political spaces in the organisation for experiments in cross-functional teamworking. The most significant example of cross-functional collaboration is the move towards simultaneous engineering in Ford's product development process. But, however hesitant and qualified the break with Fordist management since 1979, the cumulative impact has been decisive and irreversible.

NOTES

The research reported in this paper was supported by the Economic and Social Research Council. We gratefully acknowledge the co-operation of the Ford Motor Co. Unless otherwise indicated, all quotations are from K. Starkey and A. McKinlay, *Strategy and the Human Resource: Ford and the Search for Competitive Advantage* (Oxford, 1993).

1. J. Womack, D. Jones and D. Roos, *The Machine that Changed the World* (1990), pp.39–43.
2. A.D. Chandler (ed.), *Giant Enterprise: Ford, General Motors and the Automobile Industry* (New York, 1964).
3. A. Nevins and F. Hill, *Ford: Decline and Rebirth 1933–1962* (New York, 1963), pp.294–328.
4. P. Drucker, *Concept of the Corporation* (Boston, 1946); and his *Adventures of a Bystander* (Oxford, 1978), p.267.
5. Drucker, *Concept of the Corporation*, p.47.
6. P. Drucker, *The Practice of Management* (Oxford, 1989 ed.), 109–10.
7. W. Hayes, *Henry: A Life of Henry Ford II* (1990), p.14.
8. D. Halberstram, *The Reckoning* (1987).
9. D. Hackett, *The Big Idea: The Story of Ford of Europe* (Brentwood, 1976), p.31.
10. For the 'personal sadness' of an American Vice-President of Product Development at the 'Byzantine' nature of corporate politics, see D. Frey, 'Learning the Ropes: My Life as a Product Champion', *Harvard Business Review* (Sept.–Oct. 1991), p.56.
11. See Starkey and McKinlay (1993), Chs. 4 and 7; A. Jardim, *The First Henry Ford* (Cambridge, MA, 1970), p.31.
12. W. Abernathy, *The Productivity Dilemma: Roadblock to Innovation in the Automobile Industry* (Baltimore, 1978).
13. See C. Bartlett and S. Ghoshal, *Managing Across Borders: The Transnational Solution* (1989).
14. M. Wilkins and F. Hill, *American Business Abroad: Ford on Six Continents* (Detroit, 1964), Chs. 17, 18.
15. J. Stopford and L. Turner, *Britain and the Multinationals* (1985), p.24; R. Church, 'The Effects of American Multinationals on the British Motor Industry: 1911–83', in A. Teichova, M. Levy-Leboyer and H. Nussbaum (eds.), *Multinational Enterprise in Historical Perspective* (Cambridge, 1986), p.120.
16. J. Bloomfield, 'The Changing Spatial Organisation of Multinational Corporations in the World Automobile Industry', in F. Hamilton and G. Linge (eds.), *Spatial Analysis, Industry and the Industrial Environment. Vol II International Industrial Systems* (1981), pp.382–5.
17. G. Turner, *Cars* (1965), pp.18–21; J. Leontiades, *Multinational Corporate Strategy: Planning for World Markets* (Lexington, 1985), p.23.
18. C. Layton, 'The Benefits of Scale for Industry', in J. Pinder (ed.), *The Economies of Europe: What the Common Market Means for Britain London* (1971), p.51; N. Owen, *Economies of Scale, Competitiveness, and Trade Patterns within the European*

204   THE MAKING OF GLOBAL ENTERPRISE

Community (Oxford, 1983), pp.52–5; M. Casson, *Multinationals and World Trade: Vertical Integration and the Division of Labour in World Industries* London (1986), p.43.
19. Y.S. Hu, *The Impact of US Investment in Europe: A Case Study of the Automotive and Computer Industries* (New York, 1973), pp.175, 178; K. Williams, J. Williams and C. Haslam, *The Breakdown of Austin Rover: a Case-Study in the Failure of Business Strategy and Industrial Policy* (Leamington Spa, 1987), p.35.
20. C. Dassbach, *Global Enterprises and the World Economy: Ford, General Motors, and IBM: The Emergence of the Transnational Enterprise* (New York, 1989), p.382.
21. For general background see, J. Laux, *The European Automobile Industry* (New York, 1992), p.182.
22. 'Face to Face: Alex Trotman of Ford of Europe', *European Motor Business*, No.14 (1988), p.4.
23. T. Beckett, to House of Commons Expenditure Committee, *The Motor Vehicle Industry: Report and Evidence* (1975), p.238.
24. Ford Interviews, Aug. 1987, 07/2.
25. Owen, *Economies of Scale*, p.52.
26. P. Geroski and A. Murfin, 'Advertising and the Dynamics of Market Structure: The UK Car Industry,' *British Journal of Management*, Vol.1 No.2 (1990), pp.82–3; S. Young, N. Hood and J. Hamill, *Foreign Multinationals and the British Economy: Impact and Policy* (1988), pp.87, 225.
27. R. Walton, 'From Control to Commitment: Transforming Work Force Management in the United States', in K. Clark, R. Hayes and C. Lorenz (eds.), *The Uneasy Alliance: Managing the Productivity-Technology Dilemma* (Boston, 1985).
28. Womack *et al.*, *Machine that Changed the World*, pp.48–65.
29. R. Shook, *Turnaround: The New Ford Motor Company* (New York, 1990), p.16; F. Zimmerman, *the Turnaround Experience: Real-World Lessons in Revitalising Corporations* (New York, 1991), pp.41–5.
30. For comparable British examples see A. Pettigrew and R. Whipp, *Managing Change for Competitive Success* (Oxford, 1991); J. Stopford and C. Baden-Fuller, 'Corporate Rejuvenation', *Journal of Management Studies*, Vol.27 No.4 (July 1990), pp.399–415.
31. D. Petersen, *A Better Idea: Redefining the Way Americans Work* (Boston, 1991), pp.44–5; R. Pascale, *Managing on the Edge* (1990), p.117, for example.
32. H. Katz, *Changing Gears: Changing Labor Relations in the US Auto Industry* (Cambridge, MA, 1985), pp.75–7.
33. P. Banas, 'Employee Involvement: A Sustained Labor/Management Initiative at the Ford Motor Company', in J. Campbell, R. Campbell and Associates, *Productivity in Organizations: New Perspectives from Industrial and Organizational Psychology* (San Francisco, 1988).
34. R. Pascale, *Managing on the Edge*, p.121.
35. K. Starkey and A. McKinlay, 'Beyond Fordism? Strategic Choice and Labour Relations in Ford UK', *Industrial Relations Journal*, Vol.20 No.2 (1989), pp.93–100.
36. A. McKinlay and K. Starkey, 'Between Control and Consent?: Corporate Strategy and Employee Involvement in Ford UK', in P. Blyton and J. Morris (eds.), *A Flexible Future? Prospects for Employment and Organization* (Berlin, 1991), pp.157–68; S. Tolliday, 'Ford and "Fordism" in Postwar Britain: Enterprise Management and the Control of Labour 1937–1987', in S. Tolliday and J. Zeitlin (eds.), *The Power to Manage? Employers and Industrial Relations in Comparative Historical Perspective* London (1991).
37. Ford Interviews, June 1987, 03/1.
38. R. Kaplinsky, 'Restructuring the Capitalist Labour Process: Some Lessons from the Car Industry', *Cambridge Journal of Economics*, Vol.12 No.4 (1988), pp.451–70.
39. N. Oliver and B. Wilkinson, *The Japanization of British Industry: New Developments in the 1990s* (Oxford, 1990), pp.110–13.
40. E. Silva, 'Labour and Technology in the Car Industry: Ford Strategies in Britain and Brazil' (Unpublished PhD thesis, Imperial College, 1988), pp.149–50; D. Jones,

'Technology and the UK Automobile Industry', *Lloyds Bank Review*, no.148 (April 1983), p.24.

41. P. Buckley and P. Enderwick, *The Industrial Relations Practices of Foreign-Owned Firms in Britain* (1985), p.114; D. Marsden, T. Morris, P. Willman and S. Wood, *The Car Industry: Labour Relations and Industrial Adjustment* (1985), pp.155-6.
42. S. Tolliday, 'Ford and "Fordism" ', pp.102-3.
43. S. Jary, 'New Technology: The Union Response at the Local Level' (Unpublished M.Sc. thesis, Imperial College, 1985), pp.72, 76.
44. P. Strebel, 'Ford of Europe', *Journal of Management Case Studies*, Vol.3 No.3 (1987), pp.138-57.
45. Petersen, *A Better Idea*, pp.55-6 *et seq*.
46. P. Seidler, *Let's Call it Fiesta: The Autobiography of Ford's Project Bobcat* (Lausanne, 1976), p.11.
47. R. Rothwell and P. Gardiner, 'Design and Competition in Engineering', *Long Range Planning*, Vol.17 No.3 (1984), pp.88-9.
48. H. Mintzberg and J. Quinn, *The Strategy Process* (Englewood Cliffs, NJ, 1991), p.493.
49. P. Bianchi and G. Volpato, 'Flexibility as the Response to Excess Capacity: The Case of the Automotive Industry', in C. Baden-Fuller (ed.), *Managing Excess Capacity* (Oxford, 1990), p.231.
50. R. Lutz, cited in C. Lorenz, *The Design Dimension* (Oxford, 1986), p.91.
51. J. Butman, *Car Wars: How General Motors Europe Built 'The Car of the Future'* (1991).
52. K.B. Clark and T. Fujimoto, *Product Development Performance: Strategy, Organisation and Management in the World Auto Industry* (Cambridge, MA), pp.67-96.

INDEX

For Product Safety Concerns and Information please contact our EU
representative GPSR@taylorandfrancis.com
Taylor & Francis Verlag GmbH, Kaufingerstraße 24, 80331 München, Germany